a
# SOURCEBOOK
on
child
sexual
abuse

a

# SOURCEBOOK

on
child
sexual
abuse

## david finkelhor

with

Sharon Araji
Larry Baron
Angela Browne
Stefanie Doyle Peters
Gail Elizabeth Wyatt

**SAGE** PUBLICATIONS
*The International Professional Publishers*
Newbury Park   London   New Delhi

*For information address:*

SAGE Publications, Inc.
2455 Teller Road
Newbury Park, California 91320

SAGE Publications Ltd.
6 Bonhill Street
London EC2A 4PU
United Kingdom

SAGE Publications India Pvt. Ltd.
M-32 Market
Greater Kailash I
New Delhi 110 048 India

Printed in the United States of America

**Library of Congress Cataloging-in-Publication Data**


Main entry under title:

Finkelhor, David.
    A sourcebook on child sexual abuse.

    Bibliography: p.
    Includes index.
    1. Child molesting.   2. Sexually abused children.
3. Child molesters.   I. Title.   [DNLM: 1. Child Abuse.
2. Sex offenses.   WA 320 F499s]
HQ71.F52   1986        362.7′044        85-27773
ISBN 0-8039-2748-7
ISBN 0-8039-2749-5 (pbk.)


92  93  94  15  14  13  12

# Contents

# Acknowledgments

My best and most edifying interactions with colleagues and friends over the last two years have revolved around preparations for this book. I have been touched and gratified by the help they have given, the excitement they have shown, and the very personal kind of consideration they have extended to me. I continue to be reinforced in my conviction that people working in the field of child sexual abuse have a special quality of openness, commitment, and generosity that one does not find in other fields.

I want to express special appreciation to my coauthors. The work on many of the chapters has been arduous, painstaking, and time-consuming, and they stuck with it. I have learned from each of these collaborations.

Among the things that make work in this field so exciting and rewarding are a particular group of colleagues who have taken special interest in my work—Lucy Berliner, John Briere, David Corwin, David Chadwick, Anne Cohn, Jon Conte, Jim Garbarino, Judy Herman, Gerry Hotaling, Mark David Janus, Kee MacFarlane, Lynn Sanford, Roland Summit, Murray Straus, and especially Diana Russell. All of them have contributed greatly to my general understanding of the problem of sexual abuse, and have given me specific help with the issues touched upon in this book.

Many others, in addition, have read chapters and given me extremely valuable comments and ideas: Chris Bagley, Jo Bulkley, Cordelia Anderson, Jack Fowler, William Friedrich,

Mary Ellen Fromuth, Jim Garbarino, Jill Korbin, Mary Koss, Chris Holmes, Karin Meiselman, Eli Newberger, Carolyn Moore Newberger, Karl Pillemer, Robert Prentky, Desmond Runyon, Dan Saunders, and Rich Snowden. Also among my most loyal chapter readers are present and past members of the Family Violence Research Seminar.

The conduct of the research and the preparation of the manuscript have been vastly simplified by a few key support staff, who have been indispensable to me. Linda Gott, with her meticulous attention to detail, zealous commitment to the project, cheerfulness, and plain good sense, made the process of readying the manuscript easier and more enjoyable than ever before. She has been of incalculable assistance at many stages of the work. Sigi Fizz came to the rescue on occasions too numerous to count. Heidi Gerhardt and Ruth Miller both worked conscientiously on many sections.

The whole project owes its existence to the National Center on Child Abuse and Neglect, which provided the bulk of the funding (under grant 90CA840/01). Aeolian Jackson, the project officer, and Helen Howerton, the director of NCCAN, with their moral support and administrative assistance, have given the undertaking a special meaningfulness. Several other sources of financial support have played a crucial role at crucial times. The Eden Hall Farm Foundation has helped my work with their generous support. Some of that thanks goes to Sherman McLaughlin. The National Center for Prevention and Control of Rape and Mary Lystad provided some very timely financial assistance for the research on Chapter 8. Finally, the National Institute of Mental Health, which funds the Family Violence Research Training Program (under grant MH15161), has helped support my collaborations with Sharon Araji, Larry Baron, and Angela Browne.

Portions of chapters in this book have appeared earlier: in David Finkelhor and Larry Baron (1986) "Risk factors for child sexual abuse: a review of the evidence," *Journal of Interpersonal Violence*; Sharon Araji and David Finkelhor (1985) "Explanations of pedophilia: review of empirical research,"

*Bulletin of the American Academy of Psychiatry and the Law*; Angela Browne and David Finkelhor (1986) "Impact of child sexual abuse: a review of the research," *Psychological Bulletin*; copyrighted (1986) by the American Psychological Association and adapted by permission of the publisher; David Finkelhor and Angela Browne (1985) "The traumatic impact of child sexual abuse: a conceptualization," *American Journal of Orthopsychiatry*; and David Finkelhor (1984) "The prevention of child sexual abuse: an overview of needs and problems," *SIECUS Report XIII*: 1-5. I appreciate the permission granted for adaptation by each of these sources.

The two years of work on this book have been engrossing ones, but they easily could have been otherwise. I was fortunate during that time to have a person who challenged me to embark on other adventures, as well, which worked miraculously to replenish my energies for work on this one. I want Carole, my partner in adventures, both inward and outward, to know how important she has been.

*—David Finkelhor*

# Introduction

**David Finkelhor**

This book is a decade review of scientific knowledge about the problem of child sexual abuse. It was not until the mid-1970s that child sexual abuse first began to appear on the agenda of mental health and child welfare professionals. Since then, however, the field has developed rapidly. The number of cases reported to agencies of all types has soared. Public awareness and concern about the problem, as reflected in media attention, has intensified. More and more professionals and their academic counterparts have become interested. An extensive literature on the subject has developed, ranging from first-person accounts to clinical textbooks to research monographs. Government funding has increased, coming from such agencies as the National Institute of Mental Health, National Center on Child Abuse and Neglect, and the Office of Juvenile Justice and Delinquency Prevention. It has been a hectic decade.

Happily, all this has activity has given a boost to new scientific inquiry about the problem. But long-awaited knowledge from this research has been slow to materialize and be disseminated. At the end of a decade of intense professional concern, many have the feeling that the same old unsatisfying answers are being given to the same old nagging questions and that nothing new really has been learned.

The problems of accumulating new knowledge in this field are very real. Sexual abuse is an extremely difficult problem to study. Because of the shame and stigma that surround it, victims, offenders, and their families are not eager and cooperative research subjects. Ethical dilemmas hamper and complicate many direct and simple approaches to answering important questions.

But beyond these basic difficulties, other obstacles have inhibited the accumulation and dissemination of new knowledge. First, the flood tide of cases coming to professional attention has taxed and exhausted all available resources. In the face of constant clinical emergencies, little time and attention has been left over for painstaking scientific tasks, such as developing instruments, conducting evaluations, following up clients, and formulating results.

Second, this problem has come to the fore at a time of general retrenchment in levels of government-sponsored research. Particularly because the problem is primarily in the realm of social relationships rather than medicine or physiology, child sexual abuse has suffered from the relative unavailability of research funding.

However, more research has been done than is generally recognized. Part of the problem is that what research exists has not been widely disseminated. This has stemmed from several factors. First, the dissemination of all research is slow. It takes a long time for papers and books to be published, read, and assimilated into professional awareness. In a research perspective 10 years is not a lot of time.

But sexual abuse research has some particular difficulties. Sexual abuse does not fall clearly within the domain of one particular discipline. Professionals approach the problem from psychology, sociology, nursing, psychiatry, pediatrics, social work, criminology, law, counseling psychology, and elsewhere. Although this diversity has stimulated innovative approaches to the problem, it has posed problems of communication. Research published in nursing journals does not reach the psychologists, and vice versa. Few professionals can monitor the wide diversity of professional domains in which research reports on sexual abuse can appear. This can give the impression of less research than is really the case.

Another problem stemming from the interdisciplinary character of interest in sexual abuse is that the topic is seen as somewhat peripheral to all disciplines and not squarely in the domain of any. Thus many of the prestigious, mainstream publications in various fields have not tried to put any focus on sexual abuse. What papers these publications do receive are often rejected, because much of the submitted research is exploratory and lacking in the rigor and acceptability that come from being part of a better-developed research tradition.

This book is intended to address the obvious need for a review of the available research in the field. We have tried to gather as much of the current literature as possible, both unpublished and recently published, to bring it together with the older literature. Curiously, it is this older literature that provides many of the most interesting findings in the book. Apparently, due to the fragmented character of the field, much of the old research (for example on offender recidivism) has been overlooked.

A major drawback in the field is that the available research, even the newest research, is of such variable quality. It is plagued by inadequate samples, oversimplistic research design, conflicting definitions, and unsophisticated analyses. However, when the research is brought together and considered as a whole, as this book has tried to do, some problems recede. In certain areas (for example, the question of which children are at high risk) the same findings are replicated again and again, with different types of samples, different types of designs, and different levels of research sophistication. Conclusions emerge in spite of the methodological problems. This book attempts to look at what patterns are visible when the whole body of research is viewed simultaneously.

However, the methodological problems are not to be ignored. The field is in desperate need of methodological reevaluation.

Still another objective of the book is to make suggestions about ways to improve the research currently being done or planned for the future.

The book considers five main topics: prevalence of sexual abuse, children at high risk, offenders, effects, and prevention. Chapter 1 tries to unravel the puzzle presented by the availability of more than a dozen surveys concerning the prevalence of sexual abuse, all with very disparate findings. The conclusions should be of interest to the public and policymakers who want to know the dimensions of child sexual abuse. Moreover, they should also be of interest to researchers and clinicians, both of whom need to take accurate histories of abuse in the course of their work.

Chapter 2 assembles the available evidence about which children seem to be at highest risk for sexual abuse. It finds a remarkable degree of convergence among the variety of studies that have been done. These findings are perhaps the most striking and deserving of dissemination of any in the book.

Chapter 3 reviews a wide range of theories and findings concerning child molesters. Much of this material is old, but, curiously, has never been assembled before in one place. When brought together, it falls into a conspicuous pattern that suggests four major factors that contribute to the development of molesting behavior.

Chapter 4 critiques some of the main problems in the literature on offenders, including the popular "intergenerational transmission" notion. It also summarizes what has been learned about the likelihood that child molesters, once caught, will reoffend.

Chapter 5 is an extensive review of the large literature on both the initial and long-term effects of sexual abuse. In spite of the sheer quantity of current and unpublished literature and the pace at which new material is appearing, there are still serious gaps. It is clear that sexual abuse is a serious mental health problem. However, the exact dimensions and locations of its impact are still very sketchy.

Chapter 6 is an effort to build some coherence out of the mass of data in Chapter 5. It presents a conceptual framework of four basic "traumagenic dynamics" that relate the nature of the sexual abuse experience to anticipated outcomes. It is a framework without, as yet, any empirical support, but one that could prove useful for clinical evaluation and the planning of research.

Chapter 7 examines methodological issues, particularly related to the study of the effects of sexual abuse. It offers a variety of suggestions for improving research by discussing such topics as how to define sexual abuse, how to choose samples, what kinds of comparison or control groups to include, what kinds of instruments to use, and how to deal with ethical dilemmas.

Chapter 8 takes up the newly expanding field of sexual abuse prevention education. Early sections of the chapter lay out the rationale for and the content of current prevention programs. Later sections review the small amount of research evaluating these educational programs and make suggestions for future research.

These topics represent the key areas that have emerged in this active decade of research in child sexual abuse. It is worthwhile to pause and review what we have learned so far and consider directions for future research. It is also important, at this early stage of the field, to examine our methodology and research techniques critically so that we might do better research in the future. If the implications of what we have accomplished up until now can be fully assimilated and utilized, we believe they can form the foundation for major new developments in our understanding of and intervention into this profound and troubling problem.

# 1

# Prevalence

Stefanie Doyle Peters
Gail Elizabeth Wyatt
David Finkelhor

E ver since cases of child sexual
abuse began to appear in large
numbers in the late 1970s, there
has been a fervent interest in establishing the true scope of the
problem. Child molestation, although the concern of many parents in a previous era, was nonetheless thought to be relatively
rare. The sudden flood of cases prompted a genuine concern on
the part of professionals, parents, and policymakers to know its
real dimensions.

The demand for such a measure inevitably produced some
statistics. It turned out that studies with information about the
prevalence of child molestation had been done as far back as
1929 (Hamilton, 1929; Landis et al., 1940). Such studies
clearly had shown child molestation to be not uncommon in the
lives of children. However, for a variety of reasons, including
the skepticism of psychoanalysts (Masson, 1984) and the caution of sex reformers (Finkelhor, 1979), these statistics had
never been given wide public notice. But in the late 1970s some
of them were rediscovered. Estimates such as "one in four girls
and one in nine boys," usually attributed to unnamed experts,
got passed around from article to article, and took on authority
simply from being cited so often. (The estimate of one in four
girls probably comes from Kinsey, Pomeroy, Martin, and
Gebhard, 1953.) Then suddenly, in the early 1980s, a rash

of conflicting numbers began to appear. In the morass of contradictory estimates many people became confused and simply skeptical of any numbers at all.

The situation is confusing. The reality is that there is not yet any consensus among social scientists about the national scope of sexual abuse. No statistics yet exist that fully satisfy the request that journalists and others so frequently make for an accurate national estimate. However, by 1985 there had been a variety of attempts to estimate the scope, and, although the statistics are often very conflicting, the studies have revealed a great deal about the problem of sexual abuse, and how to go about measuring it.

The task of this chapter is to review and assess the available research on the incidence and prevalence of child abuse, including some of the earliest and the most recent work. The primary focus will be on comparing the ways in which different researchers have approached this problem, with an eye to determining what are the most accurate estimates and formulating some guidelines and suggestions for the design of future studies.

The discussion delves deeply into the realm of methodology at times, but it is a discussion well worth understanding. First, it has many implications about how future research on sexual abuse should be conducted. Second, it also has implications about fundamentally clinical issues, such as how to frame questions about a history of sexual abuse. Finally, all professionals who work with the problem need to be critical consumers of the research to which they are exposed.

### Prevalence and Incidence

Efforts to document the scope of sexual abuse can be categorized as two types. What we will call "incidence studies" are attempts to estimate the number of *new cases* occurring in a given time period, usually a year. What we will call "prevalence studies" are attempts to estimate the proportion of a population that have been sexually abused in the course of their childhood. Incidence figures are usually expressed as a number (44,600) per year or a rate (.07 per 1,000 children) per year. Prevalence figures are expressed as a percentage (35% of all girls).

There have been two attempts to gather nationwide incidence figures. The American Humane Association (AHA), under contract from the government, served until 1985 as a clearinghouse for statistics on child abuse and neglect gathered by individual states. Most of the states collect certain basic statistics on child abuse and neglect from their child protective agencies using a standardized form, and report at least the summary statistics from these forms to the AHA. From these reports, the AHA extrapolates some national estimates, shown for the years 1976 through 1983 in Table 1.1. It should be noted that the numbers in Table 1.1 refer to *cases*, not children, because some cases involve more than one child.

It is generally acknowledged, however, that many reports of child abuse are never passed on to child protective agencies. In an effort to get an even broader measure of the true scope, the National Incidence Study (NCCAN, 1981) examined a random

TABLE 1.1
Estimates of Sexual Abuse Cases Reported to
State Reporting Agencies for United States
(1976-1983)

| Year | Estimate[a] |
|------|-------------|
| 1976 | 7,559 |
| 1977 | 11,617 |
| 1978 | 12,257 |
| 1979 | 27,247 |
| 1980 | 37,366 |
| 1981 | 37,441 |
| 1982 | 56,607 |
| 1983 | 71,961 |

SOURCE: American Humane Association.
a. These estimates are not based on complete figures, but are extrapolated on the basis of the states who participate in the AHA reporting system. The percentage of American children covered by the reporting system was as follows: 1976, 27%; 1977, 36%; 1978, 43%; 1979, 42%; 1980, 43%; 1981, 47%; 1982, 40%; 1983, 46%.

sample of 26 U.S. counties and tried to count all the cases that came to the attention of other professionals, in addition to child protection agencies. This study estimated that 44,700 children were sexually abused in the year starting May 1, 1979, equivalent to an incidence rate of 0.7 per 1,000 children.

These kinds of incidence studies have some usefulness for keeping track of the number of cases professionals and public agencies are called upon to handle. But they have a major and widely recognized shortcoming in terms of estimating the "true scope" of the problem (Finkelhor & Hotaling, 1983): Most cases of sexual abuse do not come to the attention of any child welfare agency or any professional. The nature of the problem— its secrecy and shame, the criminal sanctions against it, and the young age and dependent status of its victims—inhibits discovery and discourages voluntary reporting. Professional efforts at case detection can alter vastly the number of cases coming to public attention. Thus most people consider the rise in incidence figures (noted in Table 1.1) to be primarily a product of new education, awareness, and professional attention to the problem. And most people consider the scope of the problem reflected in such figures to be a substantial underestimate. A comparison of incidence figures with prevalence figures suggests this to be true. Therefore, throughout the rest of the chapter we will focus on matters of prevalence.

### Prevalence Studies of Sexual Abuse

Prevalence studies have started from the premise that because most sexual abuse is never reported, the most valid measures of scope would have to come from victim or offender self-reports. Victims have seemed more promising prospects for self-disclosure, so researchers have devised a variety of studies to try to elicit such self-reports in a variety of populations. Prior to 1960, there were four such studies, and no fewer than 15 have been conducted in the last decade. However, the number of such studies has increased particularly rapidly since 1980, and many of the findings are just being published. (There may also be studies that we overlooked in our review.) This has provided a "rush" of data in the area of sexual abuse, without the opportunity to digest the findings of other investigators and to improve upon their methodologies.

Table 1.2 presents a summary of the available findings from the prevalence studies of child sexual abuse. The studies have been grouped into three broad categories, according to the type of sample involved, and arranged alphabetically within each category. The earliest studies utilized volunteers recruited from various sources. Beginning in the mid-1950s and continuing through the present, researchers have made use of college student populations. Since the late 1970s, investigators have attempted prevalence surveys on probability samples of the general population, including one of the entire United States (Lewis, 1985; Timnick, 1985a, 1985b). It should be noted that two of the studies included are Canadian (Bagley & Ramsay, in press; Badgley et al., 1984). There have been some prevalence studies in other countries, notably Sweden (Ronstrom, 1985) and England (Baker, 1983), but these have not been included.

It is evident from Table 1.2 that there is considerable variation in the prevalence rates for child sexual abuse derived from the various North American studies. Reported rates range from 6% to 62% for females and from 3% to 31% for males. Although even the lowest rates indicate that child sexual abuse is far from an uncommon experience, the higher reported rates would point to a problem of epidemic proportions.

Several possible factors could account for the variation in prevalence rates. First, variations may reflect differences in the definitions of sexual abuse used in various studies. Some studies clearly used more restrictive definitions than others. Second, these discrepant findings may reflect true differences in the prevalence of sexual abuse among various segments of the population. Certain geographic regions or certain ethnic groups, for example, may have more abuse. A third possibility is that the lower rates are the result of methodological factors: how respon-

TABLE 1.2
Prevalence of Child Sexual Abuse

| *Study* | *Types of Experiences* | Prevalence Rates (percentages) | |
|---|---|---|---|
| | | *Females* | *Males* |
| Volunteer samples | | | |
| Hamilton (1929) 100 married women and 100 married men in New York City | prepubertal sexual aggressions | 20 | 22 |
| Kinsey et al. (1953) 4,444 adult women | preadolescent sexual contact with older male | 24 | — |
| Landis et al. (1940) 153 "normal" women and 142 psychiatric patients in New York City | prepubertal sexual aggressions | 24 | — |
| College student samples | | | |
| Finkelhor (1979) 530 female and 266 male college students in New England | sexual experiences with older partners (prior to age 17) | 19 | 9 |
| Fritz et al. (1981) 540 female and 412 male college students in Seattle, Washington | prepubertal sexual encounters with adults involving physical contact | 8 | 5 |
| Fromuth (1983) 482 female college students from Auburn University in Alabama | same as Finkelhor (1979) | 22 | — |
| Landis (1956) 1,800 college students | experiences with adult sexual deviates (no upper age limit) | 35 | 30 |
| Seidner & Calhoun (1984) 595 females and 490 male college students from University of Georgia | sexual experiences with older partners (prior to age 18) | 11 | 5 |
| Community samples | | | |
| Badgley et al. (1984) Random sample of 1,006 females and 1,002 males from 210 communities in Canada | unwanted sexual acts before 18 including exposures | 34[a] | 13 |
| Bagley and Ramsay (in press) Random sample of 401 women in Calgary | serious sexual abuse in childhood (prior to age 16) | 22 | |

TABLE 1.2  (Continued)

| Study | Types of Experiences | Prevalence Rates (percentages) Females | Males |
|-------|---------------------|--------|-------|
| Burnam (1985)<br>Random sample of 1,623 females and 1,459 males in Los Angeles | sexual assault (prior to age 16) | 6 | 3 |
| Finkelhor (1984)<br>Random sample of 334 females and 187 males in the Boston Metropolitan area | sexual experiences with older partners (prior to age 17) | 15 | 6 |
| Keckley Market Research (1983)<br>Random sample of 603 adults in Nashville area | sexual abuse (during childhood) | 11 | 7 |
| Kercher and McShane (1984)<br>Random sample of 593 females and 461 males in Texas | sexual abuse (during childhood) | 11 | 3 |
| Lewis (1985)<br>[Timnick, 1985a, 1985b]<br>National random sample of 1,252 males and 1,374 females | sexual abuse (during childhood) | 27 | 16 |
| Miller (1976)<br>Random sample of 3,185 Illinois adolescents (14-18) | sexual molestation | 14 | 8 |
| Murphy (1985)<br>Random sample of 415 women and 403 men in Central Minnesota | forced unwanted sexual activity by an adult (prior to age 18) | 13 | 3 |
| Russell (1983)<br>Random sample of 930 women in San Francisco | intrafamilial and extrafamilial sexual abuse including noncontact (prior to age 18) | 54 | |
| Wyatt (1985)<br>Quota sample of 248 women in Los Angeles County | sexual abuse (prior to age 18) | 62 | |

a. Figures recalculated from tables on page 182 in Badgley et al. (1984).

dents were recruited, how they were interviewed, who interviewed them, or the wording of the questions they were asked.

These explanations are not mutually exclusive and each may
play some part in accounting for the widely discrepant findings
presented in Table 1.2. Let us examine how such differences
may contribute to the variation in reported prevalence rates.
Understanding the implications of such differences is important,
not just for the researcher who is planning new investigations,
but also for the consumer of research, who needs to evaluate the
merits of various statistics and studies.

For purposes of this discussion, we will focus on prevalence
rates for child sexual abuse among female children only. There
are several reasons for this decision. First, the literature on the
prevalence of abuse of boys has been reviewed very recently
(Finkelhor, 1984). Second, the studies that have included males
have less methodological variation. Of the eight most recent
studies with male subjects, all but two have relied on self-
administered questionnaires to collect data on abuse experiences. As a result, the possibilities for methodological
comparison are somewhat limited. Finally, issues pertaining to
definitions and to methodological strategies may be different for
boys.

In restricting our discussion to prevalence rates for females,
we do not mean to imply that the sexual abuse of boys deserves
less attention. However, we believe that focusing on abuse
among women will make for clearer comparisons between studies and help us to identify the key issues in the areas of definition
and methodology. The research on sexual abuse among males
deserves to be evaluated in its own right, to allow for the possibility that different issues may emerge.

### Definition

Prevalence studies differ to some extent according to what
ages, acts, and types of relationships are included in their definitions of child sexual abuse. Unfortunately, in a number of early

studies no definition was specified (Fritz, Stoll, & Wagner, 1981; Hamilton, 1929; Landis, 1956; Landis et al., 1940; Walters, 1975), and even some more recent studies provide only a general definition (Keckley Market Research, 1983; Kercher & McShane, 1984). Another problem with some studies is the failure to specify upper age limits to the concept of childhood. In more recent studies, fortunately, there is a trend toward detailed operational definitions that clearly specify the criteria used to evaluate experiences as sexual abuse (Burnam, 1985; Finkelhor, 1979, 1984; Fromuth, 1983; Kinsey et al., 1953; Russell, 1983; Seidner & Calhoun, 1984; Wyatt, 1985). Such definitions have obvious advantages for purposes of comparisons among studies. For the most part, we will be excluding from consideration studies in which the operationalization of the concept of sexual abuse was unavailable (such as Hamilton, 1929; Landis, 1956; Walters, 1975).

The operational definitions used in nine studies in which they were clearly specified are presented in Table 1.3. These definitions have been broken down along three common dimensions to facilitate comparisons among studies. The first column indicates the upper limit placed on the victim's age at the time the incident occurred, which was 16 or 17 in seven of the studies. Kinsey and his associates (1953) collected data only on incidents occurring before puberty, and Burnam (1985) set the upper limit at age 15. The second column describes the types of sexual behavior included in each definition. The term *noncontact abuse* refers, for the most part, to two types of experiences: (1) encounters with exhibitionists and (2) solicitation to engage in sexual activity, where no physical contact occurred. The term *contact abuse* applies to all behaviors that do involve sexual contact, including fondling of breasts and genitals, intercourse, and oral or anal sex. All but one study (Burnam, 1985) encompassed the full range of contact and noncontact forms of abuse. The third column of the table summarizes the criteria used to define a sexual encounter as abusive. In most cases, these criteria pertain to the difference in age between the perpetrator and the victim.

### TABLE 1.3
### Definitions of Child Sexual Abuse

| Study | Age Limit | Types of Behavior | Defining Characteristics |
|---|---|---|---|
| Burnam (1985) | 15 | all types of contact abuse, plus verbal propositions | sexual experience occurred as a result of pressure or force |
| Finkelhor (1979) | 16 | all types of contact and noncontact abuse | age discrepancy: 5 years up to age 12 10 years ages 13-16 |
| Finkelhor (1984) | 16 | all types of contact and noncontact abuse | age discrepancy of 5 years *and* respondent considered the experience to have been sexual abuse |
| Fromuth (1983) | 16 | all types of contact and noncontact abuse | age discrepancy: 5 years up to age 12 10 years ages 13-16 *and* perpetrator at least 16 years old |
| Kinsey et al. (1953) | Pre pubertal | all types of contact and noncontact abuse | age discrepancy of 5 years *and* perpetrator at least 15 years old |
| Lewis (1985) | 17 | all types of contact and noncontact abuse | respondent considered it to be sexual abuse |
| Russell (1983) | 17 | narrow definition: Intrafamilial—All types of contact abuse Extrafamilial—All types of contact abuse up to age 13; completed or attempted forcible rapes only, ages 14-17 broad definition: adds all types of noncontact abuse to above | sexual experience was unwanted (extrafamilial) or exploitative (intrafamilial) |
| Seidner and Calhoun (1984) | 17 | all types of contact and noncontact abuse | age discrepancy of 5 years |
| Wyatt (1985) | 17 | all types of contact and noncontact abuse | age discrepancy of 5 years *or* sexual experience was wanted and involved some degree of coercion |

However, several studies also focused on whether the experience was considered to be abusive (Finkelhor, 1984), unwanted (Russell, 1983), coercive (Wyatt, 1985), or the result of pressure or force (Burnam, 1985).

Some of the differences in Table 1.3 reflect unsettled questions concerning the definition of sexual abuse. The first of these involves whether or not noncontact abuse should be included in reports of the prevalence of sexual abuse. Until recently, the practice has been to include noncontact experiences in definitions of sexual abuse, largely for two reasons. First, exhibitionism is widely considered a criminal act, the intent of which is to shock and frighten, and therefore merits the same consideration as contact abuse, which may, in some cases, be less intimidating to a child. Second, certain sexual propositions, when they come from an inappropriate source such as a brother, father, or teacher, can presumably have a significant psychological impact on a child.

On the other hand, some people consider exhibitionism to be primarily a nuisance act, and do not believe that purely verbal experiences are in the same category of seriousness as acts that violate a child's body. Moreover, some recent research does suggest that noncontact experiences are not as likely to cause long-term effects (Peters, 1984; Sorrenti-Little, Bagley, & Robertson, 1984). Researchers who are interested in a conservative definition of sexual abuse sometimes tend to want to exclude noncontact experiences. Two researchers, Russell (1983) and Wyatt (1985), resolved this issue by reporting prevalence rates both ways: with noncontact included and excluded.

Another definitional issue that various investigators have handled in different ways concerns the inclusion or exclusion of incidents involving peers as perpetrators. Some investigators have interpreted the notion of sexual abuse to mean exclusively experiences that occurred with adults (Kinsey et al., 1953) or at least older partners (Finkelhor, 1979, 1984; Fromuth, 1983; Seidner & Calhoun, 1984). Research does indicate that experiences with peers, even when they involve force, are perceived as less traumatic (Finkelhor, 1979). However, peers are certainly capable of committing extremely abusive, violent, forced acts of sexual assault. Moreover, girls do encounter, especially in adolescence, an enormous quantity of intrusive and unwanted sexual aggressions, which, because they are abusive and occur in childhood, could be considered "child sexual abuse." Recent investigators have increasingly opted to include some portion of these peer aggressions in their tally of child sexual abuse. They have generally required that the experiences be unwanted (Russell, 1983), forced (Burnam, 1985), or coercive (Wyatt, 1985) in order to distinguish them from sexual exploration with peers.

A third and related issue concerning definitional differences involves the use of different criteria for determining which relationships are abuse simply because of age difference. All definitions of sexual abuse acknowledge that sexual contact even in the absence of coercion constitutes sexual abuse when it involves a young child and an adult. Children are deemed to lack the capacity to consent to such relationships (Finkelhor, 1984). However, at some point in adolescence children acquire the ability to consent. It is doubtful that many people consider a consenting relationship between a 17-year-old and a 19-year-old to be abuse, even though it may qualify as statutory rape in some states.

Many operationalizations of sexual abuse have required a five year age difference, where no force was involved. Finkelhor (1979) and Fromuth (1983) dealt with this issue by increasing the required age discrepancy from *five years* in childhood (up to age 12) to *ten years* in adolescence (ages 13 to 16). Wyatt (1985) simply excluded all voluntary experiences between the ages of 13 and 17, no matter what the age difference. Since this is an area in which law, custom, and social mores are in transition, no rule may be completely satisfactory to everyone.

Given all these definitional differences, some variation in the prevalence rates found in different studies is to be expected. It is clear that the inclusion or exclusion of noncontact forms of abuse made a difference. Russell (1983), for instance, reports prevalence rates of 54% *with* noncontact sexual abuse and 38% *without*. Wyatt's (1985) figures show a similar discrepancy, with rates of 62% and 45%, respectively. Badgley et al.'s (1984) figures drop from 39% to 22% if exposers are excluded. However, Russell's, Wyatt's, and Badgley et al.'s figures excluding noncontact are still much higher than a number of studies that included noncontact. Thus the inclusion of noncontact experiences does not explain some of the largest variations.

What about the inclusion of peer experiences or the use of different criteria for defining abuse during adolescence? Because Wyatt's (1985) study used a slightly less restrictive definition of abuse, we were able to recompute prevalence rates based on the definitions of other researchers (Wyatt & Peters, 1986). When Finkelhor's (1979) criteria were imposed, the prevalence rate dropped from 62% to 54%. A decrease of similar magnitude, to 53%, occurred as a result of recomputation in accordance with Russell's criteria. Although this brings Wyatt's findings into close approximation to Russell's, the result is still nearly three times the prevalence rate of Finkelhor's findings. The exclusion of peer experiences reduced rates by 9% at most. This suggests that other factors, such as sample characteristics, sampling techniques, or data collection procedures, must be accounting for the bulk of the variation in the reported prevalence.

## Sample Characteristics

Some of the variation in prevalence rates may stem from differences in the populations sampled. For example, college students tend to come from more protected, middle-class families, and community samples include a greater diversity of individuals in terms of age, education, and ethnicity. In this section we will examine whether sample characteristics such as age, educational level, ethnicity, or region might be related to the prevalence of child sexual abuse.

*Age of Subjects.* If child sexual abuse occurred at different rates for different age groups, then studies limited to younger samples, such as college students, might have different rates than studies with broader samples. However, comparisons between studies are not very suggestive on this point. College student samples composed primarily of young adults do not have consistently higher or lower prevalence rates than community samples that include a greater age range. Wyatt and Russell had similar rates even though Wyatt's respondents were all below the age of 37.

Moreover, within studies, there are no clear trends according to age. Russell's (1985) findings suggest a slightly higher prevalence among women aged 18 to 36 (59%) compared to women 37 and older (50%).[1] However, Wyatt's (1985) prevalence rates were slightly lower among the younger women (18 to 26) (60%) compared to a somewhat older group (27 to 36) (64%). In the Canadian National Population Survey (Badgley et al., 1984), the prevalence of child sexual abuse was quite consistent across age groups, with the exception of higher rates among the youngest group—women between the ages of 18 and 20. Overall, the evidence available at this time does not suggest that age of respondents makes a major difference in prevalence rates.

*Education and Socioeconomic Status.* There has been some speculation that the education level of respondents might affect prevalence rates for child sexual abuse (Finkelhor, 1979; Kilpatrick, 1984). For example, victims of sexual abuse might be underrepresented among college student samples because college students are middle class and because the psychological impairment of abuse may interfere with educational attainment.

Empirical findings, however, do not support this hypothesis. Within the community studies (Finkelhor, 1984; Keckley Market Research, 1983; Russell, 1986; Wyatt, 1985), rates of sexual abuse have not varied significantly by social class and education.[2] Moreover, the college student studies, as we pointed out, do not have consistently lower rates than community studies. Of course, various studies measured socioeconomic status in different ways (for example, Russell, 1984a, and Keckley, 1983, using income, and Wyatt, 1985, using the Hollingshead measure of social class). But even with this diversity, it does not appear that SES or education is responsible for the variations in prevalence findings.

*Ethnicity.* Findings on ethnicity as a risk factor for sexual abuse are discussed at length in Chapter 2. However, we will summarize them here as well, because the ethnic composition of a sample would appear to be a potentially important factor in relation to prevalence rates. In earlier studies of cases obtained through medical facilities or social service agencies (DeFrancis, 1969; Peters, 1976), children from ethnic minority backgrounds constituted the majority of sexual abuse victims. If these findings represented true differences in base rates, then ethnicity would have a significant impact on prevalence rates.

There is growing evidence that the prevalence of sexual abuse is no higher among Afro-Americans than among the white population. The results of five community surveys, conducted independently in diverse locations, consistently show similar prevalence rates for Afro-Americans and whites (Keckley Market Research, 1983; Kercher & McShane, 1984; Russell, 1986; Wyatt, 1985). For other ethnic groups, there are only isolated and often inconsistent findings (see Chapter 2).

Overall, the available data indicate that differences in the ethnic composition of samples would not be expected to affect prevalence rates. However, two methodological issues in this area should be noted. First, only two of the studies reviewed here (Burnam, 1985; Wyatt, 1985) were designed to recruit comparable numbers of participants from minority and nonminority groups. In most of the community surveys, the number of subjects from ethnic minority groups is small in proportion to the number of white subjects, even though the distribution of ethnic groups may be representative of the larger population. Second, within a given sample, ethnic minority subjects may differ from white subjects on a number of demographic and familial characteristics. With the exception of Wyatt's (1985) study, few studies examine prevalence rates by economic status and ethnicity, especially because the ethnic minority samples tend to be relatively small. The confounding of these variables has been cited as a frequent problem in studies of Afro-Americans (Myers, 1982). Researchers need to be aware of these issues when comparing the prevalence of sexual abuse across ethnic groups.

*Region.* In addition to class and ethnic differences, it is possible that regional differences may affect study findings. In the past decade, prevalence studies have been conducted in a number of areas of North America, including New England (Finkelhor, 1979, 1984), the Midwest (Walters, 1975), the South (Fromuth, 1983; Keckley Market Research, 1983; Kercher & McShane, 1984; Seidner & Calhoun, 1984), the West (Burnam, 1985; Fritz et al., 1981; Russell, 1983; Wyatt, 1985), and Canada (Badgley et al., 1984; Bagley & Ramsay, in press). If there are regional variations in the prevalence of child sexual abuse, studies carried out in different areas would be expected to yield different prevalence rates. However, the figures presented in Table 1.2 do not indicate any strong regional trends, with the exception of the high prevalence rates reported by two of the three studies conducted in California. Because of a popular perception that California harbors a greater degree of sexual license, the question has been raised whether or not the high rates in California studies might reflect a true regional difference in sexual abuse.

At least one study suggests that California could indeed harbor a higher prevalence of sexual abuse, although another dissents. In a national telephone survey of 2,627 adults, Lewis (1985) found that although the sexual abuse prevalence rates for other regions were 26%, for the Pacific region (which includes California, Oregon, Washington, Alaska, and Hawaii) the rate was 38%. Although this significant difference might well reflect higher prevalence rates in California, by far the most populous state in the region, the Lewis study was not designed to make comparisons between individual states.

Wyatt addressed the question of California's deviation in her study in a different fashion, by comparing subgroups of women who had spent the majority of their childhood (up to age 12) inside and outside California. The prevalence rates for both these groups were identical, suggesting no higher levels of abuse in California.

The apparently differing findings from the Wyatt and Lewis studies, however, are not as contradictory as they might at first seem. Among other factors that may be at work, migration may play a role. For example, it might in fact be true, as Wyatt finds, that women who spent their childhood in California were no more likely to be abused than women elsewhere. However, if abused women from other parts of the country are more likely to leave (to get away from abusers, from the stigma, or simply from bad memories), then areas like California that have large inmigrant populations might have higher prevalence rates. It must be cautioned that this is speculative; other factors may be at work as well in explaining the discrepancy, and there is no current evidence that victims of sexual abuse are more likely than others to migrate.

Nonetheless, this speculation points out that in future research on regional differences in sexual abuse, investigators should be careful to distinguish three distinct issues: (1) where victims are currently residing, (2) where they actually grew up, and (3) where they were when they were sexually abused. To aid in our understanding of regional patterns, studies should gather information on all these matters. In interpreting regional differences, another factor to be taken into account is that of regional differences in respondent candor. What may be ostensibly different prevalence rates reported by persons living in different regions may actually reflect a differential willingness to confide in researchers. In any case, evidence of possible regional differences is an argument for national or multiregional studies in future assessments of prevalence.

## Methodological Factors

Given that differences in definitions and sample characteristics do not fully explain differences in prevalence rates, we turn now to methodological factors. The various prevalence studies have differed dramatically in terms of the methodologies they have used: their sampling techniques, participation rates, mode of administration, and the types of questions that were asked. Some of the differences in reported rates, we believe, are best explained by these methodological considerations.

*Sampling Techniques.* Over time, sampling techniques for studies of the prevalence of sexual abuse have grown increasingly sophisticated. The earliest studies relied simply on groups of volunteers recruited through social networks or community organizations (Hamilton, 1929; Kinsey et al., 1953; Landis et al., 1940). Later, college student samples became popular (Landis, 1956; Finkelhor, 1979). More recent research has used a variety of probability samples and professional survey research organizations.

A description of the sampling techniques for 13 of the most contemporary of studies is given in Table 1.4. The main division is between those with probability samples and those without. The probability samples themselves are a quite heterogeneous group, including household, telephone, and mail surveys, self-administered and interviewer-administered surveys, and surveys with and without professional interviewers. The nonprobability samples, by contrast, are much more homogeneous, consisting almost entirely of student surveys, using variations of Finkelhor's (1979) methodology and questionnaire. This helps explain the general consistency of the rates from the nonprobability studies, almost all falling within the range of 11% to 22%, compared to the enormous variation of the probability samples, ranging from 6% to 62%. It does suggest that similar methodologies tend to yield similar rates, but it certainly does not appear to be the case that probability samples intrinsically obtain higher or lower rates.

## TABLE 1.4
## Description of Sampling Techniques for
## Selected Sexual Abuse Prevalence Studies

Random Sample Studies

*Badgley et al.* Survey was conducted by Gallup Canada with professional interviewers. Stratified probability sample was drawn for entire country of Canada. Interviewer went to door, asked respondent to complete a self-administered questionnaire, waited as it was completed. Questionnaire devoted entirely to sexual assault.

*Bagley and Ramsay:* Part of the follow-up of mental health survey. Stratified probability sample for Calgary based on reverse telephone directory. Interviewers were nonprofessionals specially hired and trained for survey. Follow-up interview completed approximately one year after first interview. Both interviews took approximately an hour and a half and contained many standard mental health epidemiology scales. Sexual abuse question came toward end of follow-up.

*Burnam:* The study used a multistage clustered sampling design to identify households for a probability sample of two mental health catchment areas in Los Angeles. Interviews were conducted face to face with respondents in their households. Interviewers were nonprofessionals hired and trained for the study matched for language (Spanish/English) but not sex or ethnicity. Questionnaire was lengthy (60-90 minutes) and consisted primarily of questions about mental health status. Sexual abuse question was at the very end.

*Finkelhor:* Sample and interviewing conducted by professional interviewers with Center for Survey Research. Statified probability sample for Boston SMSA. All respondents were parents of a child age 6 to 14. Main body of survey concerned attitudes and knowledge about sexual abuse. Sex abuse victimization question was contained in a self-administered questionnaire at end of interview.

*Keckley Market Research:* Sample and interviewing conducted by market research firm. Random digit dial sample for telephone exchanges in Nashville. The 25 question survey was entirely devoted to sexual abuse. Question about sexual victimization came in the middle.

*Kercher and McShane:* The survey was conducted by Criminal Justice Center at Sam Houston State University. Systematic random sample of 2,000 names of persons 17 or older holding valid Texas drivers licenses. Questionnaires were mailed and two follow-up packets sent if no response was received. The whole questionnaire concerned knowledge and attitudes concerning sexual abuse. The sexual abuse victimization question came at the end.

*Lewis:* The survey was conducted by the *Los Angeles Times* Poll, using an in-house staff of professional survey researchers. A random sample of telephones in the entire U.S. (including Alaska and Hawaii) was constituted through random sample of area codes, telephone exchanges, and random digit dialing. Both men and women were interviewed over the phone by a mixed group of male and female interviewers with no matching by sex. The interview, which lasted a half hour, was almost entirely devoted to attitudes and knowledge concerning the problem of child sexual abuse. The four questions on the respondent's own victimization came near the end.

*Miller:* The survey was conducted by the Institute for Juvenile Research. The sample consisted of a stratified random probability sample of Illinois households. Nineteen thousand households were screened to locate adolescents age 14 to 18. Most interviewers were experienced survey research staff, who delivered question-

TABLE 1.4 (Continued)

naires to households and waited as they were filled out. The main body of the self-administered questionnaire, which required an hour to complete, concerned self-reported delinquent behavior. The question about sexual molestation came near the end.

*Murphy:* Survey was conducted by trained student interviewers. Random-digit dialing was used to select a sample for the area within a 20-mile radius of St. Cloud, Minnesota. Interview consisted of a variety of subjects including sexual abuse.

*Russell:* Sample drawn by Field Research Corporation. Key addresses from telephone directory were used to start a household listing procedure ending with probability sample of San Francisco. Face-to-face interviews were conducted at households by female interviewers specially hired and trained for the study, and matched to respondent ethnicity where possible. Entire questionnaire, average length 80 minutes, was devoted to sexual assault.

*Wyatt:* A multistage stratified probability sample was drawn by the Institute for Social Science Research. Random-digit dialing was used to recruit roughly equal numbers of Afro-American and white women, ages 18 to 36, in Los Angeles County. To increase the comparability of the two ethnic groups within the sample, quotas based on age, education, marital status, and the presence of children were used. Female interviewers were hired and trained for the survey and matched to the subject's ethnicity. Interviewers made appointments and conducted interviews at a location of the subject's choice. A lengthy interview consisted of a detailed sexual history. Sexual victimization questions came near the end of the interview.

### Student Surveys

*Finkelhor* (1979): Sample was drawn from six New England colleges and universities. Self-administered questionnaire was given to whole classes (primarily in social sciences) to fill out during class time. Questionnaire took approximately one hour to complete, and was entirely devoted to questions concerning child sexual experiences. Questions on abuse came in the middle.

*Fromuth:* Sample was drawn from women students in undergraduate psychology courses at Auburn University, who filled out the questionnaire in groups of 4-37. Questionnaire was a modified version of one used by Finkelhor (1979).

*Seidner & Calhoun:* Sample was drawn from volunteers in the undergraduate psychology research pool at the University of Georgia. Self-administered questionnaire consisted of standard measure of psychological adjustment.

However, the high rates achieved by some of the probability methodologies are significant. Before probability samples had been done, it had been speculated that it would be very difficult to obtain candid reports of sexual abuse in a random sample community survey, in which a complete stranger appears at the door or telephones, compared to volunteer studies or student studies in which researchers have more leverage for motivating participants (Finkelhor, 1979). Nonetheless, it appears that some survey researchers have been able to overcome whatever obstacles there are to candor in community probability samples. Given the advantages of probability samples—they constitute a group that is representative of the community and they produce findings that are generalizable to that community—this success suggests that, whenever possible, probability samples should be the method of choice.

However, the variability in rates for probability samples also suggests caution. It appears to be that under some conditions, probability samples have generated very low prevalence rates. The success of probability samples may depend on other aspects of the methodologies—their response rate, mode of administration, interviewer training, and wording of questions—aspects to which we now turn.

*Response Rates.* One can formulate two plausible, yet contradictory, hypotheses about how response rate might affect reports about such a sensitive subject as sexual abuse. The more common hypothesis is that sexual abuse victims will, if given the opportunity, decline to participate in surveys because they are embarrassed or because they are traumatized in a way that makes them distrustful. The implication is that low response rates mean artificially low prevalence rates as victims screen themselves out. This reasoning was part of what made researchers skeptical of the possibility of valid surveys of sexual abuse. The second, opposing, hypothesis is that these same low response rates mean inflated prevalence rates. This would be because sexual abuse victims select themselves preferentially into surveys because they are looking for an opportunity to confide their history to someone who appears to be interested and concerned about this subject. However, the response rate remains low because nonvictims with nothing to discuss select themselves out.

It is possible to examine the various prevalence studies according to their response rates, particularly the studies done with probability samples in which this factor may be so important. This comparison is shown in Table 1.5. Unfortunately, however, response rates are not easy to compare, especially

TABLE 1.5

Prevalence Rates for Women and Response Rates

(percentages)

| Study | Prevalence | Response Rate[a] | |
| *(in order of prevalence rates)* | *Rate* | *Overall* | *Refusals Only* |
|---|---|---|---|
| Burnam (1985) | 6 | 69 | na |
| Keckley Market Research (1983) | 11 | 61 | na |
| Kercher & McShane (1984) | 11 | 53 | na |
| Murphy (1985) | 13 | na | 71 |
| Miller (1976) | 14 | 64 | 74 |
| Finkelhor (1984) | 15 | 61 | 74 |
| Bagley & Ramsay (in press) | 22 | na | 74 |
| Badgley et al. (1984) | 35 | na | 94 |
| Russell (1983) | 54 | 50 | 64 |
| Wyatt (1985) | 62 | 55 | 75 |
| r with prevalence | | ns | ns |

a. Response rates express the number of respondents as a percentage of the total number of respondents and nonrespondents combined. However, these rates can be calculated in different ways, depending on how the nonrespondent group is defined. For the figures presented here as overall response rates, the nonrespondent group includes potential respondents whose eligibility could not be determined, as well as eligible persons who refused to participate. For the rates labeled "refusals only," the nonrespondent group was restricted to actual refusals.

across different methodologies, because they can mean different things. Another problem is that response rates have different implications depending on what respondents knew at the time they chose to participate. A respondent agreeing to participate in a study of sexual abuse has made a different decision than one agreeing to participate in a study of crime. Unfortunately, this information is not available for all the studies.

Keeping these cautions in mind, an examination of the figures in Table 1.5 does not reveal any obvious pattern. The response rates, with some exceptions, tend to be lower on the average than those obtained in most sociological surveys, but this is perhaps due to the sensitive subject matter. However, it cannot be said that low response rates are consistently associated with either low or high prevalence. The lowest response rate, Kercher and McShane's (1984) mail survey, resulted in one of the lowest prevalence estimates. However, the studies with the highest prevalence rates (Wyatt, 1985; Russell, 1983) also had relatively low response rates. Thus even if sexual abuse is a topic sensitive enough to discourage some respondents, the current data do not suggest that victims react consistently differently from others. Some victims may decline to participate to avoid embarrassment, but the subject may be embarrassing for an equal number of nonvictims who also decline. Thus although researchers should continue to try to improve their response rates as a good practice, and readers should be cautious about the generalizability of findings based on particularly low response rates, at the present, at least, we cannot ascribe differences in prevalence figures to differences in response rates.

*Mode of Administration.* Table 1.6 illustrates the modes of administration used in 14 of the most recent prevalence studies. These methods have been categorized into three types: self-administered questionnaires (SAQ), face-to-face interviews (FFI), and telephone interviews (TI).

Until recently, SAQs were the most frequently utilized method of data collection. All of the studies of college students used them (Finkelhor, 1979; Fromuth, 1983; Seidner & Calhoun, 1984), as did Kercher and McShane's (1984) mail survey, and Miller's (1976) survey of adolescents. The Canadian National Population Survey (Badgley et al., 1984) also used self-administered questionnaires to collect data, although an "interviewer" came to the door and waited while it was filled out. Finkelhor's 1984 study involved a combination of methods. The bulk of the interview, regarding attitudes and knowledge of child sexual abuse, was conducted via FFI, but then SAQs were used to ask about the respondent's own abuse experiences.

In four studies (Bagley & Ramsay, in press; Burnam, 1985; Russell, 1983; Wyatt, 1985), subjects were interviewed face to face concerning sexual abuse. Finally, telephone interviews were used in the studies conducted by Keckley Market Research (1983) and Murphy (1985) and in the national *Los Angeles Times* survey (Lewis, 1985).

TABLE 1.6
Prevalence Rates for Women by Mode of Administration
(percentages)

|  | Rate |
|---|---|
| Self-administered questionnaire | |
| Badgley (1984) | 34 |
| Finkelhor (1979) | 19 |
| Finkelhor (1984) | 15 |
| Fromuth (1983) | 22 |
| Kercher & McShane (1984) | 11 |
| Miller (1976) | 14 |
| Seidner & Calhoun (1984) | 11 |
| Face-to-face interviews | |
| Bagley & Ramsay (in press) | 22 |
| Burnam (1985) | 6 |
| Russell (1983) | 54 |
| Wyatt (1985) | 62 |
| Telephone interview | |
| Keckley Market Research (1983) | 11 |
| Lewis (1985) | 27 |
| Murphy (1985) | 13 |

NOTE: $F(2, 11) = 1.95$, $p = .18$.

Examining the prevalence rates reported in these various studies, we can see some evidence for a relationship between method of data collection and prevalence rates (Table 1.6). With one exception, the studies that utilized self-administered questionnaires yielded prevalence rates of 22% or less. Out of the three telephone surveys, two reported extremely low rates, under 13%. In contrast, of the four studies that involved face-to-face interviews, three yielded rates of 22% or more and two were more than 50%. This suggests an advantage in favor of face-to-face interviews.

Interestingly, however, this pattern of higher rates for FFI is not consistent with the previous literature on survey research techniques. In general, no one method has been found to be superior for all types of questions (Sudman & Bradburn, 1974). With sensitive questions, one reviewer reports, "the more anonymous methods of administration [SAQs] appear to work somewhat better; that is, they lower the degree of under- or over-reporting" (Bradburn, 1983). However, another reviewer (DeLamater, 1982) found no differences. At least one recent study (Mangione, Hingson, & Barret, 1982) found SAQs inferior to FFIs for sensitive subjects. The findings from the survey research literature are ambiguous at best. Nonetheless, sexual abuse may be a special type of sensitive topic in which mode of administration does make a difference. The findings from studies about other sensitive subjects, which primarily concern self-reported delinquency, bankruptcy, or drunk driving, do not necessarily pertain.

In collecting data about sexual abuse, FFI may have certain important advantages. First, in FFI there is a possibility for rapport to develop in the course of the interview, which may enhance the subject's motivation to respond candidly (Bradburn, 1983.) A second advantage is that face-to-face contact can provide the interviewer with greater opportunity to identify and attend to cues that the subject is uncomfortable or is misinterpreting a question (DeLamater, 1982).

Additionally, researchers need to consider what implicit messages may be communicated to subjects by various methods of data collection. Face-to-face contact with a sympathetic, nonjudgmental interviewer can be used to convey a message about the acceptability and importance of discussing abuse experiences, and at the same time acknowledge the possibility of some discomfort. A more impersonal method, such as self-administered questionnaires, may reinforce the idea that sexual abuse is a topic too uncomfortable to be discussed. The risk of communicating such a message may be increased in situations in which the interviewer is actually there, but gives the respondent a SAQ instead of asking questions forthrightly (for example, Badgley et al., 1984; Finkelhor, 1984).

Maybe the most important fact about FFI is that it gives the interviewer the maximal opportunity to have an effect. It may be possible to boost or inhibit the level of candor substantially in sexual abuse surveys, depending on the skills and characteristics of interviewers (Cannell, Miller, & Oksenberg, 1981). There is some evidence that interviewers who expect difficulty in asking about sensitive topics obtain fewer reports of such behaviors as drug use and sexual activity (Sudman, Bradburn, Blair, & Stocking, 1977). Thus it is probably not coincidence that in both of the higher prevalence FFI sexual abuse studies (Russell, 1983; Wyatt, 1985), interviewers were specially selected for the study and received extensive training designed to sensitize them to the issues involved in asking about sexual abuse. If FFI allows for the possibility of better reporting, it may be because of the possibility of using well-selected and trained interviewers to enhance candor. Without this special component, FFI may be no different from the other modes.

*Specific Questions on Sexual Abuse.* Another crucial difference among the surveys concerned the kinds of questions each used to elicit reports of abuse. All the surveys used one or more "screen" questions (listed in Appendix 1.A) to ask about possible abuse experiences (for example: "Were you ever sexually abused as a child?" or "Has anyone ever touched the sex parts of your body when you didn't want this?"). The differences in these screen questions seem to account for some of the variation in rates obtained.

One important difference was simply the number of screen questions used, which varied from one to fourteen, with the majority of studies using four or fewer. Examination of the prevalence rates according to the number of screen questions (Table 1.7) shows a definite connection between the number of questions asked and the prevalence rates reported. The six studies that relied on a single general question to elicit reports of abuse (Bagley & Ramsay, in press; Burnam, 1985; Keckley Market Research, 1983; Kercher & McShane, 1984; Miller, 1976; Murphy, 1985) obtained relatively low rates of 6% to 22%. Prevalence rates were somewhat higher (ranging from 11% to 35%) among the studies that utilized two to four questions (Badgley et al., 1984; Finkelhor, 1979, 1984; Fromuth, 1983;

TABLE 1.7
Prevalence Rates for Women by Number of Screen Questions
(percentages)

|  | *Rate* |
|---|---|
| 1 question | |
| Bagley & Ramsay (in press) | 22 |
| Burnam (1985) | 6 |
| Keckley Market Research (1983) | 11 |
| Kercher & McShane (1984) | 11 |
| Miller (1976) | 14 |
| Murphy (1985) | 13 |
| 2-4 questions | |
| Badgley (1984) | 34 |
| Finkelhor (1979) | 19 |
| Finkelhor (1984) | 15 |
| Fromuth (1983) | 22 |
| Lewis (1985) | 27 |
| Seidner & Calhoun (1984) | 11 |
| More than 4 questions | |
| Wyatt (1985) | 62 |
| Russell (1983) | 54 |

NOTE: $F_{(2, 11)} = 31.27$; $p < .0001$.

Lewis, 1985; Seidner & Calhoun, 1984). Finally, the two studies that included eight or more questions (Russell, 1983; Wyatt, 1985) both report prevalence rates substantially higher than those of other studies, ranging from 54% to 62%.

Another difference in the screen questions concerns the *amount and type of specifics* that they give the respondent concerning the experience being asked about. Many of the single question screens were what we would call "general" questions. General questions inquire about a category of events, using simply a label such as "sexual abuse" or "molestation" without providing clear boundaries as to what is included in the category. A good example of such a question is, "As a child were you ever sexually abused?" (Kercher & McShane, 1984)[3] or "Has anyone ever tried to sexually molest you?" (Miller, 1976).

In most of the surveys that used multiple screens, in contrast, the questions usually gave a more specific description of the type of experience that was being asked about. These specifics were of two sorts: (1) about the relationship or (2) about the activity. "Relationship-specific" questions focused on some aspects of the perpetrator, such as age discrepancy or relationship to the victim. For example:

- "During the time before you were 16, were any sexual things done to you or with you by a person at least 5 years older than you?" (Finkelhor, 1984, p. 71)
- "At *any* time in your life, has an uncle, brother, father, grandfather, or female relative ever had *any kind of* sexual contact with you?" (Russell, 1983, p. 136)

"Activity-specific" questions frame the inquiry in terms of particular types of sexual behaviors, such as fondling or exposure. For example:

- "During childhood and adolescence, did anyone ever expose themselves to you?" (Wyatt, 1985: 512)
- "Did anyone ever try or succeed in touching your breasts or genitals against your wishes before you turned 14?" (Russell, 1983, p. 137)

Obviously, some of these specific questions (such as "at any time in your life . . . " and Russell's questions 6, 7, 10–14) drew accounts of experiences that were not child sexual abuse as these studies defined it. The standard procedure in these (and other studies) was to get specific details on any experience mentioned in response to a screen question. Thus if a person said in response to a screen that someone had molested him or her, or that someone had exposed himself or herself, the interviewer or questionnaire asked for the respondent's age at the time; the age, sex, and relationship of the offender; and more detail about the exact nature of the sexual activity that occurred. Only if the experience met the previously established definition of sexual abuse was it included in the reported prevalence rate.

Studies that used specific rather than general questions varied in their mix of types. Finkelhor (1979, 1984), Fromuth (1983), and Seidner and Calhoun (1984) relied exclusively on relationship-specific questions. Wyatt (1985) and the Canadian

Survey (Badgley et al., 1984) relied exclusively on activity-specific questions. Russell (1983) incorporated both types into her interview.

It is clear that the studies using specific questions obtained higher prevalence than those using general questions. The range for the general questions was 6% to 14%; the range for specific questions was 11% to 62%. There was also something of a tendency among the multiple-question surveys for studies with at least some activity-specific questions (Badgley et al., 1984; Russell, 1983; Wyatt, 1985) to produce more reports.

The question then arises, Why do multiple, specific screens elicit more reports of sexual abuse than single, general ones? We see three factors involved.

(1) The general questions may not work so well because the labels they use may not match the way the respondents think about their own experiences. For a variety of reasons, many people resist thinking about their own experiences in terms of negatively charged labels such as "abuse" or "molestation." When dealing with potentially embarrassing personal experiences, respondents may be reluctant to put a lot of effort into "matching" each one of a set of possible personal experiences with the ambiguous and highly charged concept provided by the interviewer. In fact, they may be looking for opportunities to excuse themselves from the obligation to disclose. If the label provided by the interviewer—that is, "sexual abuse" or "molestation"—doesn't fit their own label, the respondents may feel relieved, say no, and stop scanning.

(2) The multiple screens may work better because they provide a longer time period during which a disclosure can occur. If a respondent has some embarrassment and hesitation about an experience, her first impulse may be to avoid disclosure. In fact, the shock of the first question about sexual abuse may prompt an almost automatic denial. However, as the conversation continues with other questions about possible abuse, the respondent may recognize the persistence of the interviewer, the seriousness of the interviewer's interest, and this may give the respon-

dent courage to reveal, when subsequent questions allow the opportunity.

(3) Perhaps most important, the multiple, specific screens may work better because they provide many cues that assist in recall and matching. They give information that reminds respondents that what they should scan for includes "family members," "fondling," "unwanted sex," "authority figures," "exposures," and so on. Sexual abuse experiences may be stored in memory in association with a variety of topics. The more of these topics that are mentioned, the more likely that the respondent will be directed toward the memories. Moreover, the sheer persistence of the interviewer in making so many probes may encourage the respondent to continue the search and thus uncover more relevant memories.

This question of recall and matching may also explain some of the value of activity-specific questions. It may be that activity-specific questions are among the ones that best clue the respondents where to search. However, more research needs to be done on this before the process is clear.

Of all the differences among the studies we have reviewed, the matter of question type seems to be among the most important. However, it also must be pointed out that the type of questions asked and the method of data collection are to some extent confounded in the sample of surveys we have examined. All but one of the studies that utilized self-administered questionnaires relied on either general or relationship-specific questions to elicit reports of abuse experiences. The only exception to this is the Canadian National Population Survey (Badgley et al., 1984), which asked four activity-specific questions and reported a relatively higher prevalence rate. Thus we cannot be certain that the advantages of the multiple specific questions necessarily operate in the self-administered format, in which avoidance may be easier no matter what the question format. But the advantages of the multiple specific questions seem very apparent at our current level of knowledge.

### Recommendations

We believe that some recommendations can be drawn from the foregoing review of efforts to survey childhood sexual abuse.

(1) It is eminently possible and scientifically preferable to conduct studies of sexual abuse with general population surveys. The research to date demonstrates that a high degree of candor can be achieved in random sample surveys, and given that they have great advantages over college student and other special population studies in terms of representativeness and generalizability, they should be the method of choice for future prevalence studies when resources allow.

(2) The trend of the evidence at the moment points to the advantage of interviews over self-administered questionnaires. The personal interview appears to allow for greater rapport, gives opportunities for clarification, and reminds the respondent of the expectation of honesty. The supposed advantages of self-administered questionnaires, their confidentiality, have not been evident, although the use of SAQs has not been by any means disastrous and future studies may make improvements over the efforts to date.

(3) We believe that the advantages of the interview mode are contingent upon the use of interviewers who are both comfortable with and knowledgeable about the problem of sexual abuse. Given the subject matter, it seems possible that interviewers may discourage candor by even slight and unconscious gestures of discomfort. We strongly recommend that interviewers for sexual abuse studies receive intensive training about the subject matter. We also recommend some screening of interviewers to ferret out those who cannot deal with the subject matter, although it has not yet been established just what the best screening criteria are.

(4) The evidence appears most convincing that studies containing multiple screening questions, each of which can elicit reports of sexual abuse, are preferable over a single screening question. These multiple screens (a) avoid labels, like "sexual

abuse," that respondents may not have applied to their own experiences, (b) give respondents a longer block of time and more opportunities to either remember forgotten experiences or gather courage to reveal embarrassing ones, (c) tell respondents more about the types of experiences the researchers are looking for, and (d) assist recall of experiences with a variety of cues to elicit memories. Single-question screens do not provide these opportunities and are particularly deficient when they are piggybacked onto questionnaires full of other unrelated or only marginally related subjects. There is also some indication that recall is aided when the multiple screens include a mixture of relationship-specific questions with activity-specific questions. For suggestions of specific questions to use, we recommend that investigators consult the instruments used by Badgley et al. (1984), Russell (1983), and Wyatt (1985).

(5) Finally, we recommend that investigators gather information on sexual abuse by *peers* as well as older partners and about noncontact experiences as well as contact experiences. Even though the studies to date do not provide convincing evidence in favor of any one definition of sexual abuse, it makes sense, for research purposes at least, to gather data about a broader rather than more restricted definition. Information once collected can always be ignored, but information not gathered is simply unavailable. With the broader definition, at least, samples can be trimmed for comparability to other samples using a somewhat different definition. This need to adjust for different definitions, we believe, will be present for some time in this field because no consensus about definitions has yet developed.

### *Unresolved Questions*

The above recommendations should all be regarded as tentative because research specifically aimed at confirming them is needed. Moreover, this new research should be done in the context of answering even broader questions aimed at evaluating and improving prevalence studies of sexual abuse.

For example, any study comparing the interview mode of administration with the self-administered questionnaire should also look at the question of telephone interviewing. Telephone surveys achieve enormous cost savings over household surveys, and although many people harbor a strong prejudice against telephone interviewing, the methodological data in other subject areas have not in general found it to be inferior. However, with a topic as sensitive as sexual abuse, it is not clear whether or not telephone interviewing can achieve the rapport and sense of individual responsibility that may lie behind the success of face-to-face interviews. Two of the telephone interview studies of sexual abuse to date have produced quite low rates, but this may stem from other factors. The one national telephone survey (Lewis, 1985) is promising, but a full report on its methodology is not yet available. If telephone interviews could be used in sexual abuse research it would be a boon to the field. Further research is needed to see if telephone interviews, done well, can consistently generate prevalence rates equivalent to those of face-to-face interviews.

More research is also needed about question choice and question wording. Although multiple questions seem preferable to single questions, it is not yet clear just which combination of multiple questions works the best. It may be that certain types of specific questions (such as about family members or about unwanted fondling) tap the realms that are least likely to come to awareness with general screens. Given the need for economy in virtually all surveys, research should also try to determine the smallest number of specific questions that can elicit the most reports. The survey research literature also shows important effects of question wording and length (Bradburn, 1983). Investigators in designing screens need to experiment with preambles, with the use of different words for various sexual activities and sexual organs, and with questions of different length.

There are several other aspects of the interview besides the specific screen questions that may also make a difference in the level of candor. For example, how much difference do the attitudes and knowledge of interviewers make? Are respondents affected by how the goals and the subject of the study are presented, and by how much they are told about the study at the time they are recruited? Does placement at the beginning, middle, or end of the interview affect the number of revelations? Is candor about sexual abuse affected by the subject matter that precedes it in the interview? Methodological studies have demonstrated that many of these factors, such as interviewer attitudes, reminders about honesty, placement of questions, and prior subject matter, do make a difference. How they affect surveys related to sexual abuse has not yet been shown.

In general, it would be of great assistance to research on sexual abuse if the problem of underreporting could be broken down and analyzed in its component parts. Conceptually, underreporting of sexual abuse can be seen as having at least four components: (1) experiences that are blocked and not accessible to retrieval, (2) experiences that are partially forgotten but retrievable with the right prompting, (3) experiences that are in memory but are not defined according to the terms referred to in survey questions and (4) experiences that are in memory but are not volunteered due to embarrassment or to other conscious withholding.

Each of these components calls for a different strategy. The first problem, unfortunately, is not solvable within the confines of a survey approach. The second problem requires techniques to stimulate memory. The third problem necessitates the development and use of terms that more accurately fit respondents' conceptual frameworks. And the fourth problem calls for techniques to increase comfort and rapport. If we could better understand which of these components is the main source of underreporting, we would be able to address it with the most appropriate strategy. Moreover, we might be better able to understand the type of distortions that underreporting introduces.

Another problem with prevalence studies as they are being done is that, because the respondents are all adults, the information they generate does not necessarily apply to the current cohort of children. It is possible that social conditions may have changed such that the rates of abuse or types of abuse done to people who are now adults may not be the same as what is being done to children today. One way to try to deal with this problem is to concentrate studies on youthful populations. Thus it may make sense to focus studies on cohorts ages 18 to 25, because their childhood experiences are the most proximate. Attempts should also be made to design prevalence studies that talk to children directly. Such an approach would require sensitivity to the dependent position of children within their families, as well as to issues of cognitive development. It remains to be seen whether or not valid information can be elicited from children and, more important, whether or not human subject protections can be met under these conditions, but the possibilities need more consideration.

Another issue in need of research concerns the validity of these retrospective surveys of prevalence. It is well established in survey research that the validity of reports declines with the distance from the event. In most crime surveys, investigators are reluctant to ask about events that occurred more than a year in the past. Unfortunately, because of the difficulty of gathering contemporaneous reports, researchers on childhood sexual abuse have little alternative. But the consequences of gathering information on events that may have happened as many as 30 years ago have not been adequately considered. One question is whether or not accuracy of memory is related to ease of recall. Are the least accurate reports likely to come from the respondents who have to be prodded most to reveal their experiences? If this were true, then the very techniques that might be used to increase reporting might also decrease validity. Studies are needed to check the validity of sexual abuse reports and to associate different interview techniques with degrees of validity as well as with higher prevalence.

Sexual abuse investigators have to deal with an additional question not faced so frequently by other survey researchers. Because the findings of widespread undisclosed child sexual victimization seem so at odds with many people's personal world-views, skeptics have continued to raise the possibility that sexual abuse surveys are eliciting many fabricated or embellished reports of child sexual abuse. However, researchers have found little evidence of this kind of problem (Russell, 1986). Like researchers on other sensitive topics, they find the problem of underreporting because of embarrassment or memory loss much more apparent in dealing with interviewees than fabrication or embellishment. However, because of the persistence of some skepticism, researchers should try to gather as much evidence as possible to evaluate this concern.

### *Suggestions for Future Studies*

The issues raised here certainly point to the need for a series of studies specifically directed toward answering methodological questions about sexual abuse prevalence. Among the techniques that might be used on this line of research, we would like to suggest the following:

(1) Studies should be done with experimental designs that systematically vary the mode of administration (such as personal interview, telephone, self-administered questionnaire), the question type, the question length, the question placement, question preambles, interviewer variables, and the way in which the survey is presented. Prevalence rates can be used as the dependent measure, but the studies should also examine whether or not the alternatives affect the types of reports as well as quantity of reports. Possible interaction effects need to be noted.

(2) Studies should consider, especially in pretesting, the use of probes (Belsen, 1981) to gauge a respondent's reactions to specific questions. Thus after a selected question or series of questions about sexual abuse, an item might ask, "How comfortable did you feel in answering the previous question(s)?" These probes need not imply a questioning of respondents' honesty, but simply ask about reactions respondents have. They give some measure of the degree of threat or candor provoked by different questions under different conditions.

(3) Investigators should consider the possibility of intensive laboratory pretesting of questions and protocols, under condi-

tions that allow for lengthy introspection and debriefing. Respondents could be interviewed in depth about the precise meaning questions have for them and about the precise cognitive processes they go through to "search for" answers. They may be asked to reflect on all the sources of discomfort and distractions in the interview process. This may be one of the best ways to find the optimal mix of questions.

(4) Systematic studies can be done about the meaning of key terms such as "sexual abuse" and "child molestation," and this may provide information about how best to define these terms operationally and what types of experiences people are likely to include under each term. For example, Finkelhor and Redfield (1984) and Shrum and Halgin (1984) have used systematically varied vignettes in surveys to assess the common meaning of the term *sexual abuse*. Studies that further define the boundaries of this term are needed.

(5) Studies need to be done on the reliability of reports of sexual abuse. The same individuals need to be questioned at different times to see if they report the same experiences and if they give the same information about the experiences they do report.

(6) One way to investigate the validity of reports is to try to perform a records check. Individuals can be asked whether their abuse experiences were reported to police, social agencies, or health professionals, and a search could be performed for these records. Conversely, with appropriate protections, it might even be possible to try to follow up some years later individuals for whom there are established police or child welfare records to see what proportion will report their abuse in response to the type of survey questions that are currently in use. It is important to recognize that official reports may contain inaccuracies and that some agencies do not retain records for more than a few years. Therefore, when discrepancies are found, it is difficult to determine whether it is the official report or the survey report that is in error.

(7) Another more subjective assessment of validity involves simply asking respondents how confident they are of the information they are providing, in light of the time that has passed

since the event. Although it is routine to ask about details such as age at time of abuse and identity of abuser, no one has ever inquired how confident respondents are about these facts. Although it would not be by any means conclusive, it would carry some weight if it turned out that some high proportion (say, 97%) of respondents felt certain of the details of these events.

## The Future of Prevalence Studies

Many more prevalence studies of sexual abuse are certain to be done, particularly because there is strong demand for such studies by politicians, policymakers, and the news media. The U.S. Congress, for example, when it reauthorized the Child Abuse and Neglect Act in 1984, added a requirement for a new national study of the scope of the child abuse problem, even though the National Center for Child Abuse and Neglect was not enthusiastic about such a study.

This highlights a potential problem. The motivation behind prevalence studies can sometimes be more political than scientific, leading to unnecessary numbers of expensive studies. At the moment, the need is valid because there is just one national study, and estimates from other studies are so divergent. But once prevalence figures have been targeted accurately within a range, knowing if the "real" figure is 5% one way or the other has only marginal scientific value. Thus political considerations should not be allowed to waste money in search of absurdly refined estimates when there are other more important scientific and policy questions that could be of more immediate benefit in addressing the problem. To put prevalence studies in their proper perspective, and at the same time make sure that they are effectively used, we would like to make some recommendations.

First, before many more large-scale prevalence studies are done, money should be invested in the study of methodological issues. We can learn the answers to questions about interviewing mode, question design, and validity by mounting smaller, less expensive studies. These preliminary studies will ensure that the larger-scale studies have more of a payoff and not make mistakes that could invalidate their results. Moreover, money invested in methodology will have additional benefits for other kinds of etiologic and clinical investigations besides prevalence studies.

Second, there is a need for more nationwide prevalence studies. All prior studies but one have been local and therefore lacking in relevance to some national issues. National policy considerations certainly justify other nationwide studies, but only after important methodological issues have been settled.

Third, prevalence studies are currently well justified if they are focused on looking for differences in rates and characteristics of abuse in various population subgroups. For example, although we have data on black-white differences, we could use more studies on the question of whether or not there are differences among other ethnic subgroups. We could also use more studies to determine if there are regional, state, and urban-rural variations. Rates for states or SMSAs (standard metropolitan statistical areas) could be used in ecological studies that might give insight about the social correlates of sexual abuse.

Fourth, other scientific and policy questions should be built into prevalence studies. An obvious example is to do prevalence studies that also examine the long-term mental health effects of sexual abuse. All these goals could be accomplished within one sophisticated national prevalence study.

A matter for consideration is whether or not sexual abuse prevalence studies can be incorporated into other types of large-scale survey efforts. It might be possible, for example, to gather prevalence figures on sexual abuse in the National Crime Victimization Survey, which interviews approximately 60,000 individuals every year, or the National Health Survey, or the National Youth Survey. However, there are some serious questions about whether or not this is feasible, especially because some of the available studies that have grafted sexual abuse questions onto other surveys (Miller, 1976; Burnam, 1985) have seemed quite ineffective. One concern is that asking about sexual abuse in the context of other topics, such as crime in the NCVS, may limit and distort the responses. Another concern is that such an approach does not give respondents adequate preparation for being asked about sexual abuse. However, the idea of piggybacking is attractive because of the cost saving and the generation of trend data from repeated waves. Even though it may be a slim possibility, feasibility studies should be done to explore it.

## Conclusion

Of all the research on sexual abuse, the results from the prevalence studies have been the most impressive. Ten years ago most clinicians, policymakers, and social scientists doubted that people would be willing to report histories of sexual abuse to survey researchers. Since then it has become clear that people will not only report such histories, but also that they will do so in large numbers. This discovery has made possible whole new research agendas. Many questions about the causes of sexual abuse, the effects of sexual abuse, trends over time, and the connection between sexual abuse and a variety of other social problems are now closer than ever to scientific resolution as a result of prevalence studies. Having established that the task of asking about histories of sexual abuse is feasible, the next step is to refine what has been done, and push on to the next stage. In so doing, social science is making available a powerful tool to aid in the understanding, prevention, and treatment of a serious social problem.

### Appendix 1.A: Questions Used in Surveys to Elicit Histories of Sexual Abuse

**Badgley et al. (1984)**

For this section, we define the sex parts of your body as:

— a *vagina* is a woman's sexual part of her body
— a *penis* is a man's sexual part of his body

— a *crotch* is the area between a person's legs
— an *anus* is a person's rear opening
— the *buttocks* are a person's seat or bottom

Has anyone ever *exposed* the sex parts of their body to you when you didn't want it?

Has anyone ever *threatened* to have sex with you when you didn't want this?

Has anyone ever *touched* the sex parts of your body when you didn't want this?

Has anyone ever *tried to have sex* with you when you didn't want this, or *sexually attacked you*?

## Bagley and Ramsay (in press)

When you were a child (up to the age of 16) did you ever experience a serious sexual assault by an older person?

## Burnam (1985)

In your lifetime, has anyone ever tried to pressure or force you to have sexual contact? By sexual contact I mean their touching your sexual parts, your touching their sexual parts, or sexual intercourse.

How many times did this happen before you were 16 years of age?

## Finkelhor (1979)

It is now generally realized that most people have sexual experiences as children and while they are still growing up. Some of these are with friends and playmates, and some with relatives and family members. Some are very upsetting and painful, and some are not. Some influence people's later lives and sexual experiences, and some are practically forgotten. Although these are often important events, very little is actually known about them.

We would like you to try to remember the sexual experiences you had while growing up. By "sexual," we mean a broad range of things, anything from playing "doctor" to sexual intercourse—in fact, anything that might have seemed "sexual" to you.

Did you have any of the following experiences *before the age of 12* (6th grade) (circle any that apply).

    a. An invitation or request to do something sexual.
    b. Kissing and hugging in a sexual way.
    c. Another person showing his/her sex organs to you.
    d. You showing your sex organs to another person.

    e. Another person fondling you in a sexual way.

    f. You fondling another person in a sexual way.

    g. Another person touching your sex organs.

    h. You touching another person's sex organs.

    i. Intercourse, but without attempting penetration.

    j. Intercourse.

    k. Other:

Choose three sexual experiences—or however many up to three—that you had before the age of 12 with other children, including friends, strangers, brothers, sisters, and cousins. Pick the three most important and answer the following questions about them.

Now we want to ask you to think of three sexual experiences—or however many up to three—that you had before the age of 12 with an adult (a person over 16) including strangers, friends, or family members like cousins, aunts, uncles, brothers, sisters, mother, or father. Pick the three most important to you and answer the following questions.

Now we would like you to think of sexual experiences you had after the age of twelve with a family member or relative, including cousins, uncles, aunts, brothers, sisters, grandparents, mother or father, or a guardian or close friend of a parent. (If this relationship was described in a previous section, do not repeat it.) Pick the three most important to you and answer the following questions.

Finally, we would like you to think of any sexual experience that occurred to you after the age of 12, which you did not consent to. That is, a sexual experience which was forced on you, or done against your will, or which you didn't want to happen. (Once again, do not repeat describing a relationship you described earlier.) Pick the three most important and answer the following questions.

### Finkelhor (1984)

Think back to the time when you were growing up, before you were 16 years old. We are interested in any sexual things which may have occurred during that time with someone at least 5 years older than you. These things may have been sexual abuse or may not have been sexual abuse; we are interested in both kinds of things.

During the time before you were 16, were any sexual things done to you or with you by a person at least 5 years older than you?

    1 ___YES                 2 ___ NO

                                        Before you were 16 were any
attempts made to do sexual

things to you by a person at
least 5 years older?

1 ___ YES    2 ___ NO

Do you consider these experiences to have been *sexual abuse*?

## Keckley Market Research (1984)

Thinking back on your own childhood, do you think that you were ever asked
to participate or do anything sexually as a child that you did not want to do or
felt uncomfortable about? (This excludes playing among peers and dates.)

## Kercher and McShane (1984)

"Were you ever sexually abused as a child?"

Earlier in the survey, sexual abuse had been defined as contacts or interactions
between a child and an adult when the child is being used for the sexual stimulation of the perpetrator or another person. Sexual abuse may be committed by
a person under the age of 18 when that person is significantly older than the
victim or when the perpetrator is in the position of power or control over
another child.

## Lewis (1985)

1. When you were a child, can you remember having any experience you
would now consider sexual abuse—like someone trying or succeeding in having any kind of sexual intercourse with you, or anything like that?

2. When you were a child, can you remember having any kind of experience
that you would now consider sexual abuse involving someone touching you,
or grabbing you, or kissing you, or rubbing up against your body either in a
public place or in private—or anything like that?

3. When you were a child, can you remember any kind of experience that you
would now consider sexual abuse involving someone taking nude photographs
of you, or someone exhibiting parts of their body to you, or someone performing some sex act in your presence—or anything like that?

4. When you were a child, can you remember any kind of experience that you
would now consider sexual abuse involving oral sex or sodomy—or anything
like that?

## Miller (1976)

Has anyone ever tried to sexually molest you?

## Murphy (1985)

When you were under 18, were you ever physically or psychologically forced by an adult to engage in any unwanted sexual activity such as unwanted sexual touching of your body or sexual intercourse?

## Russell (1983)

(1) Before you turned 14, were you ever upset by anyone exposing their genitals?

(2) Did anyone ever try or succeed in having any kind of sexual intercourse with you against your wishes before you turned 14?

(3) In those years, did anyone ever try or succeed in getting you to touch their genitals against your wishes (besides anyone you've already mentioned)?

(4) Did anyone ever try or succeed in touching your breasts or genitals against your wishes before you turned 14 (besides anyone you've already mentioned)?

(5) Before you turned 14, did anyone ever feel you, grab you, or kiss you in a way you felt was sexually threatening (besides anyone you've already mentioned)?

(6) Before you turned 14, did you have any (other) upsetting sexual experiences that you haven't mentioned yet?

(7) At any time in your life, have you ever had an unwanted sexual experience with a girl or a woman?

(8) At any time in your life, have you ever been the victim of a rape or attempted rape?

(9) Some people have experienced unwanted sexual advances by someone who had authority over them, such as a doctor, teacher, employer, minister, therapist, policeman, or much older person. Did you ever have any kind of unwanted sexual experience with someone who had authority over you, at any time in your life?

(10) People often don't think about their relatives when thinking about sexual experiences, so the next two questions are about relatives. At any time in your life, has an uncle, brother, father, grandfather, or female relative ever had any kind of sexual contact with you?

(11) At any time in your life, has anyone less closely related to you such as a stepparent, stepbrother, or stepsister, in-law, or first cousin had any kind of sexual contact with you?

(12) In general, have you narrowly missed being sexually assaulted by someone at any time in your life (other than what you have already mentioned)?

(13) And have you ever been in any situation where there was violence or threat of violence, where you were also afraid of being sexually assaulted—again, other than what you (might) have already mentioned?

(14) Can you think of any (other) unwanted sexual experiences (that you haven't mentioned yet)?

## Wyatt (1985)

It is now generally realized that many women, while they were children or adolescents, have had a sexual experience with an adult or someone older than themselves. By sexual, I mean behaviors ranging from someone exposing themselves (their genitals) to you, to someone having intercourse with you. These experiences may have involved a relative, a friend of the family, or a stranger. Some experiences are very upsetting and painful while others are not, and some may have occurred without consent.

Now I'd like you to think back to your childhood and adolescence and remember if you had any sexual experiences with a relative, family friend, or stranger. Describe each experience completely and separately.

(1) During childhood and adolescence, did anyone ever expose themselves (their sexual organs) to you?

(2) During childhood and adolescence, did anyone masturbate in front of you?

(3) Did a relative, family friend or stranger ever touch or fondle your body, including your breasts or genitals, or attempt to arouse you sexually?

(4) During childhood and adolescence, did anyone try to have *you* arouse them, or touch *their* body in a sexual way?

(5) Did anyone rub their genitals against your body in a sexual way?

(6) During childhood and adolescence, did anyone attempt to have intercourse with you?

(7) Did anyone have intercourse with you?

(8) Did you have any other sexual experiences involving a relative, family friend, or stranger?

## *NOTES*

1. The prevalence rate for women 37 and older was computed based on Table 2 in Russell (1983) and Table 4.4 in Russell (1986).

2. Finkelhor (1984) reported no association with education, and a slight, but *not significant*, association with income.

3. Kercher and McShane did include a definition of child sexual abuse in the introduction to their questionnaire, but the question on the participants' own abuse experiences was not presented until the end, at which point the definition may have lost its salience.

# 2

# High-Risk Children

David Finkelhor
Larry Baron

In responding to the problem of child sexual abuse, one of our most pressing tasks is to identify any group of children who may be at high risk. Not only will such identification allow us to focus our prevention efforts where they are most needed, it will also give us valuable new clues about the causes of sexual abuse.

The task of identifying high-risk children is not a simple one, however. Because much sexual abuse is hidden, so are the risk factors. Any characteristic that appears to be common to victims who come to public attention may not apply to the vast number of victims who do not. If most reported sexual abuse victims are from impoverished, disorganized families, for example, is it because these children are at higher risk or simply because these victims are more readily detected?

Community surveys, which disclose relatively large numbers of unreported cases (reviewed in Chapter 1), provide new opportunities to look at the question of risk and vulnerability. It is true that the cases reported in these studies involved adults looking back on their childhood experiences, not children currently being abused. But they do tell about risk factors among a sample of victims that is much more representative than cases coming to the attention of social agencies and police.

In the following review of findings concerning risk factors,[1] we will rely exclusively on studies that employed samples of the general population—either whole communities or students. One crucial feature of these studies is that they also contain built-in comparison groups. (Details on all these studies can be found in Chapter 1.) The whole notion of a "risk factor" requires such a comparison between characteristics of abuse victims and characteristics of nonvictims from the same samples. We will from time to time make reference to a few studies without comparison samples, particularly when these studies are large in scope, but it will be primarily for supporting evidence.

At the outset, it should be said that the prevalence studies are most notable in demonstrating, as we saw in Chapter 1, not who is at high risk, but how large and widely distributed the risk appears to be. It may at one time have been thought that sexual abuse was confined to a small number of children in certain unusual family and social circumstances that might be readily identifiable. However, the findings from the surveys establish conclusively that this is not the case; sexual abuse is prevalent in virtually all social and family circumstances. Nonetheless, it is true that there are some important variations and it is to those that we now turn.

### Sex

Virtually all studies that included men as well as women found higher abuse rates for women. The differences range from more than 4 women for each man in the Minnesota telephone survey (Murphy, 1985) to 1.5 women for each man in one of the more obscure student surveys (Fritz, Stoll, & Wagner, 1981). There is one study listed in Table 1.2 that appears to show higher rates for men than for women (Hamilton, 1929), but it asked very ambiguous screening questions that included much more than sexual abuse; in addition, it is quite old and suffers from many other methodological problems. In general, the studies using the more careful definitions of abuse have tended to find higher proportions of abuse for women compared to

men. The mean ratio of all the eight random sample community
surveys that interviewed both men and women (Badgley et al.,
1984; Burnam, 1985; Finkelhor, 1984; Keckley Market
Research, 1983; Kercher & McShane, 1984; Lewis, 1985;
Miller, 1976; Murphy, 1985) is 2.5 women for every man. This
would translate into an expectation that among all victims 71% are
females and 29% males.

Interestingly, even the biggest differences in the ratio between
the sexes found in the community surveys tend to be lower than
the extreme differences shown in agency-based studies, where
in the past as many as 9 girls have been reported for every boy
(De Francis, 1969). In more recent years, the number of boys
appearing in agency-based studies has increased somewhat. The
National Incidence Study of Child Abuse and Neglect (NC-
CAN, 1981), based on cases known to professionals, and the
American Humane Association study (1981), based on agency-
identified cases, have reported about 5 girls for every boy, or a
distribution of about 83% girls and 17% boys.

However, the degree to which these agency surveys reveal a
smaller proportion of boys than the community studies strongly
suggests that the abuse of boys is still quite underreported. This
is also what clinicians have hypothesized (Woods & Dean,
1984). Boys, it is speculated, are reluctant to admit victimization because it clashes with the expectations of masculinity. The
homosexual character of most abuse of boys may also inhibit
disclosure. And the fact that public stereotypes have focused
primarily on the risk to girls may have made parents and professionals less apt to identify abused boys.

The fact that abuse of boys is underreported has led some to
speculate that boys may, in fact, be abused just as frequently as
girls (Kempe & Kempe, 1984; Plummer, 1984). However, the
consistent data from the surveys cast doubt on this assertion.
Nonetheless, there are those who question these survey findings, wondering whether, even in surveys, boys do not reveal
their abuse or that they are abused in ways that do not show up in
such surveys. We have examined some of these doubts else-

where (Finkelhor & Russell, 1984) and failed to find much merit in them.

Those who think boys are at equal risk frequently cite one study in particular (Tobias & Gordon, 1977), although it is hard to see why it merits attention. In 1977, police in the Detroit metropolitan area, in search of a particular molester, went into public schools and set up a procedure under which children were encouraged to report to their teachers if they had been approached by a potential molester. Actually they were asked, "Boys and girls, sometimes you may be approached by a person who asks directions, a question, takes a picture, offers you a ride, talks of a job, or suggests that you show him a particular place. . . . If anything like this has happened to you, we would like you to stop in and tell Mr. [the presenter] about it." Almost as many boys as girls (363 versus 402) reported incidents (the report called them "offenses") as a result.

It hardly needs to be pointed out that this is not a very good method for gaining information on the prevalence of abuse. Most of what the children were reporting was not sexual abuse at all, but simply "suspicious strangers." Certainly no family or intimate abuse would be reported by young children in this situation. Young boys might well be motivated to overreport to help the police to fight crime. Indeed, the informal data collection procedures of this study even cast doubt on whether it is study at all. In the face of all the other studies of much more scrupulous methodology pointing to differences in the rate of risk between sexes, the Detroit study can hardly be given much weight. The evidence that girls are at higher risk than boys seems clearly established.

Because girls are at higher risk, they have been subject to more attention, study, and analysis. This is unfortunate because it may have contributed to an already mistaken public impression that boys are rarely abused at all. It has resulted also in the collection of substantially fewer data about the abuse of boys. Although some of the studies that we review here had samples of boy victims, most did not analyze risk factors pertaining to boys. It is hoped that this will soon change. For the moment, however, not enough data exist; thus the rest of this review will focus almost exclusively on girls.

## *Age of Child at Onset*

Almost all studies report statistics showing that children are more vulnerable to sexual abuse starting in the preadolescent period between ages 8 and 12. The mean or median ages of onset stated by several of the survey studies are as follows: Finkelhor (1984), girls 10.2, boys 11.2; Russell (1983), girls 11.2; Wyatt (1985), girls 11.2.

However, mean or median statistics are not the best for conveying the true distribution of risk because they do not show the relative vulnerability at different ages. Moreover, they are affected by the choice of an upper limit (Russell, 1983, with an upper limit of 18, shows an inflated mean or median compared to Finkelhor's 1981 study, which used 16). Thus we have constructed Table 2.1 to illustrate risk on a year-by-year basis. In Table 2.1, studies are listed so as to show the risk per 100 for each year of age. When studies reported the exact number of cases that occurred for each year, these figures were simply divided by the total N and multiplied by 100 to obtain the risk per 100 for that year. When studies had only data grouped for a range of years, the number of cases in each group was divided by the total N and by the number of years in each group to obtain an estimate of the risk for that year. Then a summated average was created for all six studies (shown in the last row of Table 2.1) simply by averaging the rates for all studies that reported cases for that age.

The pattern in Table 2.1 shows an increase in vulnerability at ages 6-7 and another very dramatic increase at age 10. Ages 10 through 12 appear to be years of particularly acute risk, when children are victimized at more than double the average rate.

However, looking at studies individually, there are certain discrepancies. Four of the studies (Finkelhor, 1979, 1984; Fro-

## TABLE 2.1
## Rate of Female Childhood Sexual Abuse by Age of Onset

| Studies | | | | | | | | | Age of Onset | | | | | | | | | |
|---|---|---|---|---|---|---|---|---|---|---|---|---|---|---|---|---|---|---|
| | 1 | 2 | 3 | 4 | 5 | 6 | 7 | 8 | 9 | 10 | 11 | 12 | 13 | 14 | 15 | 16 | 17 | 18 |
| Finkelhor (1979) (N = 530) | | | | 1.06 | (17) 1.06 | 1.06 | 1.69 | (27) 1.69 | 1.69 | 3.52 | (56) 3.52 | 3.52 | .89 | .89 | (19) .89 | .89 | | |
| Finkelhor (1984) (N = 334) | | | | (1) .29 | (6) 1.79 | (5) 1.49 | (9) 2.69 | (2) .59 | (4) 1.19 | (12) 3.59 | (9) 2.69 | (6) 1.79 | (4) 1.19 | | (5) 1.49 | (2) .59 | | |
| Fromuth (1983) (N = 482) | .06 | (1) .06 | .06 | 1.03 | (15) 1.03 | 1.03 | 1.86 | (27) 1.86 | 1.86 | 4.97 | (72) 4.97 | 4.97 | 1.24 | 1.24 | (24) 1.24 | 1.24 | | |
| Keckley (1983) (N = 320) | .43 | .43 | (7) .43 | .43 | .43 | 1.93 | 1.93 | (31) 1.93 | 1.93 | 1.93 | .70 | .70 | (9) .70 | .70 | .15 | .15 | (2) .15 | .15 |
| Lewis (1985) (N = 1374) | .64 | .64 | (53) .64 | (14) .64 | (15) .64 | (26) .64 | (34) 2.47 | (41) 2.98 | (26) 1.89 | (56) 4.07 | (30) 2.18 | (53) 3.85 | (39) 2.18 | (15) 1.09 | (8) .58 | .55 | (23) .55 | .55 |
| Russell (1983) (N = 930) | | (2) .21 | (3) .32 | (14) 1.50 | (15) 1.61 | (26) 2.79 | (22) 2.36 | (23) 2.47 | (23) 2.47 | (42) 4.51 | (31) 3.33 | (76) 8.17 | (105) 11.29 | (42) 4.51 | (65) 6.98 | (81) 8.70 | (70) 7.52 | |
| Summated average | .37 | .33 | .36 | .82 | 1.09 | 1.49 | 2.16 | 1.92 | 1.83 | 3.76 | 2.89 | 3.83 | 2.91 | 1.68 | 1.88 | 2.02 | 2.74 | .35 |

muth, 1983; Lewis, 1985) show particularly high vulnerability in the preadolescent period (10 to 12) with a decline in the adolescent period. Russell's (1983) study, however, shows continuing or higher vulnerability in the adolescent period. Some of this difference is due to definitions. Russell included certain types of peer aggressions in the tallies, whereas Finkelhor (1979, 1984) and Fromuth (1983) included only experiences with older partners (see Chapter 1). Moreover, both Finkelhor (1979) and Fromuth (1983) made criteria for abuse in adolescence more restricted. This tells us that the distribution for age of onset is affected by what types of experiences are being counted.

All the studies do agree about lower rates of vulnerability for children under 6–7. Here again, however, methodological considerations urge some caution. Clinicians have pointed out how easy it is for the memories of early sexual abuse experiences to be forgotten and repressed, especially when they occur to children without a cognitive framework for interpreting their experiences. It is possible that the lower rates for younger children may simply reflect a greater loss of memory of these experiences.

In discussing the age distributions for victims of sexual abuse, it is also important to include some comment about statistics that come from studies of reported cases. In general such studies show much higher means or median ages for abused children than do the studies using survey methodology. For example, in the National Incidence Study of Child Abuse and Neglect, 60% of the sexually abused children were 12 or older. It must be remembered, though, that most studies using reported cases record the age of the child *at the time of the reporting*, which is in a great many cases some years after the *onset* of the abuse. Moreover, it is probable that older children are more likely to reveal abuse, thus biasing upward the ages of children in studies of reported cases. Thus the discrepancies between the clinical and survey studies are less contradictory than they might seem.

## Social Class

Child abuse in general has been thought to be more prevalent in lower social classes. But child welfare advocates generally have found this a politically unappealing stereotype and have tried to emphasize the fact that child abuse occurs in all social strata. For some writers, this emphasis has turned into a claim that child abuse is *unrelated* to social class. Empirical studies repeatedly have undercut these claims, however, finding rather strong associations between class and physical abuse (Pelton, 1981; Straus, Gelles, & Steinmetz, 1980). Although abuse is certainly not limited to the lower classes, as the stereotype might suggest, to most researchers it makes sense that the frustrations of poverty, joblessness, lack of education, and inadequate housing contribute to the conditions that increase violence toward children.

Child *sexual* abuse, however, may be an entirely different story. The most representative surveys of child sexual abuse in the community have been unable to find any relationship between sexual abuse and the social class of the family in which the victims grew up. For example, Russell's (1986) probability sample in San Francisco showed no association between sexual abuse and measures of father's education or occupation. Peters's (1984) community study of white and black women in Los Angeles could find no relationship between sexual abuse and either parental education or the Hollingshead measure of social class.[2] In Finkelhor's (1984) Boston survey, the victimized children did not come disproportionately from families at any income level. And Miller's (1976) survey, a probability sample of Illinois adolescents, showed only a nonsignificant trend in an unexpected direction: 24% of the girls from upper-middle-class families were victimized versus 17% of the lower-class girls.

Other retrospective community studies looked at victimization rates according to respondents' *current* social class standing and also failed to find any higher rates in lower social statuses. Unfortunately, current SES measures (such as current income or education) are not the best way to see if social class is a risk factor for abuse, because the issue at stake is whether or not coming from a lower-class background as a child (better measured by parents' education, occupation, or income) raises the risk for sexual abuse. If anything, having been abused might be a cause of downward social mobility as an adult, creating a misleading association between abuse and social class. Nonetheless, studies looking at current measures do not find such an association. The Nashville telephone survey (Keckley Market Research, 1983) showed a nonsignificant trend for higher rates not among low-income, but among the middle-income, $15,000–$35,000 group. The *Los Angeles Times* survey (Lewis, 1985; Timnick, 1985a) found somewhat higher rates among high school graduates and people with white-collar jobs. Although Finkelhor (1984) found somewhat higher rates among those adult women with current family incomes under $10,000, the finding was not quite significant. The conclusion from these community-based studies is that sexual abuse is not disproportionately prevalent in lower social classes.

However, two student-based studies have found some variation by social class. Finkelhor (1984) found higher rates among female students from families with incomes under $10,000, with blue-collar fathers, and with poorly educated mothers (33%, 26%, and 38%, respectively, compared to an overall rate of 19% for the sample). Landis (1956) also reported higher rates among students whose fathers were employed in public service, skilled, semiskilled, and unskilled jobs compared to those with business-class fathers (although no mention is given of the magnitude of difference). Fromuth (1983), in another student study, found no social class association, however. It is very likely that the social class structure in student populations is complicated by the question of who gets selected into college. Students are not the best samples to test for social class relationships.

A positive relationship exists between sexual abuse and social class among reported cases, too, but here again the data are not well suited for determining the class linkages. It is generally acknowledged that the child welfare system is heavily biased toward identifying abuse in lower social strata. The data, of course, show this bias. The National Incidence Study of Child Abuse and Neglect (NCCAN, 1981) found that 38% of all sexual abuse cases known to professionals came from families with annual incomes less than $7,000, whereas only 17% of American families had incomes in this category. This is about the same lower-class bias as for physical abuse (35% of cases from incomes less than $7,000), but not as much as for child neglect (53% of cases are from the poorest bracket). Similarly, the American Humane Association (Trainor, 1984) reports that, although only 11.9% of U.S. families were receiving public assistance in 1980, 29.3% of officially reported sexual abuse cases in 1982 came from such families. Interestingly, the report notes that there has been a marked decline since 1976 (from 39.8%) in the percentage of sexual abuse cases that involved welfare recipients. Unfortunately, these data probably tell us more about the system for identifying child abuse than they do about the true social class distribution of sexual abuse.

The currently available data on sexual abuse suggest that sexual abuse and social class are unrelated. The most representative community surveys suggest little connection (Russell, 1986; Miller, 1976; Peters, 1984). The strong overrepresentation of the poor among reported cases is readily accounted for as a reporting bias in that system.

An argument could be made that the surveys are masking a social class connection. It is possible that women from higher social classes are more candid with middle-class interviewers and report more of their abuse, thus creating an artificial parity with less candid lower-class women. But there is no evidence for this specific effect, and not much inferential support for it from the methodological studies of survey research.

### Ethnicity

Across the board, studies have consistently failed to find any black-white differences in rates of sexual abuse. Even among reported cases, in which it is thought that blacks suffer from a labeling bias (O'Toole, Turbott, & Nalepka, 1983), the percentage of black cases is no more than the percentage of blacks in the population as a whole (NCCAN, 1981). In four community surveys (Keckley Market Research, 1983; Kercher & McShane, 1984; Russell, 1986; Wyatt, 1985), rates among whites and blacks have been very similar. In the only survey showing any black preponderance (Miller, 1976), 18% for blacks and 13% for whites, the difference disappeared when controlling for city size and other demographic factors.

Among reported cases, sexual abuse has consistently been the type of abuse in which blacks have the lowest representation. In the American Humane Association National records (Trainor, 1984), for example, black families accounted for 15.3% of sexual abuse cases, almost exactly their proportion in the American population. In the National Incidence Study (NCCAN, 1981), the percentage of blacks was 11%, somewhat below their representation in the population. This is especially significant considering that discrimination, poverty, and stereotyping usually influence professionals to more readily label black families as abusive.

Wyatt's (1985) study, based on a community survey, and the related follow-up by Peters (1984) were specifically designed to look at possible black-white differences, and were remarkable in the similarities they found. Wyatt (1985) showed no overall difference in rates of abuse or types of abuse, and Peters (1984) found few differences in either risk factors or effects. The studies did show that because of different family patterns in the black community, certain factors associated with vulnerability in the white community—such as separation from father, changes in caretakers, and mother's labor force participation—did not operate in the black community (Peters, 1984). However, overall the studies were remarkable in the similarities they showed between sexual abuse in the black and white communities.

Although studies have found no black-white differences, there are hints of possible differences for other ethnic groups.

Kercher and McShane (1984), for example, in a mail survey of Texas driver's license holders, found victimization rates of 21.7% for Hispanic women, compared to 9.8% for whites and 10.4% for blacks. Russell's (1986) findings concerning Hispanic women give some possible support to the Texas study. Although not statistically significant, Russell's overall rates for incestuous victimization for Hispanic women are somewhat higher than for the sample as a whole (20% versus 16% for the whole sample), and in the case of father-daughter incest, Hispanic women have a rate of 7.5% compared to 4.5% for the sample as a whole. Russell's data also show low rates (this time statistically significant) for Asian and Jewish women, only 8% and 10% of whom were incestuously victimized. Ethnic differences should be the subject of further analysis.

### *Social Isolation*

Social isolation is a risk factor of interest to sexual abuse researchers for two reasons. First, there are anecdotal reports of concentrations of sexually abusive families in rural areas (Summit & Kryso, 1978). Second, social isolation has proven to be correlated in some research with other forms of child abuse and neglect (Garbarino & Stocking, 1980).

However, rural residence has been associated with more sexual abuse in only one study, and in two it has actually been associated with less. Finkelhor (1984) found a significantly high rate (44%) among the college student women who had grown up on farms. Russell (1986) also found rates of incestuous abuse somewhat higher among women from both rural (17%) and town (20%) backgrounds, compared to city-raised women (14%), but the relationship did not reach statistical significance. On the other hand, Miller's (1976) results were completely opposite, with adolescents from farm communities reporting the lowest rates (10%) compared to adolescents from urban (15%) and suburban (19%) areas. Wyatt (1985) also found higher rates among women raised in urban areas. So the idea that sexual abuse is more common in rural areas seems doubtful.

However, another aspect of social isolation has been confirmed empirically by three studies: Sexual abuse victims appear to be isolated among their peers. Finkelhor (1984) found that women with two or fewer friends at age 12 had more experiences of sexual abuse. Fromuth (1983) confirmed this in her student sample with the exact same question. Peters (1984) found higher rates associated with women who reported either lack of closeness with peers or lack of closeness with siblings. (The peers were a better predictor with white women and the siblings were with black women.) In fact, lack of closeness with siblings was one of three variables that best predicted sexual abuse in Peters's multivariate analysis of all risk factors.

A plausible hypothesis is that social isolation is related to abuse. If children have few friends, this may create a need for contact and friendship on which sexual abusers can capitalize. Friendless children may be easy marks. However, the friendlessness found in the three studies may, unfortunately, be the *result* of having been victimized rather than a risk factor. Children who are being abused by family members are often prohibited from having friends. Children who are feeling shame and stigma as a result of having suffered victimization often isolate themselves from others. At age 12, the year asked about in both the Finkelhor and the Fromuth studies, more than half of the respondents had already suffered their victimizations. This casts doubt on whether the friendlessness was truly a risk factor. Social isolation may indeed be a risk factor for sexual victimization, but we should find other, more sensitive, variables with which to measure it.

### Parental Absence and Unavailability

In general, the background factors that have shown the strongest connection to sexual abuse, both across and within studies, have been those relating to parents and family. We have subdivided these into four categories: (1) parental absence and unavailability, (2) poor relationship with parents, (3) parental conflict, and (4) presence of a stepfather. However, it should be kept in mind that these categories may all be measuring aspects of the same issue.

In regard to parental absence, seven studies have found higher vulnerability to sexual abuse among women who *lived without their natural mothers or fathers* at some time during childhood. In Finkelhor's (1984) student study, having lived apart from a natural mother was the most powerful risk factor, resulting in an almost threefold higher risk. Herman and Hirschman (1981) found separation from mother to be a serious risk for father-daughter incest. However, these findings were not replicated by Fromuth (1983) or Peters (1984). Finkelhor, Fromuth, and Peters all found that girls who had ever lived without their natural *fathers* were at higher risk, although Peters's finding applied only to white women. Russell (1986) also found higher rates among girls living with their biological mothers and no fathers, but the finding applied only to extrafamily abuse. Similarly, Miller (1976) found elevated risk for adolescents who were currently living without their fathers or without both natural parents. Bagley and Ramsay (in press) found that any separation from either parent for a period of six months or more before the age of 16 was correlated with the likelihood of being a victim. This is an impressive number of studies with positive findings on the question of parental absence.

Another variable that in some of its forms might be related to parental absence is the *mother's employment outside the home*. At least four studies have found this related to sexual abuse (Fromuth, 1983; Landis, 1956; Peters, 1984; Russell, 1986). Peters found the relationship held only for the white women, and Russell, whose findings were short of statistical significance for the whole sample, found that the mother's employment increased risk significantly in households with step-fathers. Finkelhor (1984) did not find any risk for mother's employment.

Parental unavailability may also be indicated by a *disabled or ill* parent. Finkelhor (1984) found higher rates of sexual victimization among girls who reported that their mothers were often ill. Peters (1984) reported somewhat higher rates (only at p = .10) for girls with one parent who was disabled by substance addiction, emotional problems, or physical ailments. Looking specifically at father-daughter incest families, Herman and Hirschman (1981) found significantly more mothers who were seriously ill (most commonly due to alcoholism, depression, or psychosis) and also mothers who were burdened with many children and pregnancies. However, Fromuth (1983), using the same variables as Finkelhor, did not confirm any association between sexual abuse and mother's illness.

## *Poor Relationship with Parents*

As impressive as the findings concerning parental absences are the findings concerning poor relationships with parents, particularly with the mother. This has been substantiated also by a large number of studies (six) and is one of the most consistent findings to date. Landis (1956) was one of the first to observe that molested women reported a more distant relationship with their mothers. Such women also were less likely to mention their mothers as their primary source of sex information. Finkelhor (1984) found in his sample of college students that those women at higher risk were the ones who said they were not close to their mothers or received little affection from their mothers or fathers. The same was true if they rated their mothers high on a scale of sexual punitiveness. All of these factors, except maternal affection, made an independent contribution in a multivariate analysis of risk factors. Peters (1984) found in her multivariate analysis that not being close to mother was the variable that was most predictive of sexual abuse. Miller (1976) also used multivariate analysis and found that poor relationships with either parent were potent correlates of abuse. Bagley and Ramsay (in press) showed an impressive correlation of .56 between sexual abuse and the EMBU, a well-validated instrument for measuring a child's recollections of harsh, punitive, and emotionally cold parenting.

One partially dissenting finding was that of Fromuth (1983), who found that only 4% of the victims and 2% of the nonvictims reported having distant relationships with their mothers. The wording of the question was perhaps not sensitive enough to discriminate problematic relationships from satisfactory ones in Fromuth's sample. However, even Fromuth found a significant association on the question of closeness with father. She also found higher risk if the father had ever been physically abusive toward the child. In another dissenting finding, Gruber and Jones (1984) actually found poor relations with mother to be a *protective* factor in a multivariate analysis of risk; but their sample consisted of 20 victimized and 21 nonvictimized girls in a delinquency intervention program, most of whom came from extremely deprived family environments. Altogether, the collection of positive findings suggests that having a poor relationship with one's parents is one of the most common correlates of sexual abuse.

### Conflict Between Parents

Besides reporting poor relationships *with* their parents, sexual abuse victims are also more likely to report poor relationships *between* their parents. Five out of five studies confirm such a risk factor. Landis (1956) found a high proportion of unhappy marriages in the families of victims of what he called "child participated" experiences. Gruber and Jones (1983), using discriminant function analysis, found poor parental relations to be the most potent predictor of sexual abuse among their group of delinquent girls. Finkelhor (1984) found that rates of sexual abuse were higher among the college student women who reported that their parents either had unhappy marriages or showed little mutual affection. Fromuth (1983) and Peters (1984) both confirmed Finkelhor's findings.

All of these findings—on parental absence, poor relationships with parents, and conflict between parents—seem to point strongly toward the idea that sexually victimized girls have disturbances in their relationships with their parents. The confirmation of the relationship through multivariate analysis in three studies adds particular weight to the idea. But the findings are subject to a number of interpretations.

One hypothesis that has to be taken very seriously is that when victimization occurs, it alienates a girl from her parents. The clinical literature is full of accounts of how victims feel estranged from their families because they have had to keep the abuse secret, or how they feel betrayed by the failure of parents to come to their support when they reveal it (Meiselman, 1978). Certainly, women who are abused by their fathers would have reason to report distance from a father. (In father-daughter incest, the daughters are often treated as special at first, but, as daughters try to extricate themselves from the abusive situation, bitterness ensues.) If the alienation is a result of the abuse, then it can hardly be considered a risk factor.

Other findings may also be interpreted as the result of abuse rather than a risk factor, particularly with intrafamily abuse. Girls who are abused may be more likely to live without a parent if they, or an offending parent, are removed from the home. If a father is removed, a mother may have to go out to work. If a girl is being abused by a father, she may certainly perceive her parents as having an unhappy relationship.

However, many of the associations related to family disturbances—parental absence, parental conflict, and poor relationships to parents—also make a great deal of sense as risk factors. It is interesting that in the studies that have measured them, variables such as closeness to mother are associated with extrafamilial as well as intrafamilial abuse (Finkelhor, 1984; Miller, 1976). It is unfortunate that more of the studies have not made sure that the family condition under question existed prior to the time that the abuse occurred.

If these clusters of variables are risk factors, there are at least two major dynamics that explain the relationship. One concerns supervision. When a child is missing a parent, has a poor relationship with a parent, or has parents who are hostile to one another, the child may be less well supervised and thus less well protected from predatory adults. The finding that abused girls received less sex education from their mothers (Finkelhor, 1984) is related here, because giving sex education may be one of the ways concerned mothers help protect their children. Although the omission may be unintentional or even well intended, not receiving sex education is a form of not being supervised and not being protected.

A second possibility is that the poor parental relationships are connected to sexual abuse through emotional disturbances in the child. If a child is unhappy, emotionally deprived, or needy, then she may be more conspicuous and more vulnerable to an adult interested in molesting her. She may be more amenable to the offers of friendship, appreciation, and the material rewards that the offender makes, and she may be less able to stand up for herself. Moreover, she may be more afraid to tell her parents about the abuse, because she has reason to believe she will not be supported. This second dynamic does not necessarily preclude the first. In fact, it seems likely that emotional disturbance and lack of supervision are both at work.

### *Stepfather Families*

Besides parental absence, conflict, and lack of support, another parental factor—the presence of a non-biologically related father—has been discussed as a risk factor for sexual abuse. Four out of six studies examining this factor have confirmed its significance. Three of these studies—Miller (1976), Finkelhor (1980), and Gruber and Jones (1983)—found that having a stepfather increased a girl's risk for all types of sexual abuse. Russell (1986) found an increased risk for father-daughter abuse only. Fromuth (1983) and Peters (1984) did not find any increased risk for any type of abuse. Although most of these studies, as mentioned earlier, indicate that simple father absence is a risk factor, both Finkelhor (1984) and Gruber and Jones (1983) used multivariate analysis and showed that the presence of a stepfather further augmented the risk.

Russell's (1986) dramatic figures on the higher rate of abuse at the hands of stepfathers are illustrative of the risk. Whereas only 2.3% of daughters growing up with natural fathers had been abused by them, 17% of the daughters growing up with stepfathers had been abused by them. Moreover, the types of abuse committed by stepfathers were more serious (involving more intercourse, fellatio, cunnilingus, analingus, and anal intercourse) and more violent. This corroborates findings from samples of reported cases, such as the National Incidence Study, in which the absolute amount of stepfather abuse sometimes exceeds the amount of natural father abuse (Study Findings, 1981).

These studies appear to point to higher risk for girls who have stepfathers, and several explanations for this risk have been offered. One is that the taboos against stepfather-stepdaughter sexual contact are less stringent and therefore have less of a deterrent effect. Another is that natural fathers are more inhibited from incestuous contact as a result of a period of parent-child bonding that occurs when the child is quite small (S. Parker, personal communication, January 1985). The intense dependency of the child during this period or perhaps the father's involvement in diapering and bodily care may block later sexualization of the relationship. Stepfathers who have not experienced this type of bonding may be more apt to see the child as a possible sexual partner.

Nonetheless, studies are not clear on whether or not the higher risk for girls with stepfathers is explained entirely by the greater predatory behavior of these stepfathers. In Finkelhor's (1980) research, girls with stepfathers were victimized at greater rates by other men as well. Finkelhor suggested that dating mothers may bring home sexually opportunistic men who exploit the daughters. Stepfathers may also bring steprelatives into the family who do not feel so constrained about becoming sexually involved with daughters. And perhaps stepfathers are less concerned and protective of stepdaughters when friends or relatives make sexual overtures to them.

The vulnerability of girls in stepfather families is clearly an issue of urgent public policy importance, given the current increase in the number of such families (Glick, 1979), and yet more research is needed to confirm clearly and even specify the risk. One caution about some of the findings reported here is that they may be historically outdated. They are based mostly on studies of women who grew up before the 1970s, when fewer children had stepfathers. It may have been very different to live in a stepfather family in an era when there were few such families compared to the current era, when such families are much more commonplace. Assuming that this vulnerability does show up even in studies of current cohorts of children, it would support a crucial new direction for social policy. A case might be made that families containing stepfathers should be the target of sexual abuse prevention efforts.

### *Summary of Risk Factors*

This review of findings concerning risk factors has been fruitful in identifying some emerging consistencies across studies. A number of background factors seem to be associated clearly with higher risk in several studies (see Table 2.2).

Not surprisingly, girls are at higher risk than boys. Also, preadolescents appear to be more at risk than either younger or older children. Girls with few friends in childhood report more abuse, but this may be an effect of abuse and not a risk factor. The strongest and most consistent associations across the studies concerned the parents of abused children. Girls who are victimized are (1) more likely to have lived without their natural fathers, (2) more likely to have mothers who were employed outside the home, (3) more likely to have mothers who were disabled or ill, (4) more likely to witness conflict between their parents, and (5) more likely to report a poor relationship with one of their parents. Girls who lived with stepfathers were also at increased risk for abuse.

**TABLE 2.2**
**Risk Factors for Child Sexual Abuse:**
**Summary of Empirical Findings from Retrospective Surveys**

| Factor | Studies Finding Association/ Studies Looking for Association | Conclusion |
|---|---|---|
| Female gender | 11/12 | girls higher risk than boys |
| Preadolescence (10-12 peak) | 5/7 | depends on definition of abuse |
| Lower SES | 2/10 | no association with social class in community studies; only student studies found relationship |
| Blacks | 0/5 | black-white risk equal |
| Rural residence | 1/4 | uncertain |
| Urban residence | 2/4 | uncertain |
| Few friends in childhood | 3/3 | possible risk factor, but possibly *effect* of abuse |
| Ever lived without natural mother | 3/6 | mixed |
| Ever lived without natural father | 6/6 | strong association |
| Mother's employment outside home | 4/5 | strong association |
| Mother disabled or ill | 2/4 | possible association |
| Poor relationship with parent | 6/7 | strong association; three studies confirm in multivariate analysis |
| Parents in conflict | 5/5 | strong association |
| Stepfather families | 4/6 | strong association |

The studies also seem to agree that two factors do *not* increase risk for abuse. Blacks have no higher rates of abuse than whites; and girls from lower social strata are at no more risk than others. In fact, sexual abuse appears to be very democratic in its social class distribution. The studies have demonstrated strong agreement on these points.

## Recommendations for Future Studies

Considering that the study of child sexual abuse is still in its early stages, it is impressive that there are so many convergent findings concerning risk factors. But the agreement on certain points should not obscure the fact that these findings are subject to many caveats. It also should not obscure the fact that to confirm fully the implications from current research, we need more research of much greater depth and sophistication. In this section, we make a variety of suggestions about the direction future research should take.

### Better Specification of Risk Factors

The research reviewed here has concentrated on confirming the importance of certain risk factors such as stepfamilies, social isolation, and poor parental relationships. But, as was pointed out earlier, we must be careful to acknowledge all that is still uncertain about these findings. First, it needs to be substantiated that these are actually *risk factors*, that they precede the sexual abuse and are not simply the result of abuse. Second, why and how these risk factors create risk must be ascertained. This can be done in part by making the variables more precise. What is meant, for example, by "poor relationship with one's parents"? This variable needs to be broken down into such specific categories as "parent did not spend enough time with the child," "parent had negative feelings toward the child," "parent used restrictive or abusive parenting practices," and so forth. In addition, what is meant by "parental conflict"? Does this mean "violence between parents," "conflict over money," "conflict over child care"? This also needs to be specified.

In some cases, the risk factor identified may be a proxy for another variable that is the actual risk factor. Is "rural residence," for example, a proxy for "less supervision"? Is "few friends in childhood" a proxy for "feeling lonely"? Given that some of the identified risk factors, such as having a stepfather, may create risk through various causal sequences ("more predatory men in household" and "alienation from mother"), some additional variables that specify these sequences need to be added to the analysis. All this will improve our understanding of how these risk factors operate.

### New Classes of Risk Variables

In addition to better specification of already identified risk factors, whole sets of new risk factors also need to be considered. For example, no one has examined whether or not physical characteristics of children—their size, their weight, their strength, or their attractiveness—make a difference in their risk for abuse. Similarly, children's temperamental characteristics— whether they are passive, aggressive, introverted, or extroverted—may play a role. There are also many psychological variables that have not yet been examined, such qualities as the child's locus of control and self-esteem. As a comparison, it should be noted that the literature on *rape* avoidance found that women who were stronger and more athletic were less likely to be raped (Bart, 1981). Such factors might have pertinence to the risk for child sexual abuse. Various cognitive factors also need to be considered: Does the level of a child's sex education influence his or her vulnerability? What about a child's understanding of child molestation? What about a child's beliefs about adults, obedience, and his or her own rights? Intelligence may also play a role; children with more intelligence may have better coping skills and might be able to avoid sexual victimization. Before the field gets too narrow in its concerns, researchers need to brainstorm about a wide range of other possible risk factors to test.

### Evaluation of Smaller Demographic Subgroups

In the analysis of possible sociodemographic risk factors, such large categories as black, white, rural, urban, lower class, and middle class have been considered. But a much more detailed analysis of subgroups is also required. Perhaps risk is particularly high or low, as some preliminary findings suggest, in various ethnic populations, such as Orientals, Hispanics, and Native Americans. Moreover, rural populations are not uniform; perhaps risk is particularly high among rural populations in particular parts of the country. Certain specialized family structures need to be assessed, such as children who live in single-father families (a rather small subgroup of all children), as well as children who live with adopted parents and children who live in institutions. Certainly given recent public concern we need to assess whether or not there is higher risk for children who participate in day-care programs. It is also important to look at the risk to children who have emotional difficulties or are handicapped in some way.

## Better Specification of Risk by Developmental Stage

Most of the risk factor studies done so far have considered childhood as a single stage. However, it is also plausible that different risk factors create vulnerability at different stages of childhood. For example, it may be that a working mother creates risk for her child's molestation only from ages 2 to 8, but not afterward. It may be that a stepfather creates risk for molestation from ages 10 to 16 but not before. Children's needs and their environments change with different developmental stages, so it is plausible that risk factors for each stage would also change. Researchers need to isolate risk factors by developmental stage.

## Multivariate Analysis

One implication of the more complex questions that we have proposed here is that researchers need to use more complex data analysis techniques. Much of the research to date has limited itself to simple bivariate relationships. As a result, it is still unknown to what extent some of these observed risk factors are simply expressions of other antecedent risk factors, and would disappear in multivariate analysis. For example, it is possible that the increased risk in stepparent families may be explained by parental unavailability or low marital satisfaction. It is imperative that in any future analysis of risk factors researchers take advantage of multivariate techniques.

## Sample Size

Many of the foregoing suggestions for improving research also dictate research designs using large samples. Large samples are needed for studies that (1) look at the risk in small subpopulations, (2) use multivariate techniques, (3) break up the dependent variable into subcategories of extrafamilial and intrafamilial abuse, and (4) look at abuse in the various stages of childhood. The majority of sexual abuse studies to date have involved fewer than 1,000 respondents. Some new studies are needed that use samples of 2,000 or more respondents. Such studies, of course, will be expensive, but there are techniques for reducing survey costs, and these need to be reviewed for their applicability to sexual abuse research. It may be possible, for example, to do surveys using the telephone, at least for the identification of subjects (Wyatt, 1985). It may be possible to combine sexual abuse research with other kinds of studies, such as health status and crime victimization surveys.

## Other Survey Designs

Large sample surveys are not the only way in which risk studies can be conducted, however. If there are small subgroups in which, as we suspect, risk may be particularly high, special studies can be done within these subgroups. For example, researchers may wish to do a study with a cohort of children who live in stepfamilies, or a cohort of children whose mothers are disabled by psychiatric illnesses. These can be done both prospectively or retrospectively. By gathering a large number of subjects from one subgroup, it may be possible to tell under what conditions this particular risk factor seems to operate. For example, it may be that children in stepfamilies that are formed when the child is very young are not at the same degree of risk as stepfamilies formed when the child is already a preadolescent.

## Studies of Child Populations

Virtually all of the risk factor studies that have been done so far have been of adults or young adults looking back on their childhoods. These studies have some important limitations, however. For example, it is very hard to get detailed and accurate information about parent-child relationships and other childhood variables from somebody who has been out of his or her family for 20 years. The validity of the data on the relationship between the parent and the child may be very poor, and there may be a loss of memory concerning other important events that might be crucial for understanding the antecedents of the sexual abuse.

There is an obvious need for more contemporaneous studies that gather information on families immediately after the abuse has occurred to assess how these families and children may differ from others. Questions about supervision, parental relationships, and parental conflict may be much more reliably evaluated in these immediate studies. Of course, one problem with such studies now is that only a small portion of abuse comes to public attention. As a result, they may not tell us about risk factors for sexual abuse so much as risk factors for sexual abuse that gets detected.

The optimal kind of design to take care of both problems is a longitudinal study that would gather information early in the family life cycle on families with young children, and then follow them and the children until the children become adults. Then it might be possible to ascertain from self-reports in interviews whether or not sexual abuse had occurred, even if it had never been reported. The data gathered early in the study would give fairly unbiased information on possible predictors of subsequent abuse.

A modified version of this design, which has advantages because it does not take as much time, would be for investigators to find groups of children and families of a previous generation who had already been the subjects of study early in the family life cycle in some other unrelated research. It might then be possible to follow up those children (now adults) and find out whether or not they had been abused during their childhoods. The data gathered in the earlier study on their families and child-hoods, if it were still available, could be used to test risk factors. It would provide a particularly good opportunity to see if it would have been possible to predict which children subsequently would be abused.

### A Final Caveat:
### Blaming the Victim

Risk factors always require cautious handling, but this is particularly so when dealing with child sexual abuse, which has been fraught with myth and misunderstanding. In the past there have been those who have taken findings such as the fact that children without friends are at higher risk and used those findings to hold victims responsible for being abused. Others have taken findings such as the fact that children with working mothers are at higher risk and used them to hold mothers responsible for abuse.

Conclusions such as these are particularly likely when victims are studied without simultaneous study of offenders. All the data in this review are based on victim surveys, which, because they gather detailed information on victims and their families, and correspondingly little about offenders and their backgrounds, tend to overemphasize the role of victims and obscure the contribution of the perpetrators.

It is important to emphasize that true causal responsibility for abuse lies with offenders. All the research suggests that it is offenders who initiate the sexual activity. In an effort to put this issue in perspective, we have developed what we call the Four Preconditions Model of Sexual Abuse (Finkelhor, 1984). This model postulates that four preconditions must exist for sexual abuse to occur: (1) There must be an offender with the motivation to sexually abuse, (2) the offender must overcome internal inhibitions against abusing, (3) the offender must overcome external obstacles against abusing, and (4) the offender must overcome resistance by the child. To "explain" sexual abuse fully, one must account for the presence of all four of these preconditions.

Most of the risk factors discussed in this chapter refer to considerations of Preconditions 3 and 4. They are situations that may reduce the supervision of the child and thus make it easier to overcome external obstacles to abuse, or they are conditions that undermine a child's emotional health and thus his or her ability to resist abuse.

But one of the values of the model is that it makes clear that Preconditions 3 and 4 make a difference only *after* Preconditions 1 and 2 have *already been met.* That is, they are relevant only once there is an offender who is predisposed to molest and who has overcome internal inhibitions against doing so. Thus many children who may suffer from risk factors at Preconditions 3 and 4 will never experience abuse.

It is important that we know about risk factors at Preconditions 3 and 4. Through knowledge of these factors we may be able to design programs to help protect children and families at higher risk. For example, if children with few friends are more vulnerable, these might be children who school personnel want to target for special attention. But the search for these risk factors should not obscure the fact that these are not the ones that *cause* abuse. Our ultimate goal should be not simply to protect high-risk children from abuse, but to eliminate abusive behavior itself.

## *Conclusion*

The study of risk factors for sexual abuse is a very promising research area. In a few short years a number of studies have produced quite convergent findings. We are now at the point at which we can readily build on these findings and obtain some very useful answers. The tools for doing this research are readily available as well. We have good experience, as Chapter 1 shows, in surveying nonclinical populations to obtain reports on abuse. Other epidemiological techniques for risk-factor analysis are also well developed. Such studies become even more important as we develop techniques of prevention education. They may mean that we can better target our education at the child population at greatest risk. It is an area in which research should soon bear results in terms of achieving concrete reductions in the number of sexually abused children.

## *NOTES*

1. "Risk factor" is a concept used widely by epidemiologists and defined by Mausner and Bahn (1974) as "factors whose presence is associated with an increased likelihood that disease will develop at a later time." Thus, although the risk factors are presumed to precede the disease temporally, they are not necessarily causal factors, but simply markers of higher susceptibility. Thus sex, age, or ethnicity may be risk factors without having any direct connection to etiology.

2. Peters's (1984) study is a companion study to Wyatt's (1985) Los Angeles survey described in greater detail in Chapter 1. However, they have somewhat different samples. Wyatt's study recruited a quota sample of 250 black and white women in Los Angeles for extensive interviews about many aspects of sexual history, including sexual abuse. Peters recontacted this sample and completed follow-up interviews with 119 of the original women using an interview much more exclusively focused on the risk factors for and effects of sexual abuse.

# 3

# Abusers:
# A Review of the Research

Sharon Araji
David Finkelhor

T his chapter reviews the empirical evidence supporting theories of why someone would
sexually abuse immature children. Many theories have been
proposed (for reviews see Langevin, 1983; Quinsey, 1977;
Howells, 1981), but there exist few comprehensive reviews of
the problem that have looked at these theories in the light of empirical research, a gap that this chapter will try to remedy.

## *Definitional Problems*

Research in the field of sexual abuse is so underdeveloped
that disagreement exists even over what to call the phenomenon
itself. Although much of the research on victims has called the
phenomenon *sexual abuse,* the research on offenders has tended
to call it *child molesting* or *pedophilia.* The term *pedophilia* has
some utility because it suggests an internal predisposition that is
independent of an actual offense. But, unfortunately, even the
meaning of *pedophilia* itself is a matter of some controversy,
with different theorists and investigators defining it in different
ways. Some have used it in what might be called an "inclusive"
fashion, considering *pedophilia* as any sexual contact with or
interest in a child, however transitory this behavior (see, for exam-

ple, Mohr, Turner, & Jerry, 1964; Friedman, 1959). Others (for example, American Psychiatric Association, 1980) have reserved the term to mean only the condition of persons having an enduring and exclusive sexual interest in children (called "fixated" offenders by Groth, 1979, or "sexual preference mediated" offenders by Howells, 1981).

In this review, in which we will be using all three terms— *sexual abuse, child molesting,* and *pedophilia*—we will use the term *pedophilia* in its broader "inclusive" definition, taking into account the behavior of any individual who has had sexual contact with children, including incest offenders. We favor this definition of the term because the other definition reflects a particular theory about pedophilia, one that has some empirical support, but is far from being fully substantiated. Moreover, the other restrictive definition makes pedophilia a complex psychological condition to deduce, requiring detailed analysis of an individual's history and motivation. We favor being able to define the category by some more readily ascertainable behavioral criteria, which is easier to do with the broader definition.

The concepts of sexual abuse and child molesting are not entirely equivalent to pedophilia, even in its broader definition. Although sexual abuse and child molesting are actual behaviors, pedophilia is essentially a state in which an individual is predisposed to use children for his or her sexual gratification. Sexual abuse and child molesting are evidence of the existence of that state.

Specifically, we define pedophilia as occurring when an adult has a conscious sexual interest in prepubertal children. We infer that sexual interest from one of two behaviors: (1) the adult has had some sexual contact with a child (meaning that he or she touched the child or had the child touch him or her with the purpose of becoming sexually aroused), or (2) the adult has masturbated to sexual fantasies involving children. Thus we are defining pedophilia to be a little broader than sexual abuse or child molesting. It includes the conscious fantasizing about such behavior, too. This makes sense to us because, in some cases, a person may have a very strong sexual interest in children and be blocked only by circumstances from acting on it. At the same time, we emphasize that this interest has to be strong enough and conscious enough that it forms the basis for masturbation, excluding such ideas as latent or unconscious pedophilia.

We also wish to emphasize that the phenomenon we are discussing can be a state and not necessarily a trait. People who engage in sexual abuse or pedophilia do not necessarily do so all their lives. Thus although we may use the term *child molester* or *pedophile,* this refers only to the people who are sexually interested in children at that specific point in time.

Although these distinctions have helped us to clarify concepts, unfortunately, in reviewing research we found such a range of usages that we could not abide by our definitions rigorously. We have not limited the review to those studies that shared our definitions, but rather included all studies that shared even some portion of that definition.

We also faced a difficulty in deciding what methodological criteria to use in the inclusion of studies. So few studies have been done that to limit such a review to strictly experimental studies would have resulted in a very short review indeed. The current review thus encompasses all studies we could find in which some effort was made to quantify offender characteristics. Beyond that, we included a few additional articles of more clinical, interpretive nature in special instances when trying to evaluate evidence for certain theories. Except when otherwise noted, our references here to child sexual abuse generally assume the abusers are men. In the next chapter, we will examine this male monopoly on child sexual abuse.

### *Need for Multifactor Explanations*

Theories of why adults become sexually interested in and involved with children have come primarily from psychoanalytic theory and, more recently, from sources such as social learning theory and feminism. What most of these approaches tend to share is that they are "single-factor theories." They identify one or, at the most, a couple of mechanisms to explain sexual interest in children. Not surprisingly, they have been inadequate to explain the full range and diversity of pedophilic behavior. This behavior ranges from the man who spends a lifetime masturbating over children's underwear ads in Sears catalogs but never touches a single child, to a man who after many years of respectable heterosexual fidelity to his wife is possessed by a strong sudden impulse to caress his granddaughter's genitals, to a man who persuades his girlfriend to help him bring a child into their bed after reading about such activities in an X-rated novel.

Such diversity of behavior defies single-factor explanations. What is needed is a more complicated model that integrates a variety of single-factor explanations in a way that accounts for the many different kinds of child molesting outcomes.

Reading through the literature, and relying particularly on excellent reviews by Howells (1981) and Langevin (1983), we developed a list of the various theories that have been proposed to explain sexual abuse behavior. One particular organizing framework stood out (Table 3.1). It appeared that most of the theories could be categorized as trying to explain one of four factors: (1) why a person would find relating sexually to a child to be emotionally gratifying and congruent (in the sense of the child fitting the adult's needs), (2) why a person would be capable of being sexually aroused by a child, (3) why a person would be frustrated or blocked in efforts to obtain sexual and emotional gratification from more normatively approved sources, and (4) why a person would not be deterred by the conventional social restraints and inhibitions against having sexual relations with a child.

Some might view the four types of theories we have grouped in this framework as competing explanations for child molesting behavior (see Table 3.1). We prefer to see them as complementary processes, many or all of which may come into play in the

## TABLE 3.1
## Summary of Empirical Evidence for
## Explanations of Child Molesting

| Theory | Evidence |
|---|---|
| **(I) Emotional congruence** | |
| Children attractive because of lack of dominance | one positive study |
| Arrested development/ immaturity | some support from psychological testing, but inferences are weak |
| Low self-esteem | some support from psychological testing, but inferences are weak |
| Mastery of trauma through repetition | several studies show frequent histories of sexual abuse in offenders' backgrounds |
| Identification with aggression | several studies show frequent histories of sexual abuse in offenders' backgrounds |
| Narcissism | untested |
| Male socialization to dominance | untested |
| **(II) Sexual arousal** | |
| Heightened arousal to children | clear experimental evidence, except for incest offenders |
| Conditioning from early childhood experience | several studies show frequent histories of sexual abuse in offenders' backgrounds |
| Modeling from earlier childhood experiences | several studies show frequent histories of sexual abuse in offenders' backgrounds |
| Hormonal abnormalities | mixed evidence |
| Misattribution of arousal | untested |
| Socialization through child pornography or advertising | untested |
| **(III) Blockage** | |
| Difficulty relating to adult females | generally positive evidence |
| Inadequate social skills | suggested by two studies |
| Sexual anxiety | some support from uncontrolled studies |
| Unresolved Oedipal dynamics | family problems evident, but not necessarily the ones Oedipal theory would predict |
| Disturbances in adult sexual romantic relationships | suggestive evidence from uncontrolled studies |
| Repressive norms about sexual behavior | suggested by two studies |
| **(IV) Disinhibition** | |
| Impulse disorder | true for some small group of offenders, but not for all |
| Senility | negative |
| Mental retardation | negative |
| Alcohol | present in grest many instances, exact role unclear |

**TABLE 3.1 (Continued)**

| | |
|---|---|
| Failure of incest avoidance mechanism | two studies show higher rates of abuse in stepfather families |
| Situational stress | only ancedotal evidence |
| Cultural toleration | untested |
| Patriarchal norms | untested |

creation of one particular person's pedophilic interest. Viewing them as complementary processes, which may work antagonistically or synergistically, may also help explain the diversity of the behavior. After describing the four factors, and the theories that comprise them, we will illustrate how they may account for some of the diversity.

We also note that explanations of sexual abuse behavior focus on two levels: the individual psychological and the sociocultural. During much of the history of research on pedophilia, it was considered to be a statistically unusual behavior, and the research, based primarily on populations of incarcerated offenders, treated the problem exclusively as one of individual psychopathology. As it has become apparent that a great deal of sexual contact occurs between adults and children, most of it undetected, a point of view has developed that broader sociocultural factors contribute to the problem. However, as we reviewed these sociocultural explanations, it was apparent that they, too, could be subdivided into the same four factors as individual psychological theories. Thus the sections that follow on the four types of theories review both individual psychological and sociocultural explanations.

### *Factor I: Emotional Congruence*

Some of the most widely cited theories about pedophilia explain that sexual abusers choose children for sexual partners because children have some especially compelling emotional meaning for them. We have called this "emotional congruence" because it conveys the idea of a "fit" between the adult's emotional needs and the characteristics of children, a fit that the theories are trying to account for.

One such theory holds that child molesters have "arrested psychosexual development" and are emotionally immature. They choose to relate to children because they are at a child's emotional level and they can respond to childlike preoccupations (for example, Hammer & Glueck, 1957; Groth & Birnbaum, 1978; Bell & Hall, 1976).

A related idea is that molesters are not just immature, but have a generally low sense of self-esteem and little efficacy in their social relationships. Relating to children is congruent because it gives them a feeling of being powerful, omnipotent, respected, and in control (for example, see Loss & Glancy, 1983, p. 323; Hammer & Glueck, 1957, p. 338).

Other theorists have surmised that relating to children allows sex abusers to try to overcome the effects of some childhood trauma. By victimizing a child, they master the trauma by reversing roles in the victimization they suffered, and through "identification with the aggressor," they combat their own powerlessness by becoming the powerful victimizer (for example, see Howells, 1981; Groth, Hobson, & Gary, 1982a; Storr, 1965).

Still another theory that can be classified under emotional congruence uses the notion of "narcissism" to explain pedophilia. In this theory, a molester, as a result of emotional deprivation or even overprotection, remains emotionally involved with himself as a child or his likenesses. He tries to give the love he misses or wished he had had to a child who resembles himself.

Finally, recent feminist ideas about sexual abuse have a surprisingly similar underlying notion. According to these theories, sexual abuse grows out of certain themes in normal male socialization that tend to make children "appropriate" objects of sexual interest. These themes include the value that male socialization puts on being dominant and the initiator in sexual relationships, as well as the value placed on partners who are youthful and subservient. Sexual abuse occurs as a natural extension of some of these values (Howells, 1981; Storr, 1965).

The idea that children have some special emotional congruence for child molesters has proven useful in many clinical accounts of the problem. Unfortunately, not much formal evidence has been marshaled to confirm these theories or demonstrate that these special meanings of children occur more frequently among sexual abusers than in other portions of the population. As far as we could find, for example, no empirical studies relating to the "narcissism" hypothesis have been completed. As for the issue of overcoming effects of childhood trauma, we will discuss this in the section on sexual arousal.

### Children Attractive Because of
### Lack of Dominance

Howells (1979) has perhaps gone further than any others to try to substantiate the idea that children have a special emotional meaning for pedophiles. Using a technique called the Repertory Grid (for a further description of the test instruments mentioned in this review, consult either the article referenced or Buros, 1970, or Woody, 1980) he found some support for two propositions: (1) that issues of dominance and hierarchy were more important in the social relationships of molesters than in those of non-sex offenders, and (2) that one of the salient characteristics that molesters point to in their victims is lack of dominance. This research gives support to the notion, common to most of the emotional congruence theories, that molesters like children because children make them feel powerful. However, Howells's methodology is somewhat vaguely described and may allow for some degree of investigator subjectivity. Extensions and replications of his very promising line of inquiry are needed.

Some other studies based on psychological tests do provide findings that could be construed as consistent with Howells (1979). For example, Langevin (1983) cites studies by Fisher (1969) and Fisher and Howell (1970) in which female-object pedophiles (pedophiles who prefer female to male children) scored higher than normals on deference, succorance, and abasement and lower on achievement, autonomy, change, heterosexuality, and aggression. These findings were based on the Edward's Personal Preference Schedule. The high score on deference, in particular, might be viewed as similar to Howells's notion that pedophiles have difficulty with dominance. However, this is a precarious inference and, most important, does not give any substantiation to the idea that children are preferred because of this difficulty.

### Immaturity and Self-Esteem

Two other hypotheses that emotional congruence theories make about molesters are that they are immature and have low self-esteem. These ideas are well suited to substantiation through conventional psychological tests, although, surprisingly, few very thorough investigations of this sort have been done. (One study that used several standardized tests and also examined hypotheses related to "immaturity" and "arrested psychosexual development" is that by Ellis & Brancale, 1956. However, because their conclusions are based on many types of sex offenders all lumped together, it seemed unwise to use their research findings to confirm or disconfirm theories about molesters. Hence, their findings were excluded from the present review.) Hammer and Glueck (1957) gave the Rorschach, House-tree-person, TAT, and Blacky picture tests to 200 sex offenders and concluded that pedophiles feel psychosexually immature and lacking in self-esteem, but they say little about which findings from the tests warranted these conclusions.

Using the Blacky pictures, Stricker (1967) was more specific and reported that pedophiles tended, in comparison to a college sample, to significantly "overuse descriptive positives (e.g., beautiful, fair, kind) on the evaluative dimension of the scale." Based on the fact that females also use more positive responses on this dimension, Stricker concluded that "pedophiles share this immature, feminine approach." This seems a weak inference and one that reflects a great deal of sex-role sterotyping, and so should be treated with caution.

Peters (1976) drew similar inferences, that sex abusers differed from normal men in that they were more immature and regressed, and had strong dependency needs and feelings of phallic inadequacy. These inferences were based on the results of the Bender Gestalt test with a sample of 224 probational male sex offenders. He also found that child sex abusers scored higher than other sex offenders on the somatic scale of the Cornell Medical Index, meaning that they had a particularly large number of physical symptoms. He take this to mean that they have "a strong tendency to somatize affective problems and thus view themselves as inferior. They seem to feel unable to compete with other men in efforts to attract adult women because of this felt inferiority." Some of these conclusions involve large conceptual leaps and should be viewed cautiously until more objective research becomes available.

Besides the above-mentioned research, it has not been uncommon for investigators to give molesters MMPI tests and make inferences from these. Among the earliest studies was one by Toobert, Bartelme, and Jones (1959), who compared pedophiles with other prisoners in general and found they scored higher on the femininity and paranoia scales. They then concluded that pedophiles were "weak and inadequate and had low self-esteem." They saw this as supporting the theoretically predicted personality of a pedophile. In this case, as before, the investigators may be making unwarranted inferences from their findings, inferences that seem also to be affected by sex-role stereotyping.

Panton (1978) compared MMPI test results of 30 rapists, 20 child rapists, and 28 nonviolent child molesters. They report that the profiles of the child molesters "implied self-alienation, low self-esteem, self-doubt, anxiety, inhibition of aggression, aversion to violence, need for reinforcement, feelings of inadequacy, insecurity, and fear of heterosexual failure." From this they concluded that "the motivation of the molester group appeared to be the satisfaction of sexual needs at an immature level of sexual development."

Cavallin (1966) also employed the MMPI in his study of twelve incestuous offenders. Although he did not report the actual MMPI findings, he indicated that, among other factors, results from the MMPI point to sex abusers having "weak psychosexual identity." There are, of course, many clinical studies that are in agreement with the above findings, including Groth et al. (1982a); Cohen, Seghorn, and Calmas (1969); and Fitch (1962).

In sum, there seem to be a number of investigators who are in agreement that child molesters are immature or inadequate. Some of these have found support for such contentions in psychological tests such as the MMPI. However, these investigators have often made broad and unwarranted inferences from test data, and we believe that the hypothesis is not much advanced beyond the status of a clinical inference. Perhaps, more important, even well-established evidence of immaturity and inadequacy on the part of pedophiles does not necessarily explain their sexual interaction with children. Immature and inadequate men might just as well be expected to be asexual as pedophilic. Howells's study does provide some initial confirmation that pedophiles may interact with children because children have special meaning for them in terms of representing weak and nonthreatening objects. However, more such studies on the meaning that children have for pedophiles are needed.

### *Factor II: Sexual Arousal*

Another group of theories about sexual abuse are essentially explanations of how a person comes to find children sexually arousing. One general theory is that some people have early sexual experiences with children that condition them when they become adults to find children to be arousing (Wenet, Clark, & Hunner, 1981, pp. 149–150).

Several suggestions exist as to what special circumstances might work to give such early childhood sexual experiences the special compelling quality they seem to have for many pedophiles. One possibility is that the critical experiences are those in which some special kind of fulfillment or frustration was involved. Another possibility is that the critical experiences might be ones associated with traumatic victimization.

McGuire, Carlisle, and Young (1965), in their general model of sexual deviation, suggest that what is important in the development of a fixation is that the early experience of arousal be incorporated into a fantasy that is repeated and becomes increasingly arousing in subsequent masturbatory repetitions (also see Wenet et al., 1981, p. 149). Any feature of the experience that makes it prominent in the person's awareness—such as being associated with great pleasure or great embarrassment or shame—will make it likely to be thought of in the course of masturbation. Because masturbation is highly reinforcing, the components of the memory (in this case the element of childhood) comes to be associated through a process like "operant conditioning" with sexual arousal, even in cases in which the original experience itself might not have been pleasurable.

In another theory of sexual arousal, Howells (1981) speculated about how a process of "attributional error" may play a role in creating arousal to children. Children elicit strong emotional reactions in many people, reactions usually labeled "parental" or "affectionate," but some individuals may mistakenly label these reactions as sexual and then come to act accordingly toward children.

Still other accounts of the origin of sexual arousal to children have focused on biological factors such as hormone levels or chromosomal makeup (Money, 1961; Goy & McEwen, 1977; Berlin, 1982).

A final theory about sexual arousal derives from speculations that some individuals might learn to become aroused to children through exposure to child pornography or other media that project children in an erotic light.

## Studies Demonstrating Heightened Arousal

In examining the above theories, the first matter to be established is whether or not child molesters are in fact persons who have unusual sexual arousal to children. There is a fairly impressive body of experimental evidence suggesting that they are indeed unusually sexually responsive to children. Most of this research has been conducted by Freund and colleagues and Quinsey and colleagues. In fact, this particular body of research represents the most methodologically and statistically sophisticated research on pedophilia.

Freund (1967a, 1967b) and Freund and colleagues (1973, 1976), in a series of studies, investigated penile responses to slides of female and male children and adults. They found significantly more arousal to children in a group of molesters, both female-object and male-object, than in either of two control groups (homosexual and heterosexual males).

Quinsey and colleagues (1975) conducted a number of similar studies and found similar results. For example, using penile and skin conductance responses to slides of children, they compared child molesters (N = 20) with nonmolesters (N = 20). Although the child molesters claimed adult females as their preferred sex object, in tests they exhibited the largest penile responses to slides of female children. The penile tests also confirmed that female-object child molesters had peak arousal to female children, and male-object pedophiles to male children. Bisexual pedophiles, interestingly, had peak arousal to female children, although the second highest peak was for adult females. (For more on bisexual pedophiles, see Freund & Langevin, 1976.) Atwood and Howell (1971) also found that the pupils of child molesters dilated to slides of children and constricted to adult females, an opposite pattern from that found for a control group.

As a whole, the above studies seem to establish the fact that some pedophiles have an arousal preference for children, but whether or not all child molesters, including incest offenders, have such a preference is not clear. There is at least one study that indicates that incest offenders do have such an arousal to children. Abel, Becker, Murphy, and Flanagan (1981) played audiotapes of sexual encounters to 6 female-object incest offenders as well as to 10 female-object pedophiles, and found that, similar to the other sex abusers, the incest offenders "developed significant erections to pedophilic cues that were not descriptions of sexual acts with their daughters or stepdaughters." However, when Quinsey, Chaplin, and Carrigan (1979) examined the penile responses of a matched sample of 16 incestuous and 16 nonincestuous child offenders, they found "that incestuous child molesters have more appropriate sexual age preferences (adults) than those who are nonincestuous.

**Early Sexual Experiences**

Although the above studies indicate that at least some groups of sex abusers are sexually aroused by children, evidence about the source of this arousal is scarce. The best researched of the arousal hypotheses is one that suggests that it may stem from early childhood sexual experiences. Many sex abusers appear to have been subjected to early sexual contact with adults themselves, as is demonstrated by a growing number of studies. In one of the earliest, Gebhard, Gagnon, Pomeroy, and Christensen (1965) found that both their male-object and female-object prison pedophile groups had higher rates of childhood sexual contacts with adults than did a group of controls. It was found, for example, that of the 199 female-object child molesters, 10% had childhood contact with an adult female, compared to only 1% for the control group. Also, 18% had had a childhood contact with an adult male, compared to 8% for controls. The male-object pedophiles in the Gebhard et al. (1965) study also had many child sexual contacts with adults, in fact, they had more childhood sexual approaches by adult males than any other sex-offender or control group—33% (N = 123). Among all the sex abusers only the incest offenders were distinct in having less sexual contact with adults during prepuberty. The Gebhard et al.

findings suggest that sexual contact with adults existed in the childhood of at least some pedophiles.

Groth and Burgess's (1979) research on child sexual contact with adults reinforced that of Gebhard et al. (1965). Groth found that 32% of a group of 106 child molesters reported some form of "sexual trauma" in their early development, compared to only 3% of a comparison group of 64 police officers. Approximately twice as many of the "fixated"-type offenders (who are also more commonly male-object) had been victimized compared to the "regressed"-type offenders. Moreover, Groth observed that these offenders tended to duplicate in age of victim and type of sex act the form of victimization they themselves had suffered. In more recent, not yet published, surveys of imprisoned sex abusers, Groth (1984) has found "sexual trauma" in 80%. Groth's concept of "sexual trauma" includes such things as witnessing sex acts, suffering from physical abnormalities, and being circumcised in addition to what is more commonly considered sexual abuse.

Langevin, Handy, Hook, Day, and Russon (1985) also show that convicted child molesters have more childhood sexual contacts with older persons than controls, but some of their specific findings differ from those of Gebhard et al. (1965). For example, among specific groups of child molesters, 21% of incest offenders had had sexual contact before age 12 with an adult male, compared to 10% of the female object molesters and 4% of the controls. Gebhard et al., in contrast, found less molestation in the backgrounds of incest offenders.

Seghorn, Binder, and Prentky (n.d.) looked for molestation in the backgrounds of both rapists and child molesters and found that significantly more child molesters (57%) than rapists (23%) had been sexual assault victims. Abel et al. (1984) also note sexual abuse in the background of child molesters (24% of female-object molesters and 40% of male-object molesters).

In sum, a number of studies support the contention that an unusual number of convicted child molesters were the subjects of molestation themselves. This is one of the most consistent findings of recent research. The exact proportion is difficult to determine, given the variation in the rates among reported studies. However, all of the studies using a conventional definition of sexual abuse, except Seghorn et al. (n.d.), report rates well below 50%. The significance of this history of molestation is somewhat hard to gauge. Most of the studies on this subject suffer from problems, most particularly related to their control groups (these and other problems with the findings are discussed in the next chapter). Unfortunately, no really good study with appropriate comparison groups has been done yet.

Dismissing methodological issues for a moment, we need to observe that if a history of sexual assault is connected to later child molesting, this evidence is consistent with several possible theories. One may be that such experiences condition an arousal to children. That is, because they have participated in, and in many cases been rewarded for, adult-child sexual contact, they may have fantasies about or arousal for such contact as part of their sexual repertoire. Another may be that the pedophiles learn the behavior through the early modeling of their own victimization. Having seen the process of someone else's arousal to children, it is a model readily available to them when they develop their own sexual scripts. The emotional congruence theories that pedophiles reenact their own victimization in an effort to "master" the trauma and take on the power of the aggressor are also consistent with these findings. To test the conditioning theories, it might be important to know whether or not pleasurable and peer-type experiences as well as traumatic sexual experiences predispose to later molesting, a matter on which we could find little data. To test the reenactment theories it might be important to know how many molesters commit acts similar to the ones they experienced. Moreover, there is a great need to specify under what conditions victimization leads to pedophilia and under what conditions it does not. This whole theoretical realm needs to be developed further.

## Biological Factors

With respect to other theories of why molesters find children arousing there has been only minimal research. Studies about biological factors are scarce, although this theory is taken seriously by many. There are reports of physiological abnormalities among some child molesters (Berlin, 1982; McAuliffe, 1983) and success in treating them with drugs. Berlin and Coyle (1981) report elevated testosterone levels in a substantial number of pedophiles seen at Johns Hopkins Hospital, but this finding is in conflict with Rada, Laws, and Kellner (1976), who report that pedophiles' testosterone levels were within normal limits. But even Berlin and Coyle concede that hormonal findings do not give much explanation of why children become arousing to pedophiles. Hormones are seen as having a generalized effect on levels of sexual interest and sexual arousability. But why this interest should focus on children is not explained.

## Pornography

The hypothesis that child molesters may learn arousal from exposure to pornography or advertising is also one that has not been investigated extensively. Goldstein, Kant, and Hartman (1973) found that pedophiles (20 male-object and 20 female-object) had had somewhat less exposure to pornography than had control groups. However, this study asked only about pornography portraying adult heterosexuality. Moreover, at the time of their research (the late 1960s) child pornography was much less available than it is at present.

In summary, empirical studies have shown that children are sexually arousing to at least some, and perhaps most, sex abusers, and that sex object preference can be determined roughly from laboratory exposure. However, it is not clear whether or not this is true of all child molesters, especially incest offenders. Early childhood experiences with adults may play a role in this process, and the data are consistent with several theories, including the "emotional congruence" theory (that the pedophile is trying to gain mastery over the trauma by repeating it) or the "sexual arousal" theory (that the earlier experience conditioned the pedophile's erotic responses).

## Factor III: Blockage

A third group of theories about pedophilia are essentially explanations of why some individuals are blocked in their ability to meet their sexual and emotional needs in adult heterosexual relationships. These theories seem to presume that normal development or normal preference would lead a person to fulfill his or her needs with adult peers. For some reason, in the child molester these normal tendencies are blocked, and thus the sexual interest orients toward children.

Individual psychological theories that rely on Oedipal dynamics fall into this category of explanation. Sex abusers are described in such theories as having intense conflicts about their mothers that make it difficult or impossible for them to relate to adult women (Hammer & Glueck, 1957; Gillespie, 1964). They are said to have "castration anxieties" as a result of early childhood experiences; their access to adult sexual behavior is blocked (Fenichel, 1945).

Sometimes the source of blockage is not seen so much in Oedipal dynamics as in early traumatic forays into sexual behavior. The man who finds himself to be impotent in his first sexual attempts, or abandoned by his first lover, may come to associate adult sexuality with pain and frustration. Because this avenue is filled with trauma, he chooses children as a substitute gratification. According to Kinsey (1948), for example, "The offenders [are] sexually thwarted, incapable of winning attention from older females and reduced to vain attempts with children who are unable to defend themselves."

Some theorists do not rely so much on the psychoanalytic explanation, but perceive the same underlying dynamic. Child molesters are described as timid, unassertive, inadequate, awkward, even moralistic types with poor social skills who have an impossible time developing adult social and sexual relationships

(Gebhard et al., 1965; Guttmacher, 1951; Hammer & Glueck, 1957; Glueck, 1965; Frisbie, 1969; Langevin, 1983). Says Storr (1965):

> A man . . . suffers from pedophilia . . . because he has been unable to find sexual satisfaction in an adult relationship. It is not from superfluity or lust, but rather because of a timid inability to make contact with contemporaries.

Theories that try to account for incest offenders rely heavily on this blockage model. In the family dynamics model of incest, for example, the marital relationship has broken down; the wife has become alienated for some reason; the father is too inhibited or moralistic to find sexual satisfaction outside the family; thus, blocked in other avenues of sexual or emotional gratification, he turns to his daughter as a substitute (deYoung, 1982; Gebhard et al., 1965; Meiselman, 1978).

This blockage model has not, to our knowledge, been developed very extensively by theorists trying to explain sex abuse at a sociocultural level (however, it is suggested by Ramer, 1977). If such theories were to be developed, we speculate that they would emphasize the role of repressive sexual norms. (We wish to thank Diana Russell for suggestions in this regard.) Repressive sexual norms, one could argue, operate to make adults feel guilty about engaging in adult sexual relationships, and this may push some into choosing child partners. For example, norms tabooing extramarital affairs may in some cases block the incestuous father from seeking out other *adult women* rather than his child (Weinberg, 1955). There is also a norm that makes masturbation seem inappropriate for adults, and this norm may block what would otherwise be another alternative and benign sexual outlet. However, it is somewhat difficult to understand why someone so sensitive to the taboo on extramarital sex or masturbation would not be sensitive to the taboo on sex with children. We leave this line of thinking for others to develop.

In general, this review of blockage-type theories suggests a further subdivision of the category into two types: developmental blockages and situational blockages. *Developmental block-*

*ages* refers to theories such as those involving Oedipal conflicts, in which a person is seen as prevented from moving into the adult heterosexual stage of development. *Situational blockages* refers more to theories, such as those related to incest, in which a person with apparent adult sexual interests is blocked from normal sexual outlets because of the loss of a relationship or some other transitory crisis.

The blockage (Factor III) theories have some similarity to and are sometimes hard to distinguish from the emotional congruence (Factor I) theories. However, there is an important difference. In the blockage theories, children do become emotionally congruent for the offender and that is why the sex abuse occurs. But the children become objects of interest for want of anything better, not because they have special attraction. In the emotional congruence theories, by contrast, children come to have an especially positive and compelling emotional connotation for the adult, for example, they allow the adult to feel a sense of mastery over trauma.

### Difficulty Relating to Adult Females

There are a wide range of studies that do indicate that male sex abusers may have many problems with adult females. In a study of 200 sex offenders, Hammer and Glueck (1957) report "fear of heterosexual contact" as a common finding. In response to a TAT card showing a seminude mature woman, they report that 85% of the pedophiles and 87% of the incest offenders did not come up with the sexual theme normally offered, but instead came up with stories such as the female was sick, dying, or dead. These researchers also had a panel of psychologists compare the responses offered by the offenders to the House-tree-person, Blacky pictures, and TAT with those given by a group of normals. The clinicians rated 90% of the offender group as having "marked" or "moderate" castration fears compared to only 55% of the control group.

Panton (1978) compared several groups of rapists with child molesters. Based on responses to the pedophile scale (a special scale derived from the MMPI), he found that child molesters tended to be anxious, inadequate individuals who felt insecure in their associations with others and who expected rejection and failure in adult heterosexual advances. In a later study (1979), he compared incestuous versus nonincestuous child molesters and found the two groups to have similar profiles, with the only significant difference occurring on the social introversion scale. He interprets this to mean that the incest sample had even greater inadequacies in social skills and difficulties in decision making.

In a study significant because it used a sample of nonincarcerated pedophiles, Wilson and Cox (1983) administered the Eysenck Personality Questionnaire and a tailor-made "Paedophile Questionnaire" to 77 members of an English pedophile self-help group, the Paedophile Information Exchange. The pedophiles scored higher than controls on introversion, psychoticism, and neuroticism scales, and were more likely to be shy, sensitive, lonely, depressed, and humorless. The authors take this to be indicative of an absence of social skills and confidence.

Gebhard et al. (1965) also noted that there were problems in the area of social relationships for the female-object, male-object, and incest offender groups. Howells (1981, p. 71) reports additional confirmation in studies by Mohr et al. (1964), Fisher (1969), Fisher and Howell (1970), Pacht and Cowden (1974), and a review by West (1977). A number of clinical-type studies have reached similar conclusions (Anderson & Mayes, 1982; Groth et al., 1982a; Marsh, Hilliard, & Liechti, 1955; Langevin, 1983; Virkkunen, 1976; Cohen et al., 1969; Bell & Hall, 1976).

Child molesters also have been shown to harbor unusual amounts of sexual anxiety, which may contribute to problems in relating to adult females. For example, Goldstein et al. (1973) found that 80% of his pedophile group reported guilt or shame from looking at or reading erotica, compared to 47% for a control group. They were "the least permissive . . . regarding premarital and extramarital intercourse." These researchers also report that male-object pedophiles expressed more opposition to talking about sex than any of the other study groups.

In sum, the evidence does seem to support the idea that many sex abusers do have problems relating to adult women and that possibly poor social skills and sexual anxiety contribute to this. Whether or not this has anything to do with family background and dynamics, as alleged in many of the theories, is, however, another matter. Gebhard et al. (1965) found evidence of poor parental relationships for his heterosexual aggressor, incest, and male-object (but not female-object) offenders. But the types of poor relationships differed. Paitich and Langevin (1976), using the Clarke Parent Child Relations Questionnaire, found problems with mothers to be characteristic of incest offenders, but not of other pedophiles. In general the evidence on this matter is very spotty and inconclusive and cannot be said to support theories about castration anxiety or Oedipal conflict.

### Disturbances in Adult Sexual or Romantic Relationships

The other component of the blockage theme is related to the adult family life of the child molesters and holds that they experience some disappointment or trauma in adult heterosexual relationships that triggers the pedophilic activity.

Fitch (1962) classified 56 (11 male-object and 45 female-object) of his sample of 139 offenders and reoffenders against children as "frustrated" in sexual relationships. Gebhard et al. (1965) found that their group's incestuous offenses always started during periods of marital stress, and, likewise, Cavallin (1966) observed that in all of his 12 cases of incest offenders the wife was seen as rejecting and threatening. (In the other sex-offender groups, marital problems were mentioned, but no specific association was drawn between marital disturbances and pedophilia). In addition, publications by Groth (1979), Cohen et al. (1969), and Peters (1976) all report similar findings. The evidence from all those studies suggests that the "disturbance in a marital or love relationship" is a factor related to pedophilic behavior more among offenders who prefer adult females ("regressed offenders" in Groth's terms). However, few of the investigations making these assertions have presented good, quantified evidence for this theory.

**Repressive Norms About Sex**

A final blockage theory is the idea that repressive norms or attitudes about such things as masturbation and extramarital sex may be related to pedophilia. Goldstein et al. (1973) found that pedophiles reported more guilt or shame from looking at or reading erotica than either rapists or controls. They also listed "fear of sex" as the main barrier to seeking more mature sexual outlets, were opposed to premarital sex, and expressed more discomfort with respect to talking about sex than any other group. Gebhard et al. (1967) also found strong moral inhibitions to premarital intercourse among the female-object pedophiles, but not among any of the other pedophile groups. In short, it seems that some sex abusers may hold repressive sexual attitudes that may predispose them toward sexual activities with children.

In summary, one blockage theory does receive most support: Sex abusers have problems relating to adult females in particular and maybe even to adults in general. As noted, there is some evidence that they have unusual sexual anxiety and also that they may suffer from frustration in love relationships. But of course many, many people in the general population have love-related or marital problems. Hence, future research needs to investigate how blockage combines with other factors to create individuals who are predisposed to interact sexually with children.

## *Factor IV: Disinhibition*

A final set of theories about sex abusers are essentially accounts of why conventional inhibitions against having sex with children are overcome or are not present in some adults. Among sex abusers, according to such theories, ordinary controls are circumvented or there is a higher level of acceptability for such behavior.

On the individual psychological level, theories have talked about child molesters as people who had generally poor impulse control (Gebhard et al., 1965, pp. 80-81; Glueck, 1965, pp. 554-559; Groth et al., 1982, p. 14; Knopp, 1982; Hammer & Glueck, 1957). In addition, a number of personality factors have been associated with molesting: senility (Cushing, 1950; Karpman, 1954, p. 106), alcoholism and alcohol abuse (McCaghy, 1968; Rada, 1976; Frisbie, 1969), and psychosis (Hammer & Glueck, 1957; Mohr et al., 1964; Marshall & Norgard, 1983; Gebhard et al., 1967). According to Storr (1965), "Some apparently normal men, when judgement and self-control have been impaired by brain damage or alcohol, are capable of making sexual advances to children." Although most researchers disclaim the idea that such conditions explain most molesting, they are seen as contributing factors or as the essential elements in at least some individuals. The presumed mechanism at work in all these conditions is the lowering or disappearance of inhibitions against acting on pedophilic impulses.

Sometimes situational factors, as well as personality factors, are used in disinhibition-type explanations to account for sexual abuse. For example, when a person with no prior history of pedophilic behavior commits a pedophilic act under conditions of great personal stress, the stressors—unemployment, loss of love, death of a relative—are viewed as factors that lowered inhibitions to deviant types of behavior (Mohr et al., 1964, p. 95; Gebhard, 1967, p. 74; Swanson, 1968).

Theories of incest also often rely on mechanisms that fall into this category. Men are seen as engaging in sexual acts with girls in their families because these girls are stepdaughters or because the men were away from their families during the children's early life (Lustig et al., 1966; Gebhard et al., 1967). Being a stepdaughter or being separated presumably works to reduce the ordinary inhibition that would exist against sex between a natural father and a daughter who had lived together continuously since the child's birth. These inhibitory mechanisms are sometimes viewed as quasi-biological in nature, coming into play merely as the result of proximity during early stages of development (Shepher, 1971; Van den Berghe, 1983). Others view them as developing out of the empathy and concern anticipatory to and resulting from a caretaking role (Herman, 1981). Incest occurs when these inhibitory mechanisms are disrupted.

Feminist theories of sexual abuse are essentially disinhibition-type arguments, too. These theories highlight certain social and cultural elements that encourage or condone sexual behavior directed toward children and thus weaken inhibitions (Densen-Gerber, 1983).

For example, Rush (1980) has written extensively about the way in which adult sexual interaction with children has been sanctioned by religion and law throughout history. Armstrong (1983) argues that the reluctance of the contemporary legal system to prosecute and punish offenders gives a green light to potential molesters. These authors and other feminists (McIntyre, 1981; Nelson, 1982) also have criticized the tendency among both the public and professionals to blame victims rather than offenders, pointing out that this feeds into the justifications that offenders use for their own violations (Russell, 1982; Rush, 1980). Anything that reinforces excuses for sexual abuse, according to these theories, acts to reduce inhibitions.

In accounting for incest, a common feminist theme has been to show how inhibitions are lowered by social approval for the excesses of patriarchal and parental authority (Rush, 1980). According to feminists, many men see families as private institutions in which parents have socially sanctioned authority to treat women and children as they wish.

> [The] seduction of daughters is inherent in a father-dominated family system, where the man expects to have his will obeyed as head of household and expects his family to provide him with domestic and sexual services. When patriarchal beliefs about

rights of fathers provide further excuse for initiating sexually gratifying relationships within the family, it is not hard to see how many "Mr. Averages" can manage to *overcome all the social and emotional barriers* to committing incest with their daughters. (Nelson, 1982; emphasis added)

Such social norms and values disinhibit offenders.

Most disinhibition theories, however, like blockage theories, are not really full explanations of sexual abuse. They have a problem standing on their own without being combined with other theories. In effect, they really take for granted some prior motive in the abuser to interact sexually with a child. If a person had no prior motive for sexually interacting with a child, then loss of inhibitions would not make a difference. So disinhibition theories are incomplete because they assume these prior sexual interests without investigating their origin. However, although they do not stand well on their own, these theories are an important contribution to a full explanation of sexual abuse, because if someone is fully inhibited from pedophilic activity, no amount of arousal or emotional congruence may provoke it. Disinhibition may best be seen not as a sufficient, but as a necessary, condition for abuse to occur.

### Lack of Impulse Control

One disinhibition-type theory for which there is some support is lack of impulse control. Based on 200 sex offenders' responses to the Bender Gestalt and Blacky pictures, Hammer and Glueck (1957) identified inadequate control of impulses as the third factor of a four-factor theory. Gebhard et al. (1965) found that 10% of their female-object pedophiles were "amoral delinquents" characterized by being "unable to defer gratification and tolerate frustration until a socially suitable situation is available." However, impulse control is not a problem for all pedophiles. For the other 70% of the pedophiles in the Gebhard et al. sample, impulsivity did not seem to be an outstanding characteristic. In fact, Gebhard et al. point out that 80% or more of the acts engaged in by all the pedophile groups were planned, not impulsive.

In summary, probably some small group of sex abusers actually suffers from impulse disorders. However, there is little evidence that it is a characteristic of abusers in general.

### Senility and Mental Retardation

A once popular disinhibition-type explanation of child molesting was that molesters were senile. As a whole, current evidence contradicts this theory. Studies show most offenders to be between 35 and 40 years of age (Chaneles, 1967; Virkkunen, 1976; Herman & Hirschman, 1980; Gebhard et al., 1965; Fitch, 1962; Marsh et al., 1955; McCaghy, 1968; Stricker, 1967), or even younger—in their mid- to late twenties (Quinsey et al., 1975, 1979, 1980; Freund, McKnight, Langevin, and Cibiri, 1972). In a two-state sample of sex offenders, Groth, Longo, and McFadin (1982b) identified two modal groups—one age 16 and the other 31. Mohr et al. (1964) also found a youthful group between 15 and 24. As with impulse disorders, there may be a small group of senile molesters, but they do not appear to be common.

The evidence is also generally negative about the stereotype of the molester as mentally retarded. Peters (1976), for example, used the revised Army Beta intelligence examination and did find molesters to have the lowest IQ of four sex-offender groups, but his findings are an exception. Mohr et al. (1964) used the Wechsler Adult IQ scale and found their 57 molesters to have normal intelligence. Their results concur with a number of other studies (Langevin, 1983, p. 274; Stokes, 1964; Julian & Mohr, 1980).

### Alcohol

Evidence for the alcohol-related disinhibition theory, however, is quite a different story. Many studies show that alcohol involvement accompanies sexual abuse, meaning that the offender was an alcoholic and/or drinking at the time of the offense. Aarens et al. (1978, pp. 541-548), for example, reviewed 11 U.S. and 2 foreign empirical studies and found alcohol involved in 30%-40% of cases in most studies, ranging from a low of 19% of the cases in a German study (Wilschke, 1965) to an overall high of 49% in a U.S. study (Rada, 1976). They also found that studies showed 45%-50% of child molesters had histories of drinking problems (low of 8% to high of 70%).

Studies by Gebhard et al. (1965), Rada (1976), and Stokes (1964) have showed female-object pedophiles to be more alcohol involved than male-object pedohiles. Gebhard et al. (1965), for example, reported that 37% of their female-object pedophiles, compared to 10% of the male group, said alcohol was a significant factor in their lives. Rada (1976) found 57% of the female-object pedophiles were involved in use of alcohol, compared to 38% of the male-object pedophiles. Stokes's (1964) comparative figures were 25% and 8%, respectively.

Aarens et al. (1978) concludes from a review of five relevant studies that incest offenders appear to be the most alcohol involved of all sex abusers. In a comparison across studies they found incestuous child molesters were characterized by larger proportions of both alcoholism and drinking at the time of the offense than were nonincestuous child molesters. Morgan (1982, p. 245) reviewed many of the same studies as Aarens et al. (1978) and reached similar conclusions.

In summary it seems safe to say that alcohol plays a role in the commission of offenses by some groups of sex abusers. Alcohol may act as a direct physiological disinhibitor or it may have some social meaning that allows a person to disregard the taboos against child molestation. This remains a somewhat unresolved question in the field of alcohol abuse (Morgan, 1982).

**Incest Avoidance Mechanism**

To our knowledge, only two studies address the "failure of incest avoidance mechanism" idea. Based on responses from a survey of a college population, Finkelhor (1980) reports that one of the strongest risk factors associated with a child's vulnerability to being sexually abused is having lived with a stepfather.

Based on responses from a probability sample of 930 female residents in San Francisco, Russell (1986) reports that approximately 1 out of every 43 women who had a biological father as a principal figure in her childhood (birth to 14 years) was sexually abused by him, compared to about 1 out of every 6 women who lived with a stepfather during these same years. There are various possible explanations for the apparently high risk of abuse at the hands of stepfathers, but one of the most plausible falls within the disinhibition theory framework: Because of different norms or different exposure to the child at an early age, stepfathers are less inhibited from having sexual feelings toward a child than are natural fathers.

The remaining disinhibition theories listed in Table 3.1 have not been subjected to any empirical examinations of which we are aware. There is no research aimed at confirming, for example, the "situational stress" notion of sex abuse. Likewise, there are no studies that have investigated a "cultural norm or attitudinal" theory of sex abuse—that abusers hold more patriarchal attitudes or have attitudes that give more legitimacy to having sex with children.

Of all disinhibition theories, it is clear that the one with the most empirical support is that of alcohol involvement. The "failure of the incest avoidance mechanism" theory as it relates to stepfathers also receives some support.

## Conclusion

This chapter reviewed empirical research to discover what support exists for theories that attempt to explain why adults become sexually interested in and involved with children. These theories are organized into four basic categories: (1) emotional congruence—why the adult has an emotional need to relate to a child; (2) sexual arousal—why the adult could become sexually aroused by a child; (3) blockage—why alternative sources of sexual and emotional gratification are not available; and (4) disinhibition—why the adult is not deterred from such an interest by normal prohibitions. The review suggests that (1) the best experimental research has been directed toward establishing that sexual abusers do show an unusual pattern of sexual arousal toward children, although no substantiated theory yet exists about why this is so; (2) a number of studies have concurred that molesters are blocked in their social and heterosexual relationships; (3) alcohol is well established as a disinhibiting factor that plays a role in a great many sexual abuse offenses; (4) at least one study gives support to the "emotional congruence" idea that children, because of their lack of dominance, have some special meaning for pedophiles; and (5) there is evidence that many sexual abusers were themselves victims of abuse when they were children. In the next chapter we discuss some of the shortcomings of this research literature and make some suggestions for how the framework and findings reviewed here might improve upon it.

# 4

# Abusers: Special Topics

**David Finkelhor**

Surveying the research makes clear that, in quantity alone, a substantial amount of research exists on sexual abusers. But at the same time, this research is so flawed with conceptual and methodological problems that there is good reason to question virtually everything this accumulated work reveals. This chapter will outline some of these major problems and make suggestions about ways of correcting them.

## *Single-Factor Theories*

A serious problem in the field of research on child molesters has been the tendency to try to explain all child molesting with single-factor theories—for example, the theory that child molesters are all immature, or that child molesters all have some kind of hormonal problem. So far the research has shown that no single factor can begin to explain fully all sexual abuse.

One current flagrant example of the problem is the attempt to explain child molesters as simply persons who were themselves the victims of molestation. As was indicated in the previous chapter, there are several studies that do suggest that many incarcerated sexual abusers have histories of sexual abuse (Gebhard et al., 1965; Groth, 1979; Langevin et al., 1985; Seghorn et al., n.d.). Such findings have been snatched hastily from the context of all the research done on sex offenders and given great emphasis by journalists and even some professionals. In recent times, whenever the question, "Why do men abuse?" is asked, the answer most frequently given is that they themselves were victims of abuse. Unfortunately, the fixation on this overly simple, single-factor explanation poses serious risks for the field. We need to discuss some of the limitations of this explanation, and some of the risks that its popularity poses.

First of all, the actual finding that many molesters were themselves victims, although replicated in several studies, is itself subject to some important qualifications. There is a serious question whether or not it is a finding that can be generalized to all molesters. The studies establishing this finding have been mostly on incarcerated child molesters. These molesters constitute a relatively small portion of all offenders—the ones who were so repetitive, compulsive, and flagrant in their molesting that they were caught, convicted, and jailed. Among this more pathological group, it may be more likely that one would find a history of sexual abuse. Among a more representative group of sex abusers, histories of sexual abuse might not be nearly so common.

A second problem with the findings is that even though the amount of sexual abuse in the backgrounds of molesters may seem high, it has not been shown conclusively that it is higher than among similar men who did not become molesters. The studies so far have not really used adequate comparison groups. It is hardly convincing to compare child molesters to police officers, as one study did. There are even problems in comparing incarcerated molesters to men selected randomly in the general population, because incarcerated offenders come disproportionately from certain disadvantaged sectors of the population. It may be that incarcerated molesters have been abused more than other men in general, but not abused more than their brothers or neighborhood friends who did not grow up to be molesters. The abuse may be related to their families or social backgrounds or even the fact that they got caught, not to the fact that they were molesters.

An adequate study of the so-called intergenerational transmission of abuse should meet a number of requirements. It should include a more representative spectrum of offenders, including intrafamily abusers and abusers who are not incarcerated. It should use a more rigorous definition of "a history of sexual abuse" than has been used previously. Finally, it should establish a control group of men from the same backgrounds— for example, neighborhood friends, schoolmates, or relatives— who did not grow up to be abusers.

Now let us suppose that the deficiencies are corrected and this more rigorous study still finds more victims of sexual abuse among molesters than among their nonmolester peers. (Based on the evidence to date, it seems probable that this will be the case, although the relationship may not be as strong or the prevalence as high as some past studies have indicated.) Nonetheless, some major qualifications still need to be observed. It is quite clear that not *all* abusers were themselves abused. Even if one generalizes from the available studies on incarcerated offenders, the maximum number one would expect with this factor in their histories would be between 30% and 60% of abusers. In a representative population of molesters, the number might be much lower. Therefore, this explanation still cannot be said to solve fully the question of why someone becomes an abuser. Other explanations are needed for the nonmolested molesters.

Moreover, other explanations also are required even for those molesters who were themselves abused. It is clear that being molested in itself is not enough to create a molester. Otherwise all those who were molested would themselves become molesters. We know from many clinical histories that this is not the case. In fact, it is probable that only a *small* percentage of victims go on to become abusers. What are the additional circumstances or events that influence a victim of abuse to become an abuser himself? These require other explanations. For example, it would seem that, given the small number of female abusers compared to the large number of female victims, the relationship between being a victim and becoming a victimizer is generally contingent on the victim being a male. This may be because male socialization puts stress on being powerful and in control. Victimizing others may be the response encouraged by male socialization to the insult to masculinity involved in being a victim of abuse. The "explanation" of molestation implied by this combination of factors could just as easily be attributed to male socialization as to a history of sexual abuse.

Other contingencies certainly are involved also in the relationship between being victimized and victimizing others. For example, it may be that only when the abuse is accompanied by intense humiliation does it create a need to reenact the molestation. When victims receive support and comfort, the relationship may be nonexistent. It may be also that only when the abuse becomes the focus of a powerful sexual fantasy does it lead to future molestations. When children are not made to feel guilty about sexual fantasies or have opportunities to develop normal fantasies, no deviant fantasy may develop and victimized children may not become molesters.

The relationship between victimization and victimizing is also clarified by the previously discussed factors of blockage and disinhibition (see Chapter 3). It is probable that victims of sexual abuse who develop the capacity for emotional and sexual intimacy of a more normative sort—for example, through later corrective experiences—do not become molesters. It is also probable that victims of sexual abuse who have well-developed social consciences and an ability to identify with others do not become molesters. Only when these capacities are lacking, due perhaps to emotional deprivation or additional developmental traumas, does the experience of being a victim form the basis for becoming an abuser.

Obviously, as these examples have been intended to show, the connection is not a simple or single-factor one. A finding that many molesters were themselves molested is not the answer to the question, but simply the framework for many new questions. Studies must examine the whole complex of factors that in conjunction with a history of molestation may go into the development of molesting behavior. The idea that abusers can be explained by the fact that they were abused is just not adequate.

The dangers of this single-factor theory about victims becoming victimizers are numerous and timely. For one, it has created in many people a premature and unfounded confidence that we understand the source of the problem. In addition to being a bad basis for public policy, it inevitably discourages the serious search for a whole host of other factors that must play a role in the creation of an abuser. Second, because the explanation places responsibility on a deviant childhood event, it has reinforced a *psychopathology-oriented* view of offenders at the expense of views that take into account sociological aspects. What is focused on as causing the abuse are factors that make the abuser different because of his childhood problem, not factors that may be shared by broad segments of society. However, the current research that shows molesting behavior to be very widespread requires a consideration of these collective aspects, especially in thinking about prevention. But because the intergenerational transmission explanation relies exclusively on a childhood experience that we cannot return and change, it breeds cynicism that we can be effective in prevention.

All the above are serious dangers stemming from the mass popularization of a simple-minded intergenerational transmission theory, but the most serious by far is the effect this theory has on victims. The idea that victims grow up to become abusers has struck terror into the hearts of victims, in particular male victims, and their parents. These people, now even more than in the past, have the unrealistic and unnecessary fear that they or their children are inevitably destined to become abusers. Although not a possibility to be ignored completely, these concerns are almost certainly exaggerated. And because we do not really know what the true probability is or what other contingencies are involved, we cannot target these concerns to the group that needs to hear them or give families much guidance about what to do. It is even possible that the fear itself has some self-fulfilling properties that may prompt some children to become molesters who would not otherwise have done so.

Because of these kinds of dangers, it is incumbent on all professionals and researchers to educate people about the true scientific status of the notion of "intergenerational transmission." They must caution that the theory still is being confirmed. More important, they need to emphasize that our understanding is that this is just one possible factor among many that contributes to the development of molesting behavior and that it is not necessarily the most important. Certainly they must insist that there is no inevitability about the relationship between being a victim and becoming a victimizer. Going beyond this particular explanation, researchers need to caution against all single-factor theories and quick explanations in general, because they can lead easily to misinformed public attitudes and short-sighted public policy.

### *The Four-Factor Model*
### *as an Alternative*

In combating single-factor theories, the four-factor model presented in the previous chapter is a healthy alternative. It encourages an appropriately complex view of the situation and at the same time gives some order to the possibly confusing array of theories that have been proposed. However, it is more than merely a classification scheme. It can also be used to generate theory about pedophilia.

First, the model shows how many single-factor theories of pedophilia really imply other processes that have not been specified fully in the theory before. For example, some theories of emotional congruence seem to imply that sexual arousal naturally follows without having to be explained: Because a man gets immature emotional satisfaction from relating to children, this explains his molesting. But many people get a great amount, perhaps even the majority, of their emotional gratification from relating to children without turning the children into sexual partners. The four-factor model suggests that, in addition to emotional congruence, arousal needs to be explained, not just taken for granted.

Similarly, theories of disinhibition seem to imply prior levels of sexual interest that would otherwise be inhibited. The fact that some fathers believe they have the right to do what they want with their children explains sexual abuse only if these fathers have some prior sexual interest in the children. But the theories do not specify where these sexual interests come from. This prior interest needs to be explained, too.

Stated somewhat differently, the four-factor model suggests that a complete theory of pedophilia needs to address issues on a number of different levels. Pedophilic behavior may not be explained adequately simply by the fact that an adult is sexually aroused by children. There may be adults who are so aroused but who have alternative sources of sexual gratification or who are inhibited by ordinary social controls from acting on their arousal. A full explanation may have to show why an adult was capable of being aroused, why he directed his impulse toward a child, and why no inhibitions halted the enacting of the impulse.

Similarly, there are many adults who are blocked in their ability to gain sexual and emotional gratification from adults. However, most of those adults may have little emotional congruence for children or little sexual arousal to children and may be inhibited from acting on such feelings even if they had them. An adequate theory needs to explain the presence of pedophilia using several, if not all, of these levels simultaneously.

This multiple-level model of pedophilia, as indicated by some of the above examples, suggests that there may be many people who have important prerequisite components for engaging in sexual abuse but who never do. Theories from only one level of the model will never accurately discriminate between those who engage and those who do not engage in such behavior. Although molesters will always show up as having many of these characteristics—for example, arousal to children, shyness, impulsivity, need for dominance, or a history of being victimized themselves—there will be large numbers of "false positives" in the population at large, people who have these characteristics too, but, because the behavior is not released by other factors, never become molesters.

## Explaining the Male Monopoly

One of the most interesting shortcomings in the literature on sexual abusers is the virtual absence of any attempt to explain a fundamental and long-recognized fact: They are predominantly men. This fact has been taken for granted and ignored as a matter of major theoretical importance, even though it suggests some very powerful explanations of why sexual abusers abuse. This fact, and theories that might explain it, can be used to better advantage in research on sexual abuse.

The male monopoly on child molesting has long been recognized, but some commentators have recently started to challenge this assumption (Plummer, 1981; Sgroi, 1982). These commentators have speculated that the number of female sex abusers might be greatly obscured and underestimated because of cultural biases against seeing the sexual behavior of adult females toward children as abuse.

However, practically no evidence supports this theory. Among reported cases of abuse, 90% or more of offenders appear to be men (Finkelhor, 1984; Finkelhor & Hotaling, 1983). Interestingly, when women are recorded as having been involved in molestation, more often than not it is at the instigation and encouragement of men. More important, however, even in general population surveys in which people reveal their own unreported childhood sexual experiences (positive or negative), 95% of the adult contacts with girls and 80% of the adult contacts with boys are made by men. (For extended review of this matter and the arguments surrounding it, see Finkelhor & Russell, 1984.)

This male preponderance among offenders needs to be explained and the explanation could serve as a touchstone for theories of sexual abuse. Gender, as a variable, appears to interact with virtually every other variable proposed by every other theory. Every theory of pedophilia needs to explain not just why adults become sexually interested in children, but why that explanation applies primarily to males and not to females.

Let us return, for example, to the earlier-mentioned idea that many abusers were themselves the victims of sexual abuse. Often a Stoller-type theory is invoked to explain this: A victimized child becomes a victimizer in an attempt to master the trauma and take on the power of the adult who victimized him (see Stoller, 1975).

The problem is that many more girls are the victims of sexual abuse than boys (McLaughlin, 1982). If being the victim of sexual abuse increases the risk of becoming an abuser, then there should be more female sexual abusers than there are. The Stoller-type theory, however, says nothing about this phenomenon. There is no reason implicit in the theory why girls should not master their trauma through an identification with the abuser, just as boys do. If this happens, at least it happens in a different way. Perhaps it has to do with the fact that males are usually the abusers and girls do not readily identify with the male abusers. However, the sex of the abuser has not been cited as an important contingency when the theory is applied to boys. Sexual victimization at the hands of both women and men is mentioned as likely to contribute to becoming an abuser among men (deYoung, 1982).

In reaction to this dilemma, some people have pointed out that although girl victims may not often grow up to be abusers, they may grow up to be the mothers of victims. The rates of victimization in the mothers of victims have been cited as being very high (Goodwin, McCarthy, & DiVasto, 1982). However, although this may be a parallel phenomenon, a different kind of theory needs to be invoked to explain it. And it does not change the fact that every theory of sexual abuse, just like this one, has to have a way of accounting for the different operation of its dynamics in males as opposed to females.

The Stoller-type theory is only one example. A host of other examples could be given, including the following:

(1) *Emotional congruence:* If arrested development leads to sexual interest in children, why not among women?

(2) *Sexual arousal:* If powerful childhood sexual experiences condition a sexual interest in children among men, why not among women?

(3) *Blockage:* If absence of adult sexual opportunities drives some men to seek out children, why does not the same hold true among women?

(4) *Disinhibition:* If impulsivity and alcohol abuse lead to acting upon pedophilic urges among men, why not among women?

The answers to all these questions are the work for a generation of researchers. A complete answer will not be attempted here. However, using the four-factor model, I would suggest a variety of the explanations that might be entertained in trying to understand the male monopoly and how it can be integrated with previous theoretical work on pedophilia.

*(1) Emotional Congruence.* There are two important reasons that women might find relating sexually to a child to be much less congruent and emotionally satisfying for them:

- Being in a position of dominance or authority is antagonistic to the role relationship that women associate with sexual behavior. Women are socialized to prefer partners who are older, larger, and more powerful than themselves.
- Women do not generally act as initiators in sexual relationships, and, because they would rarely be invited by children to engage in sex, such contacts would be unlikely to arise.

*(2) Sexual Arousal.* Men's and women's patterns of sexual arousal are very different, due both to socialization and perhaps to biological factors. Some of these factors must certainly contribute to the male monopoly.

- Men appear to be more interested in sex with a greater number of partners than women (Symonds, 1978).
- Men seem to be able to be aroused more easily by sexual stimuli divorced from any context—a case in point: men's interest in pornography (Gagnon, 1977). This may make it easier for men to be aroused by children simply because they have sex organs,

whether or not the children appear to be interested or appropriate partners.

- Women appear to be better able to distinguish situations of sexual and nonsexual affection (Person, 1980). Men may be more likely to define affectional contexts as sexual and become sexually aroused.
- Boys tend to have more childhood sexual experiences than girls (Kinsey, Pomeroy, & Martin, 1948; Kinsey et al. 1953), and, to the extent that these experiences condition a later interest in sex with children, it would be expected that women are less affected.

*(3) Blockage.* Men and women appear to react in different ways to the unavailability of sexual opportunities. Having sexual opportunities seems to be more important to the maintenance of self-esteem in men than in women (Person, 1980). Thus, when other alternatives are blocked, men may more readily turn to children (or other sexual outlets) to maintain their sense of self-esteem.

*(4) Disinhibition.* When it comes to the violation of other individuals disinhibition does appear to be more a male than a female problem as reflected in the large disparity in rates of criminal behavior of all sorts. However, there are specific inhibitions for sexual abuse that may also operate differentially.

- Because of preparation for or performance of maternal responsibilities, women may be more sensitive to the well-being of children, and may be more inhibited from sexual contact by the possibility that such contact would be harmful to the child (Herman, 1981).
- Similarly, being more often victims of sexual misuse of various kinds, women may be better able to empathize with the potential for harm that may result from such contact, and thus be inhibited from doing so.
- Sexual contact with children may be condoned more by male subculture than by female subculture (Rush, 1980).

In addition to the differences between males and females noted here, there are no doubt other factors that need to be considered in understanding why molesting is such a predominantly male domain.

## Research on Child Molester Recidivism

Another serious shortcoming in the sex-offender literature is the scant attention given to the study of sex-offender recidivism. The most important public policy question for judges, prosecutors, defense attorneys, and therapists who work with sexual abuse cases is how likely child molesters are to reoffend after they have been caught and punished. One point of view within the criminal justice community tends to see child molesters as incorrigible; long prison sentences for offenders, then, are the only way to protect the community. Others, however, take a more optimistic view. They hold that being caught deters many offenders from risking the crime again and that, especially when treated, these offenders have a fairly high probability of long-term reform. Unfortunately, there is painfully little evidence to resolve this debate fully. Only a few efforts have been made to follow up identified child molesters over a period of time to find out whether or not and under what conditions they do continue to offend.

Those few attempts are badly flawed and, probably for that reason, not well known. But they provide some measure, however crude, of the rate at which some offenders reoffend, and by examining them we may learn more about how to study this issue better in the future.

### Available Studies

Most of the follow-up studies on child molesters have similar formats. Investigators take a group of child molesters (usually together with other sex offenders) who have been released from prison and then comb criminal justice records for a period of subsequent years to find out if these offenders committed any additional offenses. A number of studies with this approach are

TABLE 4.1

**Recidivism Rates from Various Studies of Convicted Offenders**

| | Recidivism Rate (percentage) | | | | % of Sample Who Are Child Molesters |
|---|---|---|---|---|---|
| | Any Offense | Sex Offense | N | Years of Follow-Up | |
| Christiansen et al. | 24 | 11 | 3175 | 14-24 | 68 |
| Fitch | 42 | 25 | 139 | 4-9 | 100 |
| Groth | 30 | 13 | 194 | 3 | a |
| Frisbie & Dondis | | | | | |
| female victims | | 18 | 1035 | 1-7 | 100 |
| male victims | | 35 | 428 | 1-7 | 100 |
| Hall | | 23 | 313 | 5 | 100 |
| Meyer & Romero | 44 | 6 | 48 | 10 | 100 |
| Prentky | 50 | 30 | 137 | 1-24 | 100 |
| Radzinowicz | 28 | 18 | 404 | 4 | 100 |
| Soothill & Gibbens | 48 | 23 | 174 | 23 | 85 |
| Tracy et al. | 23 | 13 | 141 | 5 | <52 |

a. Combines 122 untreated and 72 treated sex offenders, exact offense unspecified.

listed in Table 4.1. All these studies used groups of incarcerated offenders, two of them from outside the United States (Christiansen, Ellers-Nielsen, Le Maine, & Sturup, 1965, used a sample from Denmark; Soothill & Gibbens, 1978, used a sample from England).

Among many problems with the studies, one is that several did not distinguish clearly between the child molesters and other kinds of sex offenders, including rapists and exhibitionists, when they calculated their recidivism figures. Thus in the fifth column of Table 4.1 we show the percentage of the study group that was made up of child molesters. Another problem is that many studies did not follow up each molester for a fixed period of time. A frequent approach was to include offenders who were released over a number of years, and to check the records up to a certain cutoff date in search of reoffenses. Thus some offenders had been followed up for substantially shorter periods of time than others. This accounts for the variable follow-up times shown in the fourth column of the table.

Most of the researchers looked for evidence of any new offense as well as specifically sexual offenses. Thus, in the first column of the table, we see that somewhere between 23% and 50% of the convicted child molesters or sex offenders were known to have committed some subsequent offense. The mean for the 8 studies shown, giving equal weight to each study, was 36% committing any subsequent offense. Many of these offenses, however, were thefts or violence that had nothing to do with sex. The percentage who had subsequently committed a specifically sexual offense was lower, ranging from 6% to 35%, with the mean for the 10 studies about 20%. According to 2 of the studies (Christensen et al., 1965; Frisbie & Dondis, 1965), approximately three-fourths of the later sex offenses were of the same type as the original one. These figures suggest a fairly large amount of subsequent criminality and reoffending among convicted child molesters.

**Problems with Studies**

These figures need to be taken with many cautions, however. There are serious problems that limit any conclusion that can be drawn from them. First of all, they probably gravely understate the amount of subsequent offending committed by the men who were studied. The investigators routinely used as their criteria of recidivism subsequent offenses that *came to the attention of the authorities*. In fact, in many cases, the new offense was counted only if a *conviction* occurred. We know from many other sources of evidence that the vast majority of sexual offenses never are reported, never come to the attention of the authorities, and, even when they do, the probability of conviction is still low. So it is virtually certain that some and perhaps many of the offenders committed subsequent offenses that were not detected and not counted in the studies.

Second, the findings about the men in these studies, sobering as they are, probably cannot be applied to all child molesters. The kind of individuals who would be included in these studies would probably be among the types of offenders most likely to reoffend in the first place. Because very few offenders get caught and sent to prison, those who do are men who have patterns of repetitive offending and who often have been convicted of previous offenses. Moreover, they are also men who have committed other kinds of nonsexual criminal acts along with their child molesting. So the men in these studies tend to be persons with other criminal propensities as well as with uncontrolled inclinations to molest. It might well be that a sample of nonconvicted and nonincarcerated offenders would be less likely to commit abuse again.

There have been at least two studies on these nonincarcerated individuals, and one of them found an unusually low recidivism rate. Northwest Treatment Associates (Smith & Wolfe, 1985) in Seattle reported reoffense rates of 3% for a group of 126 child molesters who had been treated as outpatients and followed up for an average of 24 months. Knowledge of new offenses was not based on a systematic records check, but rather on self-reports or reports from family members or police, which may partly explain the low rate. Abel et al. (1984), with another group of outpatient child molesters (a mixture of convicted, nonconvicted, and even some publicly undetected offenders), reported that, of 24 followed up for 12 months after treatment, 21% had committed another sexual offense, a rate more in line with the studies of incarcerated offenders. Abel et al. also relied on self-reports as their main technique for finding out about reoffenses, but, unlike Northwest Treatment, Abel et al. promised offenders complete confidentiality for their admission. This may explain their higher rates. It should be noted that in both of these cases, the child molesters under study were receiving some of the most intensive, innovative, and up-to-date therapeutic assistance available in the United States, so their rates may not be applicable to other offenders who are untreated or treated in less sophisticated settings.

Another problem with almost all these studies, both with incarcerated and nonincarcerated offenders, is the short time span over which offenders were followed up. Clinicians have noted that child molesting is like other addictive behavior in that the risk to reoffend seems to extend over a long period of time if not a whole life span (Carnes, 1983). Thus a child molester may appear to have reformed for a while, but then under conditions of stress much later he may revert to the original pattern. This clinical observation is supported by Soothill and Gibbons (1978), who completed one of the longest follow-ups (22 years) and found that the longer period dramatically increased their rates. That is, when they estimated recidivism on the basis of their figures for the first 5 years, the rate was only 11% for new sex offenses, half of the rate they obtained with the full 22-year follow-up. Meyer and Romero (1980) also point out how long a period child molesters remain at risk. Whereas for rapists, most offenders recorded 90% of their arrests by age 36, in the case of pedophiles, it was not until age 45 that 90% of their arrests had been reported. Thus studies that follow up offenders for periods as short as 5 years or less may be producing substantial underestimates of true rates of recidivism.

### High-Risk Recidivists

In addition to the absolute rates of recidivism, perhaps the most interesting and valuable information from these studies concerns who is most likely to reoffend. Here the studies show substantial consensus. For example, they are in complete agreement that abusers of boys and exhibitionists are among those most likely to repeat. Three studies found that offenders against boys were at least twice as likely to repeat the offense as offenders against girls (Frisbee & Dondis, 1965, 35% versus 18%; Fitch, 1962, 40% versus 13%; Radinowicz, 1957, 27% versus 13%). The rates of reoffenses by exhibitionists were also extremely high: for example, Frisbee and Dondis (1965), 41%; Meyer and Romero (1980), 51%. Many studies have found that offenders against boys tend to start their offending earlier, to be more exclusively pedophilic in their sexual interests, and to have more of an ideological commitment to their offending as a lifestyle (Abel et al., 1984; Groth, 1979; Quinsey, 1985). All of this may contribute to their greater propensity to reoffend.

The studies are also in agreement that incest offenders tend to have low recidivism rates: Frisbee and Dondis (1965) found

10% for fathers and stepfathers (versus 18% for other offenders against girls); Christenson et al. (1965) found 12% for "paternal incest" (versus 24% for other sex offenders); and Tracy, Donnelly, Morgenbesser, and Macdonald (1983) found 11% for "incest" offenders (versus 23% for other sex offenders). Although Abel et al.'s (1984) findings urge caution because many incest offenders have committed extrafamilial child molestations as well, nonetheless, many incestuous fathers do seem to be men who take advantage of the availability of and special relationship with their daughters. Once the daughters are older or well protected, incest offenders may be less likely than other child molesters to reoffend. However, studies of incest offenders need to have especially long follow-ups, because there is some indication that at later stages in the life cycle they again molest, this time with grandchildren and nieces (Goodwin, Cormeir, & Owen, 1983). Studies of incest offenders need also be cognizant of the especially great reluctance of families to report reoffenses, even by formerly convicted relatives.

Several of the studies also looked at other characteristics that were associated with recidivism among child molesters. Tracy et al. (1963) found that those who had prior arrests for sex offenses and those with personality disorders were most likely to reoffend. Christensen et al. (1965) found that prior offenders and younger offenders were greater recidivists. Fitch (1962) concluded that three factors—a history of previous sex offenses, being single, and being young at the time of first offense—were associated with recidivism, but the age at the time of the offense for which the person was originally incarcerated was not. Fitch also failed to find any association between length of sentence, intelligence, or occupational status and likelihood to reoffend.

In what was the most sophisticated study (and the only one to use multivariate analysis), Meyer & Romero (1980) found only two factors to predict recidivism: (1) most important, a prior arrest for a sex offense in adulthood, and (2) a self-reported history of indecent exposure. They also found that single offenders, younger offenders, those with "constricted thought flow," and those with negative feelings toward their mothers were more likely to reoffend, but these factors dropped to nonsignificance when controlling for prior criminal behavior. Factors that were not associated with recidivism, even initially, included the quality of the relationship with the father, the current level of sexual relations with women, feelings about the self, a childhood history of having been abused, or a history of alcohol problems.

The clear and unsurprising conclusion from all the studies, then, is that a history of prior offenses creates greater risk for future offenses. It also seems probable that offenders who begin offending at a younger age continue to commit more crimes. Some other factors related to personality, family background, and marital status may also play a role (each got support in some study). The findings from Meyer and Romero (1980) suggest that these types of factors are associated with a general risk for repetitive offending, thus they drop out when prior history of offenses is taken into account. But they still should be taken seriously as contributing to the pattern.

### Efficacy of Treatment

Unfortunately, the available studies tell us very little about what is perhaps the most important question: Does treatment reduce recidivism? The studies listed in Table 4.1 consist of some in which the offenders were treated, some in which they were not, and some with mixed groups. The recidivism rates for the treated groups are not consistently better than the nontreated groups, but such comparisons are unfair because of the different populations, different follow-up periods, and different criteria used by the studies. More to the point, three of the studies directly compared treatment and nontreatment groups. Meyer and Romero (1980) found no difference between the groups, following them up over 10 years. Hall (1985) found no difference between the groups over 5 years, but Groth (1983) did: Of 72 *treated* sex offenders, only 19% violated parole or were rearrested within 3 years, compared to 36% of the *untreated* group.

However, some cautions are in order about the Groth findings. First, Groth's sample included all types of sex offenders—

rapists against adults and exhibitionists against adults, as well as child molesters—and it is not clear from the report whether or not the results apply to child molesters taken alone. Second, Groth's follow-up period is relatively short—only 3 years—compared to others. In light of earlier remarks about the extended period of risk, Groth may be demonstrating only that treated offenders take longer to reoffend, not that they reoffend any less. Third, Groth's treatment groups consisted of men who volunteered from the general sex-offender population of the prison. It is likely that the offenders most motivated to get help would be the ones least likely to commit abuse again, and their rates might well have been lower even without participation in treatment. So it cannot be said that Groth's, or anybody else's, recidivism study provides strong evidence in favor of the positive effects of treatment.

This, however, does not mean that treatment is ineffective. For one thing, there are many studies showing treatment "successes" (for a review, see Kelley, 1982). Unfortunately, the outcome measures in these treatment studies have been such things as attitude change, physiological arousal measures, and very short-term self-reports of offending behavior. The fact that these measures show improvement is encouraging, but not nearly as important as the question of whether or not they reoffend in the long run. Another consideration is that there have been a great number of recent innovations in treatment techniques, and these really have not been evaluated with recidivism studies. The fairest judgment at the present time is that good treatment programs for child molesters have not been evaluated yet in terms of their ability to reduce long-term recidivism.

## What Is Needed
## in Sex Offender Research

Good studies of child molesters with long-term follow-ups are badly needed. They could answer a whole host of very important policy questions, including the following: Why does someone become a molester? What are some precursors that might help us to identify potential molesters? Does treatment work? What kind of treatment works best? Do longer sentences reduce the amount of subsequent offending? Can we effectively predict who is at high risk to reoffend? Can incest fathers safely be reunited with their families? However, we are a long way from designing good studies on child molesters to answer these questions. Such studies will take much planning, cooperation, money, and—perhaps most importantly—time. What follows are some of the difficulties with which study designs must contend.

A major problem with research on sexual abusers has to do with the fact that almost all such research is based on subjects recruited from the criminal justice system, either incarcerated offenders or probationers in treatment. This fact certainly casts doubt on the generalizability of almost all known findings about sexual abusers. Incarcerated offenders or probationers in treatment constitute at most a very tiny and unrepresentative fraction of all sexual abusers. From the studies reviewed earlier, it is clear that millions of children are subject to sexual advances and actions by older persons. We know that only a relatively small proportion of these are ever reported to the authorities. For example, in Russell's (1984) San Francisco survey, only 2% of the intrafamily and 6% of the extrafamily sexual abuse incidents were reported to the police. Even when incidents are reported to authorities, many offenders are not apprehended, many do not go to trial, and only a few are convicted. Rogers (1982), tracking reported cases within the Washington, D.C., criminal justice system, found that only half of all identified suspects would be arrested, and that less than a third subsequently would be convicted. Thus those sex abusers who are convicted or even seen within the criminal justice system are a small fraction of all offenders, and probably those who were most flagrant and repetitive in their offending, most socially disadvantaged, and least able to persuade criminal justice authorities to let them off. It seems virtually certain that such a group cannot be deemed representative of offenders.

This raises all kinds of disturbing questions about findings based on research with such groups. Could the finding that pedophiles are shy, ineffectual, and passive (Toobert et al., 1959; Langevin, 1983) result from the fact that it is primarily such sexual abusers who are apprehended? Could the finding that alcoholism is associated with sexual abuse (Gebhard et al., 1965; Rada, 1976; Stokes, 1964) result from the fact that alcoholic child molesters are more likely to be caught and convicted? There is reason for strong skepticism about the generalizability of the whole literature on sexual abusers.

There are still more problems with the samples of offenders chosen from the criminal justice system. For example, are some of the characteristics of sexual abusers not a cause of their offending, but rather a result of their contact with the criminal justice system? If offenders appear to have low self-esteem, could it be that this is what happens to anyone's self-esteem when he or she is caught and incarcerated (Zimbardo, Haney, Banks, & Jaffe, 1972)? Consideration also needs to be given to the possibility that institutionalized offenders have special incentives to provide researchers with answers that they think the researchers want to hear or that will help them get released. McCaghy (1967), for example, found that pedophiles altered their explanations of their own offenses on the basis of the concepts they learned in therapy. In short, there is a very pressing need for researchers to get away from prisons and to study as broad a group of offenders as possible, including offenders who have not been detected previously.

A good sex-offender study should start with as representative a group of offenders as possible. At the very least, this means getting beyond studies based at a single prison facility or hospital for sexually dangerous offenders. One improvement is to start with offenders who have just been arrested and are being evaluated. Such a sample would then include persons whose cases were dropped, who were not convicted, who went to diversion programs, or who did not go to prison for some other reason. Some other criteria besides an actual conviction (for example, the prosecutor's or therapist's judgment) would need to be used to determine whether or not the offense actually occurred. Although still within the criminal justice system, this would at least create a more representative molester group than the usual prison study. Even if the sample population consisted of all those convicted of an offense against children, irrespective of sentencing, the study would be more representative than most of the studies conducted to date.

For even more representative offender studies, investigators should try to include previously undetected molesters. This is not as impossible as it might at first seem. In their design, Abel et al. (1984) offered confidential treatment to any molester, and as a result obtained a population that included even molesters who had not been arrested. This is an excellent technique that can be used to include routinely some nonarrested offenders in a sample population. However, at the same time, studies should also try not to be based exclusively on a treatment program. Many molesters have no inclination whatsoever to seek treatment, and these may be some of the most repetitive offenders. A good idea would be to use a mixed group of offenders, some undetected molesters from an Abel et al.-type treatment program, along with some nontreatment arrestees from within the criminal justice system of the same jurisdiction.

If the effect of treatment is one of the variables of interest to the study, another caution must be observed: An effort needs to be made to prevent the treatment groups from being made up solely of volunteers. Ideally treatments (and no treatment) would be assigned to offenders on a randomized basis. But often this is not possible. What is to be avoided most is that the highly motivated offenders end up in treatment and others not. Thus treatments need to be applied to both motivated and nonmotivated groups in some fashion. Moreover, it will be extremely advantageous if measurements can be made at the start of the study concerning offenders' motivations for change, repetitiveness of current offending patterns, and other personality characteristics. In this way, the equivalence of treatment and nontreatment groups can be better ascertained.

As far as follow-up studies are concerned, if prior studies such as that of Soothill and Gibbens (1978) are taken into account, investigators need to plan to follow offenders for at least 10 years and preferably as many as 20. Admittedly this is an ambitious requirement. Naturally, interim data also should be collected and can be the basis of important findings. But their interim nature should be remembered; such findings may be changed by conclusions that emerge when the long-term follow-up has been completed.

Follow-up studies also need to plan to use multiple indices of recidivism. Records of arrests, convictions, and parole violations within the criminal justice system should be only one part of the evidence. Researchers need to try to collect self-report information directly from the offenders. Abel et al. (1984) have demonstrated that with guarantees of confidentiality a great number of otherwise withheld reports can be obtained. McCord (1983) also has demonstrated that a high proportion of offenders can be traced even after as many as 30 years, and that they will provide self-reports of criminal behavior. Researchers also should experiment with techniques of getting reports on recidivism from family members of offenders. Moreover, other records, such as child abuse rosters, should be used to supplement records of offenses from criminal justice sources.

Particular priority should be given to follow-up studies of incest offenders. Because incest offenders frequently are not incarcerated, previous recidivism studies may not have reliable information about their reoffense rates. The impression from several studies is that incest offenders tend to be at relatively low risk. But since the time when most of these studies were done, the number of reported cases of intrafamily sexual abuse has increased markedly and the handling of these cases has become an important matter of public policy. Debate has raged, for example, over whether or not it is safe to try to reunite daughters with their formerly sexually abusive fathers after these men have been treated. These important public policy questions require sophisticated studies of the reoffense patterns among incest offenders.

The study of child molesters is not an easy task. Such individuals do not make enthusiastic or cooperative subjects, and the matters of most interest to the researcher are often the exact ones the subjects are least interested in divulging. Yet there is perhaps no more important need in the field of sexual abuse. Research on offenders is an area in which little is known and additional findings may provide large payoffs for prevention and treatment efforts. For example, when research on physical child abusers demonstrated that single adolescent parents were at high risk of becoming abusers, it led very rapidly to prevention programs aimed at providing services to adolescent parents, thus reducing the likelihood of physical abuse before it occurred. If we had similar information on persons at high risk of committing sexual abuse, we might be able to devise similar sex abuse prevention programs. In addition, studies of offenders and their likelihood to reoffend may cast light on many crucial questions concerning the handling and treatment of child sex abuse cases. For example, after disclosure is it crucial to remove children from access to the offender? Can pretrial diversion programs be as effective as postconviction treatment? Is it important to incarcerate offenders for extended periods of time? Is any one form of offender treatment more effective than any other? All these questions require that we begin to have ways to measure the propensity of molesters to reoffend. It is of utmost importance in the effort to deal with the problem of sexual abuse that research be turned in this direction.

# 5

# Initial and Long-Term Effects: A Review of the Research

Angela Browne
David Finkelhor

Τhe clinical literature suggests that sexual abuse during childhood can play a role in the development of serious subsequent problems, ranging from anorexia nervosa to prostitution. However, empirical confirmation of these effects often has been lacking. This chapter will review the expanding empirical literature on the effects of child sexual abuse to try to sort out what has been established from what is still in the realm of speculation. The review will begin with a discussion of the initial effects of abuse, then turn to the long-term effects, and conclude with the studies on the impact of different kinds of abuse. Chapter 6 continues the topic with the presentation of a conceptual framework for thinking about the effects of sexual abuse, and Chapter 7 makes some suggestions for improving all the research in this area.

First, some caveats. As earlier chapters have pointed out, the phenomenon called *child sexual abuse* has been defined in different ways by different investigators. As might be expected, the studies reviewed here have employed diverse definitions as well. Some have focused only on experiences with older partners, excluding coerced sexual experiences with peers. Others have looked only at sexual abuse that was perpetrated by family members. Such differences in samples make comparisons among these studies difficult. However, we decided to include all the studies that looked at some portion of the range of experiences that are bounded by two criteria: (1) forced or coerced sexual behavior that is imposed on a child or (2) sexual behavior between a child and a much older person or a person in a caretaking role. (See Table 5.1 for breakdowns of the sample compositions of the studies reviewed.)

Two areas of the literature were not included in the review. First, there have been a small number of studies on the effects of "incest" (Farrell, 1982; Nelson, 1981), as well as one review of the effects of child sexual experiences in general (Constantine, 1980), that combine data on consensual peer experiences with those that involve either coercion or age disparity. Because we were unable to isolate sexual abuse in these studies, we had to exclude them. Second, we have decided to limit the review to female victims. Few clinical, and even fewer empirical, studies have been done on boys (for exceptions, see Finkelhor, 1979; Rogers & Terry, 1984; Sandfort, 1981; Wood & Dean, 1984), and it seems premature to draw conclusions at this point.[1] Under "empirical" studies, we have included any research that attempted to quantify the extent to which a sequela to sexual abuse appeared in a specific population. Some of these studies used objective measures; others were based primarily on the judgment of clinicians.

### Initial Effects

Initial effects of sexual abuse are those reactions occurring within two years of the termination of abuse. We have chosen this arbitrary cutoff to distinguish initial from long-term effects. These early reactions are often called "short-term" effects in the literature. We prefer the word *initial*, however, because *short-term* implies that the reactions do not persist—an assump-

## TABLE 5.1
## Studies of Effects of Sexual Abuse

| Author(s)/Year | Source of Sample | Sample Size (N) | Gender[a] | Age of Respondents[b] | Focus of Study[c] | Comparison Group |
|---|---|---|---|---|---|---|
| Anderson, Bach, and Griffith (1981) | sexual assault center | 227 | F = 155 M = 72 | Ad | I, E | no |
| Bagley & Ramsay (in press) | random sample | 679 | F = 401 M = 278 | A | I, E | yes |
| Benward & Densen-Gerber (1975) | drug treatment center | 118 | F = 118 | Ad, A | I | no |
| Briere (1984) | community health center | 153 | F = 153 | A | I, E | yes |
| Briere & Runtz (1985) | college students | 278 | F = 278 | Ad, A | I, E | yes |
| Courtois (1979) | recruited through ads and mental health agencies | 31 | F = 31 | A | I | no |
| DeFrancis (1969) | court cases | 250 | F = 217 M = 33 | C, Ad | I, E | no |
| deYoung (1982) | college students, therapy patients, and others | 80 | F = 72 M = 8 | C, Ad, A | I | no |
| Fields (1981) | prostitutes recruited after arrest | 85 | F = 85 | A | I | yes |
| Finkelhor (1979) | college students | 796 | F = 530 M = 266 | Ad, A | I, E | yes |
| Friedrich, Urquiza, & Beilke (1986) | sexual assault center, group therapy | 64 | F = 49 M = 15 | C | I, E | no |
| Fromuth (1983) | college students | 482 | F = 482 | Ad, A | I, E | yes |
| Harrison, Lumry, & Claypatch (1984) | dual disorder treatment program | 62 | F = 62 | A | I, E | yes |

(Continued)

145

# TABLE 5.1 (Continued)

| Author(s)/Year | Source of Sample | Sample Size (N) | Gender[a] | Age of Respondents[b] | Focus of Study[c] | Comparison Group |
|---|---|---|---|---|---|---|
| Herman (1981) | clients in therapy | 60 | F = 60 | Ad, A | I | yes |
| James & Meyerding (1977) | prostitutes selected from arrest records | | | | | |
| Study 1 | | 92 | F = 92 | Ad, A | I, E | no |
| Study 2 | | 136 | F = 136 | A | I, E | no |
| Landis (1956) | college students | 950 | F = 726 M = 224 | A | I, E | yes |
| Langmade (1983) | mental health centers, private clinics | 68 | F = 68 | A | I | yes |
| Meiselman (1978) | clinical records, psychiatric clinic | 108 | F = 97 M = 11 | C, Ad, A | I | yes |
| Oppenheimer et al. (1984) | clinical program, eating disorders | 22 | F = 22 | A | I, E | no |
| Peters, J. (1976) | rape crisis center | 100 | — | C | I | no |
| Peters, S. (1984) | follow-up, community random sample | 119 | F = 119 | A | I, E | yes |
| Russell (1984) | random sample | 930 | F = 930 | A | I, E | yes |
| Sedney & Brooks (1984) | college students | 301 | F = 301 | Ad, A | I, E | yes |
| Seidner & Calhoun (1984) | college students | 152 | F = 118 M = 34 | A | I, E | yes |
| Silbert & Pines (1981) | prostitutes recruited by ads | 200 | F = 200 | Ad, A | I, E | no |
| Tsai, Feldman-Summers, & Edgar (1979) | ads | 90 | F = 90 | A | I, E | yes |
| Tufts Study (1984) | clinical referrals | 156 | F = 122 M = 34 | C, Ad | I, E | no |

a. F = female;  M = male.
b. C = child; Ad = adolescent; A = adult.
c. I = intrafamilial;  E = extrafamilial.

tion that has yet to be substantiated. Overall, there have been rather few good empirical studies of initial effects, using widely accepted, objective measures, and large and representative samples of sexually abused children.

### Emotional Reactions and Self-Perceptions

Several empirical studies do give support to the clinical observations that children suffer negative emotional effects from childhood sexual abuse. But only two of these studies used standardized measures and compared subjects' scores to general population norms. In one of the early studies without standardized measures, DeFrancis (1969) reported that 66% of the victims were emotionally disturbed by the molestation; of these, 52% were mildly to moderately disturbed and 14% seriously disturbed. Only 24% were judged to be emotionally stable after the abuse. However, because this sample was drawn from court cases known to Prevention of Cruelty to Children services or to the police, and because the subjects came primarily from low-income and multiple-problem families who were on public assistance, these findings may have little generalizability.

In another study without standardized measures, Anderson, Bach, and Griffith (1981) reviewed clinical charts of 155 female adolescent sexual assault victims who had been treated at the Harborview Medical Center in Washington, D.C., and reported psychosocial complications in 63% of the subjects. Reports of "internalized psychosocial sequelae" (for example, sleep and eating disturbances, fears and phobias, depression, guilt, shame, and anger) were noted in 67% of female victims when the abuse was intrafamilial and 49% when the offender was not a family member. "Externalized sequelae" (including school problems and running away) were noted in 66% of intrafamilial victims and 21% of extrafamilial victims. However, it is possible that some of the judgments of these effects may be subjective.

In one of the better studies to date and one of the first to use standardized measures, researchers affiliated with the Division of Child Psychiatry at the Tufts New England Medical Center gathered data on families involved in a treatment program that was restricted to those children who had been victimized or revealed their victimization in the prior six months (Gomes-Schwartz, Horowitz, & Sauzier, 1985). Well-established measures—the Louisville Behavior Checklist (LBC), the Piers-Harris Self-Concept Scale, the Purdue Self-Concept Scale, and the Gottschalk Glesser Content Analysis Scales (GGCA)—with published norms and test validation data were used, so that characteristics of sexually abused children could be contrasted with norms for general and pyschiatric populations. Subjects ranged in age from infancy to 18 years and were divided into preschool, latency, and adolescence age groups. Data were gathered on four areas: overt behavior, somaticized reactions, internalized emotional states, and self-esteem.

In evaluating the initial effects of child sexual abuse, Tufts researchers (1984) found differences in the amount of pathology reported for different age groups. Of 4- to 6-year-olds in the study, 17% met the criteria for "clinically significant pathology," demonstrating more overall disturbance than a normal population but less than the norms for other children their age who were in psychiatric care. The highest incidence of psychopathology was found in the 7- to 13-year-old age group, with 40% scoring in the seriously disturbed range. Interestingly, few of the adolescent victims were found to exhibit severe psychopathology, except on a measure of neuroticism.

Friedrich, Urquiza, and Beilke (in press) also used a standardized measure in their study of 61 sexually abused females. Subjects were referred by a local sexual assault center for evaluation or by the outpatient department of a local hospital. Children in this sample had been abused within a 24-month period prior to the study. Using the Child Behavior Check List (see Achenbach & Edelbrock, 1983, for a description of this measure), Friedrich et al. reported that 46% of their subjects had significantly elevated scores on the Internalizing Scale of the CBCL (including behaviors described as fearful, inhibited, depressed, and overcontrolled) and 39% had elevated scores on the Externalizing Scale (aggressive, antisocial, and undercontrolled behavior). Only 2% of a normal sample would be expected to score in this range. Younger children (up to age 5) demonstrated a tendency to score high on the Internalizing Scale, and older children (ages 6 through 12) were more likely to have elevated scores on the Externalizing Scale.

Breaking down emotional impact into specific reactions, the most common initial effect noted in empirical studies, similar to reports in the clinical literature, is that of fear. However, exact proportions vary from a high of 83% reported by DeFrancis (1969) to 40% in Anderson, Bach, and Griffith (1981). Because of its use of standardized measures, we would give the most credence to the Tufts study (1984), which found that 45% of the 7- to 13-year-olds manifested severe fears as measured by the LBC, compared to 13% of the 4- to 6-year-olds. On the adolescent version of the LBC, 36% of the 14- to 18-year-olds had elevated scores on "ambivalent hostility," or the fear of being harmed.

Another initial effect in children is reactions of anger and hostility. Tufts researchers (1984) found that 45% to 50% of the 7- to 13-year-olds showed hostility levels that were substantially elevated on measures of aggression and antisocial behavior (LBC), as did 35% on the measure of hostility directed outward (GGCA). Of 4- to 6-year-olds, 13% to 17% scored above the norms on aggression and antisocial behavior (LBC); 25% of the 4- to 6-year-olds and 23% of the adolescents had elevated scores on hostility directed outward (GGCA). In his study of court cases, DeFrancis (1969) noted that 55% of the children showed behavioral disturbances, such as active defiance, disruptive behavior within the family, and quarreling or fighting with siblings or classmates. DeFrancis's sample might have been thought to overselect for hostile reactions; however, these findings are not very different from findings of the Tufts study for school-age children.

Guilt and shame are another frequently observed reaction to child sexual abuse, but few studies give clear percentages. DeFrancis (1969) observed that 64% of his sample expressed guilt, although more about the problems created by disclosure than about the molestation itself. Anderson et al. (1981) reported guilt reactions in 25% of the victims. Similarly, depression is frequently reported in the clinical literature, but, here too, specific figures rarely are given. Anderson et al. (1981) found that 25% of female sexual assault victims were depressed after the abuse.

Sexual abuse also is cited as having an effect on self-esteem, but this effect has not yet been established by empirical studies. In the DeFrancis (1969) study, 58% of the victims expressed feelings of inferiority or lack of worth as a result of having been victimized. However, in a surprising finding, the Tufts (1984) researchers, using the Purdue Self-Concept Scale, found no evidence that sexually abused children in any of the age groups had consistently lower self-esteem than a normal population of children.

## Physical Consequences and Somatic Complaints

Physical symptoms indicative of anxiety and distress are noted in the empirical literature as well as in clinical reports. In their chart review of female adolescent victims, Anderson et al. (1981) found that 17% had experienced sleep disturbances and 5% to 7% showed changes in eating habits after the victimization. Peters (1976), in a study of child victims of intrafamilial sexual abuse, reported that 31% had difficulty sleeping and 20% experienced eating disturbances. However, without a comparison group, it is hard to know if this is seriously pathological for any group of children, or for clinical populations in particular. Adolescent pregnancy is another physical consequence sometimes mentioned in empirical literature. DeFrancis (1969) reported that 11% of the child victims in his study became pregnant as a result of the sexual offense; however, this figure seems high compared to other samples. Meiselman (1978), in analyzing records from a Los Angeles psychiatric clinic, found only 1 out of 47 incest cases in which a victim was impregnated by her father.

## Effects on Sexuality

Reactions of inappropriate sexual behavior in child victims have been confirmed by two studies using standardized measures (Friedrich et al., 1986; Tufts, 1984). In the Tufts (1984) study, 27% of 4- to 6-year-old children scored significantly above clinical and general population norms on a sexual behavior scale that included having had sexual relations (possibly a confounding variable in these findings), open masturbation, excessive sexual curiosity, and frequent exposure of the genitals. Of the 7- to 13-year-old age group, 36% also demonstrated high levels of disturbance on the sexual behavior measure when contrasted to norms for either general or clinical school-age populations. Similarly, Friedrich et al. (in press), using the Child Behavior Check List to evaluate 3- to 12-year-olds, found that 70% of the males and 44% of the females scored at least one standard deviation above a normal population of that age group on the scale measuring sexual problems. Interestingly, sexual problems were most common among the younger girls and the older boys.

## Effects on Social Functioning

Other aftereffects of child sexual abuse mentioned in the literature include difficulties at school, truancy, running away from home, and early marriages by adolescent victims. Herman (1981) interviewed 40 patients in therapy who had been victims of father-daughter incest, and compared their reports with those from a group of 20 therapy clients who had seductive, but not incestuous, fathers. Of the incest victims, 33% attempted to run away as adolescents, compared to 5% of the comparison group. Similarly, Meiselman (1978) found that 50% of the incest victims in her sample had left home before the age of 18, compared with 20% of women in a comparison group of nonvictimized female patients. Younger children often went to a relative, whereas older daughters ran away or eloped, sometimes entering early marriages in order to escape the abuse. Two studies, neither with comparison groups, mention school problems and truancy. Of the child victims in Peters's (1976) study, 10% quit school, although all of his subjects were under the age of 12 at the time. Anderson et al. found that 20% of girls in their sample experienced problems at school, including truancy or quitting school.

Connections between sexual abuse and running away and delinquency are also suggested by several studies of children in special treatment or delinquency programs. Reich and Gutierres (1979) reported that 55% of the children in Maricopa County, Arizona, who were charged with running away or truancy or were listed as missing persons were incest victims. And in a study of female juvenile offenders in Wisconsin (1982), researchers found that 32% had been sexually abused by a relative or another person close to them.

### Summary of Initial Effects of Child Sexual Abuse

The empirical literature on child sexual abuse, then, does suggest the presence—in some portion of the victim population—of many of the initial effects reported in the clinical literature, especially reactions of fear, anxiety, depression, anger and hostility, and inappropriate sexual behavior. However, because many of the studies lacked standardized outcome measures and adequate comparison groups, it is not clear that these findings reflect the experience of all child victims of sexual abuse or are even representative of those children currently being seen in clinical settings. At this point, the empirical literature on the initial effects of child sexual abuse would have to be considered sketchy.

## Long-Term Effects

### Emotional Reactions and Self-Perceptions

In the clinical literature, depression is the symptom most commonly reported among adults molested as children, and empirical findings seem to confirm this. Two excellent community studies are indicative. Bagley and Ramsay (in press), in a community mental health study in Calgary utilizing a random sample of 387 women, found that subjects with a history of child sexual abuse scored more depressed on the Centre for Environmental Studies Depression Scale (CES-D) than did nonabused women (17% versus 9%) as well as on the Middlesex Hospital Questionnaire's measure of depression (15% versus 7%). Peters (1984), in a community study also based on a random sample in Los Angeles, interviewed 119 women and found that sexual abuse in which there was physical contact was associated with a higher incidence of depression and a greater number of depressive episodes over time, and that women who had been sexually abused were more likely to have been hospitalized for depression than were nonvictims. In a multiple regression that included both sexual abuse and family background factors (such as a poor relationship with a mother), the variable of child sexual abuse made an independent contribution to depression.

The link between child sexual abuse and depression has been confirmed in other nonclinical samples, as well. Sedney and Brooks (1984), in a study of 301 college women, found a greater likelihood for subjects with childhood sexual experiences to report symptoms of depression (65% versus 43% of the control group) and to have been hospitalized for depression (18% of the childhood experience group versus 4% of the control group). These positive findings are particularly noteworthy in light of the fact that the researchers used an overly inclusive definition of sexual experiences that may not have screened out some consensual experiences with peers. Their results are consistent, however, with those from a carefully controlled survey of 278 undergraduate women by Briere and Runtz (1985) using 72 items of the Hopkins Symptom Checklist (HSC), which indicated that sexual abuse victims as opposed to nonabused subjects had more depressive symptoms during the 12 months prior to the study.

Studies based on clinical samples (Herman, 1981; Meiselman, 1978) have not found such clear differences in depression between victims and nonvictims. For example, although Herman (1981) noted major depressive symptoms in 60% of the incest victims in her study, 55% of the comparison group also reported depression. Meiselman (1978) reported depressive symptoms in 35% of the incest victims whose psychiatric records she reviewed, compared to 23% of the comparison group; again, this difference was not significant.

However, both clinical and nonclinical samples have shown victims of child sexual abuse to be more self-destructive. In an extensive study of 153 "walk-ins" to a community health counseling center, Briere (1984) reported that 51% of the sexual abuse victims, versus 34% of nonabused clients, had a history of suicide attempts. Also, 31% of victims, compared to 19% of nonabused clients, exhibited a desire to hurt themselves. A high incidence of suicide attempts among victims of child sexual abuse has been found by other clinical researchers as well (for example, Harrison, Lumry, & Claypatch, 1984; Herman, 1981). Bagley and Ramsay (in press), in their community study, noted an association between childhood sexual abuse and suicide ideation or deliberate attempts at self-harm. And Sedney and Brooks (1984) found that 39% of their college student sample with child sexual abuse experiences reported having thoughts of hurting themselves, compared to 16% of the control-group. Of these respondents, 16% had made at least one suicide attempt (versus 6% of their peers). The depressive and self-destructive tendencies among victims of sexual abuse thus seem very well established.

## Somatic Disturbances and Dissociation

Less attention has been paid in the empirical literature to somatic problems as a long-term effect rather than as an initial reaction among victimized children. However, Briere and his colleagues have concerned themselves especially with this issue. One reaction observed in adults who were sexually victimized as children is symptoms of anxiety or tension. Briere (1984) reported that 54% of the sexual abuse victims in his adult clinical sample were currently experiencing anxiety attacks (compared to 28% of the nonvictims), 54% reported nightmares (versus 23%), and 72% had difficulty sleeping (compared with 55% of the nonvictims). In their college sample, Sedney and Brooks (1984) found 59% with symptoms indicating nervousness and anxiety (compared to 41% of the comparison group), 41% indicated extreme tension (versus 29% of the controls), and 51% had trouble sleeping (compared to 29% of the controls). In another college student group (Briere & Runtz, 1985), abuse victims were quite strongly differentiated from other students by their scores on the somatization scale (both chronic and acute) of the Hopkins Symptom Checklist. These findings are supported by results from community samples, with Bagley and Ramsay (in press) noting that 19% of their subjects who had experienced child sexual abuse reported symptoms indicating somatic anxiety on the Middlesex Hospital Questionnaire, compared to 9% of the nonabused subjects. The presence of anxiety in sexual abuse victims has thus been widely confirmed.

Another somatic outcome connected with sexual abuse in the literature is the development of eating disorders. In a British clinical program aimed at the treatment of women with eating disorders, 34% had been sexually abused before the age of 15 (about one-third with anorexia and two-thirds with bulimia). These researchers speculated that eating disorders may be a more common long-term effect of childhood sexual molestation than is currently recognized, even in nonclinical populations, as a reaction to coping with stress in adolescent and adult sexual life (Oppenheimer, Palmer, & Brandon, 1984).

Briere and his colleagues have drawn attention also to the issue of dissociation as a frequent symptom distinguishing victims of sexual abuse. Sexual abuse victims in the clinic setting disproportionately reported symptoms of dissociation and "spaciness" (42% versus 22%), as well as "out of body experiences" (21% versus 8%), and feeling that things are unreal (33% versus 11%). In their student sample, abuse victims also scored significantly higher than nonvictims on a Dissociation Scale derived from the Hopkins Symptom Checklist (Briere & Runtz, 1985). Briere and Runtz hypothesize that dissociation is a strategy that victims use to escape from the unpleasant sensations of the abuse experience and that this later becomes an autonomous symptom.

### Effects on Self-Esteem

The idea that sexual abuse victims continue to feel isolated and stigmatized as adults also has some support in the empirical literature, although these findings come only from the clinical populations. Of the victimized women in Briere's (1984) study, 64% reported feelings of isolation, compared to 49% of the controls. With incest victims, the figures are even higher: Herman (1981) reported that all of the women who had experienced father-daughter incest in her clinical sample had a sense of being branded, marked, or stigmatized by the victimization. Even in a community sample of incest victims, Courtois (1979) found that 73% reported they still suffered from moderate to severe feelings of isolation and alienation.

Although a negative self-concept was not confirmed as an initial effect, evidence for it as a long-term effect was much stronger. Bagley and Ramsay (1985) found that 19% of the child sexual abuse victims in their random sample scored in the "very poor" category on the Coopersmith self-esteem inventory (versus 5% of the control group), and only 9% of the victims demonstrated "very good" levels of self-esteem (compared to 20% of the controls). Women with very poor self-esteem were nearly four times as likely to report a history of child sexual abuse as were the other subjects. As might be expected, self-esteem problems among clinical samples of incest victims tended to be much greater: In Courtois's (1979) community sample, 87% reported that their sense of self had been moderately to severely affected by the experience of sexual abuse from a family member. Similarly, Herman (1981) found that 60% of the incest victims in her clinical sample reported they have a "predominantly negative self-image," compared to 10% of the comparison group with seductive but not incestuous fathers. The widespread clinical impression of low self-esteem among abuse victims thus seems supported by the empirical literature.

## Impact on Interpersonal Relating

Women who have been sexually victimized as children report a variety of interpersonal problems: difficulty in relating to both women and men, conflicts with their parents, and discomfort in responding to their own children. In deYoung's (1982) sample, 79% of the incest victims had predominantly hostile feelings toward their mothers, and 52% were hostile toward the abuser. Meiselman (1978) found that 60% of the incest victims in her psychotherapy sample disliked their mothers and 40% continued to experience strong negative feelings toward their fathers. Herman (1981) also noted that the rage of incest victims in her sample was often directed toward the mother, and observed that the victims seemed to regard all women, including themselves, with contempt.

In addition, victims reported difficulty trusting others that included reactions of fear, hostility, and a sense of betrayal. Briere (1984) noted fear of men in 48% of his clinical subjects (versus 15% of the nonvictims), and fear of women in 12% (versus 4% of those who had not been sexually victimized). Incest victims seem especially likely to experience difficulty in close relationships: Of the victims in Meiselman's (1978) clinical study, 64%, compared to 40% of the control group, complained of conflict with or fear of their husbands or sex partners, and 39% of the sample had never married. These results are supported by findings from Courtois's (1979) sample, in which 79% of the incest victims experienced moderate or severe problems in relating to men, and 40% had never married.

There is at least one empirical study that lends support to the idea that childhood sexual abuse also affects later parenting. Goodwin, McCarthy, and DiVasto (1981) found that 24% of mothers in the child abusing families they studied reported incest experiences in their childhoods, compared to 3% of a nonabusive control group. They suggest that difficulty in parenting results when closeness and affection are endowed with a sexual meaning, and observed that these mothers maintained an emotional and physical distance from their children, thus potentially setting the stage for abuse.

Another serious effect on which the empirical literature agrees is the apparent vulnerability of women who have been sexually abused as children to being revictimized later in life. Russell (1986), in her probability sample of 930 women, found that between 33% and 68% of the sexual abuse victims (depending on the seriousness of the abuse they suffered) were subsequently raped, compared to an incidence of rape of 17% for women who were not childhood victims. Fromuth (1983), in surveying 482 female college students, found evidence that women who had been sexually abused before the age of 13 were especially likely later to become victims of nonconsensual sexual experiences. Further evidence of a tendency toward revictimization comes from a study conducted at the University of New Mexico School of Medicine on 341 sexual assault admittances (Miller et al., 1978). In comparing women who had been raped on more than one occasion to those who were reporting a first-time rape, researchers found that 18% of the repeat victims had incest histories, compared to only 4% of first-time victims. Sexual abuse victims' vulnerability for later sexual assault is a factor that may merit more attention.

In addition to rape, victims of child sexual abuse also seem more likely to be abused by husbands or other adult partners. In her community sample, Russell (1986) found that between 38% and 48% of the women who as children had been sexual abuse victims had physically violent husbands, compared to 17% of women who had not been victims; and between 40% and 62% of the women who had been abused had later been sexually assaulted by their husbands, compared to 21% of nonvictims. Similarly, Briere (1984) noted that 49% of his clinical sexual abuse sample reported being battered in adult relationships, compared to 18% of the nonvictim group.

**Effects on Sexuality**

One of the areas of long-term effect receiving the most attention in the empirical literature concerns the impact of early sexual abuse on later sexual functioning. Almost all clinically based studies show later sexual problems among child sexual abuse victims, particularly among the victims of incest. However, there have not yet been community-based studies on the sexual functioning of adults molested as children, as there have been of other mental health areas such as depression.

Of the clinical studies, Meiselman (1978) found the highest percentage of incest victims reporting problems with sexual adjustment. Of her sample, 87% were classified as having had a serious problem with sexual adjustment at some time since the molestation, compared to 20% of the comparison group (women who had been in therapy at the same clinic, but had not been sexually victimized as children). Results from Herman's (1981) study are somewhat less extreme: Of the incest victims, 55% reported later sexual problems, although they were not significantly different from women with seductive fathers on this measure. Langmade (1983) compared a group of women in therapy who had been incest victims with a matched control group of nonvictimized women and found that the incest victims were more sexually anxious, experienced more sexual guilt, and reported greater dissatisfaction with their sexual relationships than the controls. In his study of a walk-in sample at a community health clinic, Briere (1984) found that 45% of women who had been sexually abused as children reported difficulties with sexual adjustment as adults, compared to 15% of the control group. Briere also noted a decreased sex drive in 42% of the victims studied, versus 29% of the nonvictims.

Two nonclinical studies show effects on sexual functioning as well. Courtois (1979) noted that 80% of the former incest victims in her sample reported an inability to relax and enjoy sexual activity, an avoidance of or abstention from sex, or, conversely, a compulsive desire for sex. Finkelhor (1979), studying college students, developed a measure of sexual self-esteem and found that child sexual abuse victims reported significantly lower levels of sexual self-esteem than their nonabused classmates. However, Fromuth (1983), in a similar study also with a college student sample, found no correlation between sexual abuse and sexual self-esteem, desire for intercourse, or students' self-ratings of their sexual adjustment. Virtually all (96%) of Fromuth's respondents were unmarried and their average age was 19, so it is possible that some of the long-term sexual adjustment problems reported by women in the clinical and community samples were not yet evident in this younger population. Still, this does not completely explain the discrepancy from the Finkelhor findings.

In one other study, Tsai, Feldman-Summers, and Edgar (1979) compared three groups of women on sexual adjustment measures: sexual abuse victims seeking therapy, sexual abuse victims who considered themselves "well adjusted" and had not sought therapy, and a nonvictimized matched control group. Results indicated that the "well-adjusted" victims were not significantly different from the control group on measures of overall and sexual adjustment. But the victims seeking therapy did show a difference: They experienced orgasm less often, reported themselves to be less sexually responsive, obtained less satisfaction from their sexual relationships, were less satisfied with the quality of their close relationships with men, and reported a greater number of sexual partners. It is hard to know how to interpret findings from a group of victims solicited on the basis of feeling well adjusted. This seems far different from a comparison group of victims who were not in therapy, and thus these results are subject to question.

A long-term effect of child sexual abuse that also has received a great deal of attention in the literature is an increased level of sexual behavior among victims, usually called *promiscuity* (for example, see Courtois, 1979; deYoung, 1982; Herman, 1981; Meiselman, 1978). Herman (1981, p. 40) noted that 35% of the incest victims in her sample reported promiscuity and observed that some victims seemed to have a "repertoire of sexually stylized behavior" that they used as a way of getting affection and attention. DeYoung (1982) reported that 28% of the victims in her sample had engaged in activities that could be considered promiscuous; Meiselman (1978) found 25%. However, in her study of 482 female college students, Fromuth (1983) found no differences on this variable and observed that having experienced child sexual abuse only predicted whether or not subjects would describe themselves as promiscuous, not their actual number of partners. This potentially very important finding suggests that the "promiscuity" of sexual abuse victims may be more a function of their negative self-attribution, already well documented in the empirical literature, than their actual sexual behavior, and that researchers should be careful to combine objective behavioral measures with this type of self-report.

Another question that has received comment but little empirical confirmation concerns the possibility that sexual abuse may be associated with later homosexuality in female victims. Although one study of lesbians (Gundlach, 1977) found molestation in their backgrounds, Bell and Weinberg (1981), in a large-scale, sophisticated study of the origin of sexual preference, found no such association. Studies from the sexual abuse field have also found little connection (Finkelhor, 1984; Fromuth, 1983; Meiselman, 1978).

**Effects on Social Functioning**

Several studies of special populations do suggest a connection between child sexual abuse and later prostitution. James and Meyerding (1977) interviewed 136 prostitutes and found that 55% had been sexually abused as children by someone 10 or more years older prior to their first intercourse. Among adolescents in the sample, 65% had been forced into sexual activity before they were 16 years of age. Similarly, Silbert and Pines (1981) found that 60% of the prostitutes they interviewed had been sexually abused before age 16 by an average of 2 people for 20 months. (The mean age of these children at the time of their first victimization was 10.) They concluded that "the evidence linking juvenile sexual abuse to prostitution is overwhelming" (p. 410). However, Fields (1981) noted that although 45% of the prostitutes in her sample had been sexually abused as children, this did not differentiate them from a comparison group of non-prostitutes matched on age, race, and education, of which 37% had been abused. Although there was no difference in preva-lence between the two groups, Fields did find that the prostitutes were sexually abused at a younger age—14.5 versus 16.5—and were more apt to have been physically forced.

An association between child sexual abuse and later sub-stance abuse has also received empirical support. Peters (1984), in a carefully controlled community study, found that 17% of the victimized women had symptoms of alcohol abuse (versus 4% of nonvictimized women), and 27% abused at least one type of drug (compared to 12% of nonvictimized women). Herman (1981) noted that 35% of the women with incestuous fathers in her clinical sample abused drugs and alcohol (versus 5% of the women with seductive fathers). Similarly, Briere (1984), in his walk-in sample to a community health center, found that 27% of the childhood sexual abuse victims had a history of alcoholism (compared with 11% of nonvictims), and 21% a history of drug addiction (versus 2% of the nonvictims). College student sam-ples appear more homogeneous: Sedney and Brooks (1984) found a surprisingly low reported incidence of substance abuse, and no significant differences between groups.

### Summary of Long-Term Effects

Empirical studies with adults confirm many of the long-term effects of sexual abuse mentioned in the clinical literature. Adult women victimized as children are more likely to manifest depression, self-destructive behavior, anxiety, feelings of isola-tion and stigma, poor self-esteem, a tendency toward revictim-ization, and substance abuse. Difficulty in trusting others and sexual maladjustment, such as sexual dysphoria, sexual dys-function, impaired sexual self-esteem, and avoidance of or abstention from sexual activity has also been reported by empirical researchers, although agreement among studies is less consistent for the variables on sexual functioning.

### *The Impact of Sexual Abuse*

In light of the studies just reviewed, it is appropriate to evaluate the persistent controversy over the impact of sexual abuse on victims. It has been the continuing view of some that sexual abuse is not traumatic or that its traumatic impact has been greatly overstated (Constantine, 1977; Henderson, 1983; Ramey, 1979). Proponents of this view contend that the evidence for trauma is meager and based on inadequate samples and unwarranted inferences. It is true that, because of the general lack of research in this field, clinicians until recently have not been able to substantiate their impressions that sexual abuse is traumatic with evidence from strong scientific studies. However, as evidence now accumulates, it conveys a clear suggestion that sexual abuse is a serious mental health problem, consistently associated with very disturbing subsequent problems in a significant portion of its victims.

Findings of long-term impact are especially persuasive. Eight nonclinical studies of adults (Bagley & Ramsay, in press; Briere & Runtz, 1985; Finkelhor, 1979; Fromuth, 1983; Peters, 1984; Russell, 1986; Sedney & Brooks, 1984; Seidner & Calhoun, 1984), including three random sample community surveys, found that child sexual abuse victims in the "normal" population had identifiable degrees of impairment when compared to nonvictims. Although impairments in these nonclinical victims are not necessarily severe, all the studies that have tested for long-term impairment have found it, with the exception of one (Tsai et al., 1979).

These findings are particularly noteworthy in that the studies were identifying differences associated with an event that occurred from 5 to 25 years previously. Moreover, all these studies used fairly broad definitions of sexual abuse that included single episodes, experiences in which no actual physical contact occurred, and experiences with individuals who were not related to or not emotionally close to the subjects. In all four studies that employed multivariate analyses (Bagley & Ramsay, in press; Finkelhor, 1984; Fromuth, 1983; Peters, 1984), differences in the victimized group remained after a variety of background and other factors had been controlled. The implication of these studies is that a history of childhood sexual abuse is associated with greater risk for mental health and adjustment problems in adulthood.

Although the studies indicate higher risk, they are not so informative about the actual extent of impairment. In terms of simple self-assessments, 53% of intrafamilial sexual abuse victims in Russell's (1986) community survey reported that the experience resulted in "some" or "great" long-term effects on their lives. Assessments with standardized clinical measures show a more modest incidence of impairment: In Bagley and Ramsay's (in press) community survey, 17% of sexual abuse victims were clinically depressed as measured by the CES-D, and 18% were seriously psychoneurotic, about twice the rate for the nonvictims. Thus most sexual abuse victims in the community, when evaluated in surveys, show up as slightly impaired or normal.

Summarizing, then, from studies of clinical and nonclinical populations, the findings concerning the trauma of child sexual abuse appear to be as follows: In the immediate aftermath of sexual abuse, from one-fifth to two-fifths of abused children seen by clinicians manifest some noticeable disturbance (Tufts, 1984). When studied as adults, victims as a group demonstrate more impairment than their nonvictimized counterparts (about twice as much), but less than one-fifth evidence serious psychopathology. These findings give reassurance to victims that extreme long-term effects are not inevitable. Nonetheless, they also suggest that the risk of initial and long-term mental health impairment for victims of child sexual abuse should be taken very seriously.

## Effects by Type of Abuse

Although the foregoing sections have been concerned with the various effects of abuse, there are also important research questions concerning the effects of various kinds of abuse. These usually have appeared in the form of speculation about what types of abuse have the most serious impact on victims. Groth (1978), for example, based on his clinical experience, contended that the greatest trauma occurs in sexual abuse that (1) continues for a long period of time, (2) occurs with a closely related person, (3) involves penetration, and (4) is accompanied by aggression. To that list, MacFarlane (1978) added experiences in which (5) the child participates to some degree, (6) the parents have an unsupportive reaction to disclosure of the abuse, and (7) the child is older and thus cognizant of the cultural taboos that have been violated. Such speculations offer fruitful directions for research. Unfortunately, however, only a few studies on the effects of sexual abuse have had enough cases and been sophisticated enough methodologically to look at these questions empirically. Furthermore, the studies addressing these issues have reached little consensus in their findings.

### Duration and Frequency of Abuse

Many clinicians take for granted that the longer an experience goes on, the more traumatic it is, and this conclusion is borne out by several studies, including some of the best. But the findings are not unanimous. Of 11 studies, 6 find duration associated with greater trauma. (We are treating duration and frequency synonymously here, because they tend to be so highly correlated.) However, 3 find no relationship, and perhaps most curious, 2 even find some evidence that longer duration is associated with less trauma.

Russell's (1986) study reported the clearest association: In her survey of adult women, 73% of victims whose sexual abuse lasted for more than five years rated the experience as extremely or considerably traumatic, compared to 62% of those whose abuse lasted one week to five years and 46% of those who were abused only once. Tsai et al. (1979) found duration and frequency associated with greater negative effects, when measured by MMPI and a problems checklist, at least in their group of adult sexual abuse victims who were seeking counseling. Bagley and Ramsay (in press) found that the general mental health status of adult victims—measured by a composite of indicators concerning depression, psychoneurosis, suicidal ideation, psychiatric consultation, and self-concept—was worse for longer-lasting experiences. Peters (1985) showed duration related to worse outcome with a similar composite measure in her community study. In Briere and Runtz's (1985) student sample, duration was the variable most consistently related to higher symptom scores on a variety of Hopkins Symptom Checklist scales. Finally, Friedrich et al. (1986), studying children, found that both duration and frequency predicted disturbances measured by the Child Behavior Checklist, even in multivariate analysis.

However, in spite of this consensus among some excellent studies, other studies have been unable to find such relationships. Finkelhor (1979), in a retrospective survey of college students, used a self-rating of how negative the experience was in retrospect and found no association with duration. Langmade (1983) reported that adult women seeking treatment who had had long- or short-duration experiences did not differ on measures of sexual anxiety, sexual guilt, or sexual dissatisfaction. And the Tufts (1984) study, looking at child victims, could find no association between duration of abuse and measures of distress, using the Louisville Behavior Checklist and the Purdue Self-Concept scale, as well as other measures.

Finally, some studies indicate a completely reversed relationship. Courtois (1979), surprisingly, found that adult victims with the longest lasting experiences reported the least trauma. And in their college student sample, Seidner and Calhoun (1984) reported that a high frequency of abuse was associated with higher self-acceptance (but lower social maturity) scores on the California Psychological Inventory.

In summary, then, the available studies do not uniformly show duration related to a worse outcome. However, all the community-based studies do find the relationship. Moreover, several of these studies that found a connection between duration of abuse and outcome reported it to be very strong and to persist across various measures. The studies with positive findings also used good outcome measures and multivariate analysis. Given that the relationship between duration and impact is widely endorsed by clinicians as well, there is strong, if not conclusive, evidence to establish the connection.

### Multiple-Abuse Incidents

Somewhat related to the issue of duration is the issue of multiple incidents. Some children experience abuse at the hands of several different people in the course of their childhood. Interestingly, not many investigators have looked at the effects of multiple abuse, but those who have unanimously found it predictive of more trauma. Peters (1984) found that the number of contact incidents involving different perpetrators was the most important single contributor to a multivariate analysis predicting outcome on a composite measure that included depression and substance abuse. Chronic depression and anxiety, measured by the Hopkins Symptom Checklist, were significantly higher among students who had experienced multiple perpetrators in the Briere and Runtz (1985) student study. And these findings were confirmed by Bagley and Ramsay's (in press) multivariate analysis of effects in a community sample. As all three of these were excellent studies, the idea that multiple abuse yields greater trauma seems generally confirmed.

### Relationship to the Offender

Popular and clinical wisdom holds that sexual abuse by a relative is more traumatic than abuse outside the family. Empirical findings suggest that this may be the case for some types of family abuse, especially fathers, but it may not be so generalizable to all family members. Three studies have found more trauma resulting from abuse by relatives in general: Landis (1956), in an early study asking students about how they had recovered; Anderson et al. (1981), in a chart review of adolescents in a hospital treatment setting; and Friedrich et al. (1986), in their evaluation of young victims. However, other studies and more systematic studies (Finkelhor, 1979; Peters, 1985; Russell, 1986; Seidner & Calhoun, 1984; Tufts, 1984) found no difference in the impact of abuse simply comparing abuse by all family members with abuse by others.

It must be kept in mind that how closely related a victim is to the offender does not necessarily reflect how much betrayal is involved in the abuse. Abuse by a trusted neighbor may be more devastating than abuse by a distant uncle or grandfather. Also, although abuse by a trusted person involves betrayal, abuse by a stranger or more distant person may involve more fear, and thus may be rated more negatively. These factors may help to explain why the relative/nonrelative distinction does not seem to be a predictor of trauma.

What has been reported more consistently is greater trauma from experiences involving fathers or father figures compared to all other types of perpetrators, when these have been separated out. Russell (1986), Finkelhor (1979), and Briere and Runtz (1985) all found that abuse by a father or stepfather was significantly more traumatic for victims than other abuse occurring either inside or outside the family. Bagley and Ramsay (in press) also found abuse by a father or stepfather to be more serious, but it dropped to just slightly below the significance level in multivariate analysis. Tufts (1984) also reported that children abused by stepfathers showed more distress, but for some reason the Tufts study did not find the same elevated level of distress among victims abused by natural fathers. These studies appear to confirm a traumatic effect for father figures that has not been found for relatives in general.

### Type of Sexual Act

Results of empirical studies have not, surprisingly, been consistent in demonstrating that the type of sexual activity involved in the sexual abuse is related to the degree of trauma in victims. Among the studies that did, Russell's findings on long-term effects in adult women are among the most clear-cut: Of those reporting completed or attempted intercourse, fellatio, cunnilingus, analingus, or anal intercourse, 59% said they were extremely traumatized, compared to only 36% of those who suffered manual touching of unclothed breasts or genitals and 22% of those who suffered from unwanted kissing or touching of clothed parts of the body. Bagley and Ramsay's (in press) data were also strong: In a multivariate analysis, penetration was the single most powerful variable explaining severity of mental health impairment, using a composite of standardized instruments.

However, other studies have been more ambiguous. Three confirm some relationship between type of sexual contact and subsequent effects by demonstrating that the least serious forms of sexual contact are associated with less trauma (Landis, 1956; Peters, 1984; Seidner & Calhoun, 1984; Tufts, 1984). However, several studies, such as Briere and Runtz (1985), did not find the clear differentiation that Russell and Bagley and Ramsay did between intercourse and other types of contact abuse.

Several additional studies (Anderson et al., 1981; Finkelhor, 1979; Fromuth, 1983) do not show any consistent relationship at all between type of sexual activity and effect. Thus it is premature to conclude that molestation involving more intimate contact is necessarily more traumatic than less intimate contact.

### Force and Aggression

Seven studies, three of which had difficulty finding expected associations between trauma and many other variables, did find an association between trauma and the presence of force. With Finkelhor's (1979) student sample, use of force by an abuser explained more of a victim's negative reactions than any other variable, and this finding held up in multivariate analysis. Fromuth (1983), in a replication of the Finkelhor study, found similar results. In Russell's (1986) study, 71% of the victims of force rated themselves as extremely or considerably traumatized, compared to 47% of the other victims. Briere and Runtz (1985) noted force to be associated with more acute somatization on the Hopkins Symptom Checklist. Finally, Bagley and Ramsay (in press) found force predictive of more trauma, although this relationship slipped to slightly below significance in multivariate analysis.

Both studies of children related the presence of force to symptomatology. The Tufts (1984) study found force to be one of the few variables associated with children's initial reactions: Children subjected to coercive experiences showed greater hostility and were more fearful of aggressive behavior in others. The Tufts researchers reported that physical injury (that is, the consequence of force) was the aspect of sexual activity that was most consistently related to the degree of behavioral disturbances manifested in the child, as indicated by the Louisville Behavior Checklist and other measures. Similarly, Friedrich et al. (1986) found the use of physical force to be strongly correlated with both internalizing and externalizing symptoms on the Child Behavior Checklist.

Two studies do present dissenting findings, however. Anderson et al. (1981, p. 7), in studying initial effects, concluded that "the degree of force or coercion used did not appear to be related to presence or absence of psychosocial sequelae" in the adolescents they evaluated. Seidner and Calhoun (1984), in an ambiguous finding, noted force to be associated with the victim's lower social maturity but higher self-acceptance. In spite of these findings, we think the overall evidence gives credence to the idea that force is a major traumagenic influence, given the number of studies showing this and the strength of the relationships found. Although some have argued that victims of forced abuse should suffer less long-term trauma because they could more easily attribute blame for abuse to the abuser (MacFarlane, 1978), the evidence does not seem to provide support for this supposition.

## Age

There has been a continuing controversy in the literature about how a child's age might affect his or her reactions to a sexually abusive experience. Some have contended that younger children are more vulnerable to trauma because of their impressionability. Others have felt that their naiveté may protect them from some negative effects, especially if they are ignorant of the social stigma surrounding the kind of victimization they have suffered. Unfortunately, findings from the available studies do not resolve this dispute.

Two studies of long-term effects do suggest that younger children are somewhat more vulnerable to trauma. Meiselman (1978), in her chart review of adults in treatment, found that 37% of those who experienced incest prior to puberty were seriously disturbed, compared to only 17% of those who were victimized after puberty. Similarly, Courtois (1979), in her community sample, assessed the impact of child sexual abuse on long-term relationships with men and the women's sense of self, and also found more effects from prepubertal experiences. On the other hand, one study finds older children to be more traumatized. Among Peter's (1985) sample of abuse victims in the community, women who were older at age of onset and older at the time of last abuse incident manifested more depression and more drug abuse.

The bulk of the studies, however, found no significant relationship between age at onset and impact. Finkelhor (1979), in a multivariate analysis, found a small but nonsignificant tendency for younger age to be associated with trauma. Russell (1986) also found a small but nonsignificant trend for experiences under age 9 to be associated with more long-term trauma. Langmade (1983) could find no difference in sexual anxiety, sexual guilt, or sexual dissatisfaction in adults related to the age when they had suffered the abuse. Age at time of victimization made no difference to any of the Hopkins scales in the Briere and Runtz (1985) analysis. And although Bagley and Ramsay (in press) found an association between younger age and trauma, that association dropped out in multivariate analysis, especially when controlling for acts involving penetration.

The Tufts (1984) study gave particular attention to children's reactions to abuse at different ages. The Tufts researchers concluded that age at onset bore no systematic relationship to the degree of disturbance. They did note that latency-age children were the most disturbed, but this finding appeared more related to the age at which the children were evaluated than the age at which they were first abused. They concluded that the age at which abuse begins may be less important than the stages of development through which the abuse persists.

In summary, studies tend to show little clear relationship between age of onset and trauma, especially when other factors are controlled for. If there is a trend, it is possibly for abuse at younger ages to be more traumatic. Both of the initial hypotheses about age of onset may have some validity, however: Some younger children may be protected by naivete, although others are more seriously traumatized by impressionability. However, age interacts with other factors such as relationship to offender and, until more sophisticated analytical studies are done, we cannot say whether these current findings of weak relationship mean that age has little independent effect or that it is simply still masked in complexity.

**Sex of Offender**

Perhaps because there are so few female offenders (Finkelhor & Russell, 1984), very few studies have looked at impact according to the sex of the offender. Two studies that did (Finkelhor, 1984; Russell, 1986) both found that adults rated experiences with male perpetrators as much more traumatic than those with female perpetrators. A third study (Seidner & Calhoun, 1984) found male perpetrators linked with lower self-acceptance, but higher social maturity, in college-age victims.

## Adolescent and Adult Perpetrators

There are also few studies that have looked at the question of whether or not age of the perpetrator makes any difference in the impact of sexual abuse on victims. However, three studies using college samples (Finkelhor, 1979; Fromuth, 1983; Briere & Runtz, 1985) found that victims were significantly more traumatized when abused by older perpetrators. In Finkelhor's multivariate analysis (which controlled for other factors such as force, sex of perpetrator, type of sex act, and age of the victim), age of the offender was the second most important factor predicting trauma. Fromuth (1983) replicated these findings. Briere and Runtz (1985) noted that abuse by older perpetrators was very highly associated with more acute dissociation. Russell (1986), with a community sample, reported consistent, but qualifying, results: In her survey, lower levels of trauma were reported for abuse with perpetrators who were younger than 26 or older than 50. The conclusion that experiences with younger perpetrators are less traumatic seems supported by all four studies.

### Telling or Not Telling

There is a general clinical assumption that children who feel compelled to keep the abuse a secret in the aftermath suffer greater psychic distress as a result. However, studies have not confirmed this theory. Bagley and Ramsay (in press) did find a simple zero-order relationship between not telling and a composite measure of impairment based on depression, suicidal ideas, psychiatric consultation, and self-esteem. But the association became nonsignificant when other factors were controlled for. Finkelhor (1979), in a multivariate analysis, also found that telling or not telling was essentially unrelated to a self-rated sense of trauma. And the Tufts (1984) researchers, evaluating child subjects, reported that the children who had taken a long time to disclose the abuse had the least anxiety and the least hostility. Undoubtedly, the decision to disclose is related to many factors about the experience, which confounds a clear assessment of its effects alone. For example, although silence may cause suffering for a child, social reactions to disclosure may be less intense if the event is long past. Moreover, the conditions for disclosure may be substantially different for the current generation than it was for past generations. Thus any good empirical evaluation of the effects of disclosure versus secrecy needs to take into account the possibility of many interrelationships.

### Parental Reaction

Only two studies have looked at children's trauma as a function of parental reaction, even though this is often hypothesized to be related to trauma. The Tufts (1984) study found that when mothers reacted to disclosure with anger and punishment, children manifested more behavioral disturbances. However, the same study did not find that positive responses by mothers were systematically related to better adjustment. Negative responses seemed to aggravate, but positive responses did not ameliorate the trauma. Anderson et al. (1981) found similar results: They noted 2.5 times the number of symptoms in the children who had encountered negative reactions from their parents. Thus, although only based on two studies, both of initial effects, the available evidence indicates that negative parental reactions serve to aggravate trauma in sexually abused children.

### Institutional Response

There is a great deal of interest in how institutional response may affect children's reactions to abuse, but, as yet, little research has been done. Tufts researchers (1984) found that children removed from their homes following sexual abuse exhibited more overall behavior problems, particularly aggression, than children who remained with their families. However, the children who were removed in the Tufts study were also children who had experienced negative reactions from their mothers, so this result may be confounded with other factors related to the home environment.

## Summary of Contributing Factors

From this review of empirical studies, it would appear that there is no contributing factor that all studies agree upon as being consistently associated with a worse prognosis. However, there are trends in the findings. A number of good studies agree that longer-lasting experiences are more traumatic. Children who suffer more than one incident of abuse also seem to have more long-term effects. The preponderance of studies indicate that abuse by fathers or stepfathers has a more negative impact than abuse by other perpetrators. Presence of force seems clearly to result in more trauma for the victim. In addition, when the perpetrators are males rather than females, and adults rather than teenagers, the effects of sexual abuse appear to be more disturbing. When families are unsupportive of the victims, and/or victims are removed from their homes, the prognosis also has been shown to be worse. However, these last findings are somewhat tentative, being based on only two studies.

In regard to other matters, findings are contradictory or negative. Concerning the age of onset, the more sophisticated studies found no significant relationship, especially when controlling for other factors; however, the relationship between age and trauma is especially complex and has not yet been studied carefully. There are ambiguous findings on the matter of the type of sex act; most studies have not been able to distinguish clearly the effects of intercourse from other kinds of abuse. In regard to the impact of revealing the abuse, as opposed to the child's keeping it a secret, current studies also suggest no simple relationship. And studies have not been able to demonstrate that abuse by relatives in general, apart from fathers and stepfathers, creates more serious trauma.

## *Problems with the Literature*

Conclusions from the foregoing review must be tempered by the fact that they are based on a body of research that is still in its infancy. Most of the available studies have sample, design, and measurement problems that could invalidate their findings. The study of the sexual abuse of children would greatly benefit from some basic methodological improvements.

*Samples.* Many of the available studies are based on samples of either adult women seeking treatment or children whose molestation has been reported. These subjects may be very self-selected. Especially if sexual abuse is so stigmatizing that only the most serious cases are discovered and only the most seriously affected victims seek help, such samples could distort our sense of the pathology most victims experience as a result of this abuse. New studies should take pains to expand the size and diversity of their samples, and particularly to study victims who have not sought treatment or been reported. Advertising in the media for "well-adjusted" victims, as Tsai et al. (1979) did, however, does not seem an adequate solution, because this injects a different selection bias into the study.

*Control Groups.* Some of the empirical studies cited here did not have comparison groups of any sort. Such a control is obviously important, even if it is only a group of other persons in treatment who were not sexually victimized (for example, see Briere, 1984; Meiselman, 1978). Using other clinical populations as controls, however, may actually underestimate the types and severities of pathology associated with sexual abuse, because problems that sexual abuse victims share with other clinical populations will not show up as distinctive effects.

*Sexual Abuse in Deviant Subpopulations.* Some of the studies purporting to show effects of child sexual abuse are actually reports of prevalence among specialized populations, such as prostitutes (James & Meyerding, 1977; Silbert & Pines, 1981), sex offenders (Groth & Burgess, 1979), or psychiatric patients (Carmen, Rieker, & Mills, 1984). To conclude from high rates of abuse in deviant populations that sexual abuse causes the deviance can be a misleading inference. Care needs to be taken to demonstrate that the discovered rate of sexual abuse in the deviant group is actually greater than in a relevant comparison group. In at least one study of sex offenders, for example, although abuse was frequent in their backgrounds, even higher rates of prior abuse were found for prisoners who had not committed sex crimes (Gebhard et al., 1965). It is important to recognize that such data do not indicate that sexual abuse caused the deviance, only that many such offenders have abuse in their backgrounds.

*Developmentally Specific Effects.* In studying the initial and long-term effects of sexual abuse, researchers must also keep in mind that some effects of the molestation may be delayed. Although no sexual difficulties may be manifest in a group of college student victims (as in Fromuth, 1983), such effects may be yet to appear and may become manifest in studies of older groups. Similarly, developmentally specific effects may be seen among children that do not persist into adulthood, or that may assume a different form as an individual matures. The Tufts (1984) study clearly demonstrated the usefulness of looking at effects by defined age groupings.

*Disentangling Sources of Trauma.* One of the most imposing challenges for researchers is to explore the sources of trauma in sexual abuse. Some of the apparent effects of sexual abuse may be due to premorbid conditions, such as family conflict or emotional neglect, that actually contributed to a vulnerability to abuse and exacerbated later trauma. Other effects may be due less to the experience itself than to later social reactions to disclosure. Such questions need to be approached using careful multivariate analyses in large and diverse samples, or in small studies that match cases of sexual abuse that are similar except for one or two factors. Unfortunately, these questions are difficult to address in retrospective long-term impact studies, because it may be difficult or impossible to get accurate information about some of the key variables (for example, how much family pathology predated the abuse).

*Political Pressures.* The current priority for many in the field is to convince policymakers that sexual abuse has serious immediate and long-term consequences, which then contribute to other public and mental health pathologies for its victims. However, it is important that advocates not exaggerate or overstate the intensity or inevitability of these consequences. In addition to policymakers, victims and their families wait for research findings on the effects of sexual abuse and they may be further victimized by exaggerated claims about the effects of sexual abuse. It is not possible to maintain two sets of conclusions about the effects of sexual abuse: a dire one for political purposes, and a hopeful one for family members. Thus the presence of both audiences requires that those who conduct and interpret research in this field maintain a posture of objectivity and balance.

*Preoccupation with Long-Term Effects.* Finally, there is an unfortunate tendency in interpreting the effects of sexual abuse (as well as in studies of other childhood trauma) to overemphasize long-term impact as the ultimate criterion. Effects seem to be considered less "serious" if their impact is transient and disappears in the course of development. However, this tendency to assess everything in terms of its long-term effects betrays an "adultocentric" bias. Adult traumas such as rape are not assessed ultimately in terms of whether or not they will have an impact on old age: They are acknowledged to be painful and alarming events, whether their impact lasts one year or ten. Similarly, childhood traumas should not be dismissed because no "long-term effects" can be demonstrated. Child sexual abuse needs to be recognized as a serious problem of childhood, if only for the immediate pain, confusion, and upset that can ensue.

## NOTE

1. The whole literature on sexual abuse poses problems for differentiating according to gender of victims. As can be seen from Table 5.1, many studies contain a small

number of males included in a larger sample of females. Unfortunately, many of these studies do not make specific mention of which effects apply to males, so it is possible that some of the sequelae described apply only to the males. However, we believe that most of the sequelae described relate primarily to females.

# 6

# Initial and Long-Term Effects: A Conceptual Framework

**David Finkelhor**
**Angela Browne**

As we have seen in the previous chapter, the literature on child sexual abuse is full of observations about problems that are thought to be associated with a history of abuse, such as sexual dysfunction, depression, and low self-esteem. However, such observations have not yet been organized into a clear model that specifies how and why sexual abuse might result in this kind of trauma. In this chapter we attempt to formulate such a model that can be used in both research and treatment.

The model proposed here postulates that the experience of sexual abuse can be analyzed in terms of four trauma-causing factors, or what we will call *traumagenic dynamics*—traumatic sexualization, stigmatization, betrayal, and powerlessness. These traumagenic dynamics are generalized dynamics, not necessarily unique to sexual abuse; they occur in other kinds of trauma. But the conjunction of these four dynamics in one set of circumstances are what make the trauma of sexual abuse unique, different from other childhood traumas such as the divorce of a child's parents or even being the victim of other physical child abuse.

These dynamics, when present, alter the child's cognitive and emotional orientation to the world, and create trauma by distorting a child's self-concept, worldview, and affective capacities. For example, the dynamic of stigmatization distorts children's sense of their own value and worth. The dynamic of powerlessness distorts children's sense of their ability to control their lives. When victims attempt to cope with the world through these distortions (in childhood and later as adults), it results in the problems detailed in the previous chapter. In the sections that follow, we will attempt to describe the model and suggest some of its ramifications and uses. First we will describe each of the four dynamics. Then we will show how each dynamic is associated with some of the commonly observed effects of sexual abuse. Finally, we will illustrate how the model can be used in clinical work and in research.

## Four Traumagenic Dynamics

*Traumatic sexualization* refers to a process in which a child's sexuality (including both sexual feelings and sexual attitudes) is shaped in a developmentally inappropriate and interpersonally dysfunctional fashion as a result of the sexual abuse. This can happen in a variety of ways in the course of the abuse. Traumatic sexualization can occur when a child is repeatedly rewarded by an offender for sexual behavior that is inappropriate to his or her level of development. It occurs through the exchange of affection, attention, privileges, and gifts for sexual behavior, so that a child learns sexual behavior as a strategy for manipulating others to get his or her other developmentally appropriate needs met. It occurs when certain parts of a child's anatomy are fetishized and given distorted importance and meaning. It occurs through the misconceptions and confusions about sexual behavior and sexual morality that are transmitted to the child from the offender. And it occurs when very frightening memories and events become associated in the child's mind with sexual activity.

Sexual abuse experiences can vary dramatically in terms of the amount and kind of traumatic sexualization they provoke. We would hypothosize that various factors are associated with greater degrees of traumatic sexualization. Experiences in which the offender makes an effort to evoke a sexual response from the child, for example, would be more sexualizing than those in which an offender simply uses a passive child to masturbate with. Experiences in which the child is enticed to participate are also likely to be more sexualizing than those in which brute force is used. However, even with the use of force, a form of traumatic sexualization may occur as a result of the fear that becomes associated with sex in the wake of such an experience. The degree of a child's understanding may also affect the degree of sexualization. Experiences in which the child, because of young age or developmental level, understands few of the sexual implications of the activities may be less sexualizing than when a child has full awareness. Children who have been traumatically sexualized emerge from their experiences with inappropriate repertoires of sexual behavior, with confusions and misconceptions about their sexual self-concepts, and with unusual emotional associations to sexual activities.

*Betrayal* refers to the dynamic in which children discover that someone on whom they are vitally dependent has caused them harm. This may occur in a variety of ways in a molestation experience. For example, in the course of abuse or its aftermath, children may come to the realization that a trusted person has manipulated them through lies or misrepresentations about moral standards. They may also come to realize that someone whom they loved or whose affection was important to them treated them with callous disregard. Children can experience betrayal not only at the hands of offenders, but also with family members who were not abusing them. A family member whom they trusted but who was unable or unwilling to protect or believe them—or who has a changed attitude toward them after disclosure of the abuse—may also contribute to the dynamics of betrayal.

Sexual abuse experiences that are perpetrated by family members or other trusted persons obviously involve more potential for betrayal than those involving strangers. However, we would hypothesize that the degree of betrayal is affected by how tricked the child feels, whoever the offender is. A child who was suspicious of a father's activities from the beginning may feel less betrayed than one who initially experienced the contact as nurturing and loving, and then is suddenly shocked to realize what is really happening. Obviously, the degree of betrayal is also related to a family's response to disclosure. Children who are disbelieved, blamed, or ostracized undoubtedly experience a greater sense of betrayal than those who are supported.

*Powerlessness*—or what might also be called "disempowerment," the dynamic of rendering the victim powerless—refers to the process in which the child's will, desires, and sense of efficacy are continually contravened. Many aspects of the sexual abuse experience contribute to this dynamic. We theorize that a basic kind of powerlessness occurs in sexual abuse when a child's territory and body space are repeatedly invaded against the child's will. This is exacerbated by whatever coercion and manipulation the offender may impose as part of the abuse process. Powerlessness is then reinforced when a child sees his or her attempts to halt the abuse frustrated. It is increased when the child feels fear, when he or she is unable to make adults understand or believe what is happening, or when he or she realizes how conditions of dependency have him or her trapped in the situation.

In terms of degrees of powerlessness, we would hypothesize that an authoritarian abuser who continually commands the child's participation by threatening serious harm will instill more of a sense of powerlessness. But force and threat are not necessary: Any kind of situation in which a child feels trapped, if only by the realization of the consequences of disclosure, can create a sense of powerlessness. Obviously, a situation in which a child tells and is not believed will also create a greater degree of powerlessness. On the other hand, when a child is able to bring the abuse to an end effectively, or at least exert some control over its occurrence, he or she may feel less disempowered.

*Stigmatization,* the final dynamic, refers to the negative connotations—for example, badness, shame, and guilt—that are communicated to the child about the experiences and that then become incorporated into the child's self-image. These negative meanings are communicated in many ways. They can come directly from the abuser, who may blame the victim for the activity, denigrate the victim, or, simply through his furtiveness, convey a sense of shame about the behavior. When there is pressure for secrecy from the offender, this can also convey powerful messages of shame and guilt. But stigmatization is also reinforced by attitudes that the victim infers or hears from other persons in the family or community. Stigmatization may thus grow out of the child's prior knowledge or sense that the activity is considered deviant and taboo. It is certainly reinforced if, after disclosure, people react with shock or hysteria, or blame the child for what has transpired. The child may be additionally stigmatized by people in his or her environment who now impute other negative characteristics to the victim (loose morals, spoiled goods) as a result of the molestation.

Stigmatization occurs in various degrees in different abusive situations. Some children are treated as bad and blameworthy by offenders and some are not. Some children, in the wake of a sexual abuse experience, are told clearly that they are not at fault, whereas others are heavily shamed and it may be implied the child seduced the abuser. Some children may be too young to have much awareness of social attitudes and thus experience little stigmatization, whereas others have to deal with powerful religious and cultural taboos in addition to the usual stigma. Keeping the secret of having been a sexual abuse victim may increase the sense of stigma, because it reinforces the sense of being different. By contrast, those who find out that such experiences occur to many other children may have some of their stigma assuaged.

These four traumagenic dynamics, then, account in our view for the main sources of trauma in child sexual abuse. They are not in any way distinct, separate factors, or narrowly defined.

Each dynamic can be seen, rather, as a clustering of injurious influences with a common theme. They are best thought of as broad categories useful for organizing and categorizing our understanding of the effect of sexual abuse.

### Traumagenic Dynamics in
### the Impact of Sexual Abuse

With the four traumagenic dynamics as an organizing framework, it is useful to reconsider the literature on the effects of sexual abuse reviewed in Chapter 5. As we saw, a great many behavioral and emotional problems have been related to a history of sexual abuse in the clinical literature, and many confirmed in empirical studies. What we end up with, however, is simply a list of possible problems to which sexual abuse victims are vulnerable, some confirmed in research and some not. This list is important to furthering our work with victims of abuse, but it is conceptually shallow and does not encourage deeper understanding of the phenomenon.

The notion of traumagenic dynamics, however, offers a way both to organize and to theorize about many of the observed outcomes. Most of the outcomes, it will be noted, can be conveniently categorized according to one or two of these dynamics. This we have illustrated in Table 6.1. It would seem as though certain traumagenic dynamics are more readily associated with certain effects. Obviously, there is no simple one-to-one correspondence; some effects seem logically associated with several dynamics. But there are clear general affinities. In this section, we will briefly describe the effects that seem to be associated with the four dynamics. For purposes of Table 6.1, we have tried to divide these effects roughly into psychological impact and behavioral manifestation. However, it is not always easy to separate the two.

There are many observed effects of sexual abuse that seem readily connected to the dynamic we have called *traumatic sexualization*. Among young child victims, clinicians often have

**TABLE 6.1**

**Traumagenic Dynamics in the Impact of Child Sexual Abuse**

(I)    TRAUMATIC SEXUALIZATION

Dynamics
child rewarded for sexual behavior inappropriate to developmental level
offender exchanges attention and affection for sex
sexual parts of child fetishized
offender transmits misconceptions about sexual behavior and sexual
  morality
conditioning of sexual activity with negative emotions and memories

Psychological impact
increased salience of sexual issues
confusion about sexual identity
confusion about sexual norms
confusion of sex with love and care-getting or care-giving
negative associations to sexual activities and arousal sensations
aversion to sex or intimacy

Behavioral manifestations
sexual preoccupations and compulsive sexual behaviors
precocious sexual activity
aggressive sexual behaviors
promiscuity
prostitution
sexual dysfunctions; flashbacks, difficulty in arousal, orgasm
avoidance of or phobic reactions to sexual intimacy
inappropriate sexualization of parenting

(II)   STIGMATIZATION

Dynamics
offender blames, denigrates victim
offender and others pressure child for secrecy
child infers attitudes of shame about activities
others have shocked reaction to disclosure
others blame child for events
victim is stereotyped as damaged goods

Psychological impact
guilt, shame
lowered self-esteem
sense of differentness from others

Behavioral manifestations
isolation
drug or alcohol abuse
criminal involvement
self-mutilation
suicide

TABLE 6.1 (Continued)

(III)   BETRAYAL

Dynamics
   trust and vulnerability manipulated
   violation of expectation that others will provide care and protection
   child's well-being disregarded
   lack of support and protection from parent(s)

Psychological impact
   grief, depression
   extreme dependency
   impaired ability to judge trustworthiness of others
   mistrust, particularly of men
   anger, hostility

Behavioral manifestations
   clinging
   vulnerability to subsequent abuse and exploitation
   allowing own children to be victimized
   isolation
   discomfort in intimate relationships
   marital problems
   aggressive behavior
   delinquency

(IV)   POWERLESSNESS

Dynamics
   body territory invaded against the child's wishes
   vulnerability to invasion continues over time
   offender uses force or trickery to involve child
   child feels unable to protect self and halt abuse
   repeated experience of fear
   child is unable to make others believe

Psychological impact
   anxiety, fear
   lowered sense of efficacy
   perception of self as victim
   need to control
   identification with the aggressor

Behavioral manifestations
   nightmares
   phobias
   somatic complaints; eating and sleeping disorders
   depression
   disociation
   running away
   school problems, truancy
   employment problems
   vulnerability to subsequent victimization
   aggressive behavior, bullying
   delinquency
   becoming an abuser

noted sexual preoccupations and repetitive sexual behavior such as masturbation or compulsive sex play. Some children display knowledge and interests that are inappropriate to their age, such as wanting to engage school-age playmates in sexual intercourse or oral-genital contact (Adams-Tucker, 1981, 1982; Benward & Densen-Gerber, 1977; Finch, 1967; Friedrich et al., 1986; Justice & Justice, 1979; Kaufman, Peck, & Tagiuri, 1954; Tufts, 1984). Some children who have been victimized, especially adolescent boys but sometimes even younger children, become sexually aggressive and victimize their peers or younger children. At older ages, clinicians remark about promiscuous and compulsive sexual behavior that sometimes characterizes victims when they become adolescents or young adults, although this has not been confirmed empirically (Browning & Boatman, 1977; Kaufman et al., 1954; Weiss, Roger, Darwin, & Dutton, 1955). There are also several studies suggesting that victims of sexual abuse have a high risk for entering into prostitution (Brown, 1979; James & Meyerding, 1977; Silbert & Pines, 1981).

With adult victims of sexual abuse, sexual problems, as we saw in Chapter 5, have been among those effects that have been most researched and best established. Clinicians report that victimized clients often have an aversion to sex, flashbacks to the molestation experience, difficulty with arousal and orgasm, and vaginismus, as well as negative attitudes toward their sexuality and their bodies (Briere, 1984; Burgess & Holmstrom, 1978; Courtois, 1979; Finch, 1967; Herman, 1981; Langmade, 1983; Meiselman, 1978; Rosenfeld, Nadelson, Krieger, & Backman, 1979; Steele & Alexander, 1981; Tsai & Wagner, 1978). The frequently demonstrated higher risk of sexual abuse victims to later sexual assault may also be related to traumatic sexualization (deYoung, 1982; Fromuth, 1983; Herman, 1981; Miller et al., 1978; Russell, 1984), and some victims apparently find themselves inappropriately sexualizing their children in ways that lead to sexual or physical abuse (Gelinas, 1983; Herman, 1977; Justice & Justice, 1979; Steele & Alexander, 1981; Summit & Kryso, 1981). All these observations seem connected to the traumagenic dynamic of sexualization.

These problems and behaviors, as well as the self-reports from victims, suggest the various psychological effects that traumatic sexualization produces. At its most basic level, the trauma of sexual abuse often results in an increased salience of sexual issues. This may be true particularly among young children who might not otherwise be concerned with sexual matters at their stage of development. Part of the salience is associated simply with the sexual stimulation of the abuse and the conditioning of behavior that may go along with it. However, the salience is also very much a function of the questions and conflicts about the self and interpersonal relations that the abuse provokes. Confusion often arises especially about sexual identity. Victimized boys, for example, may wonder whether or not they are homosexuals. Victimized girls wonder whether or not their sexual desirability has been impaired, and whether or not later sexual partners will be able to "tell."

Traumatic sexualization is also associated with confusion about sexual norms and standards. Many sexually victimized children have misconceptions about sex and sexual relations, which are a result of things offenders may have said and done. One common confusion concerns the role of sex in an affectionate relationship. If child victims have traded sex for affection from the abuser over a period of time, this may become their view of the normal way to give and obtain affection (Jones & Bentovim, n.d.; Herman, 1981; Meiselman, 1978). Some of the apparent sexualization in the behavior of victimized children may stem from this confusion.

Another impact that traumatic sexualization may have is in the negative connotations that come to be associated with sex. If sexual contact is associated in a child's memory with revulsion, fear, anger, a sense of powerlessness, or other negative emotions, this can contaminate all later sexual experiences. These feelings may generalize to an aversion to all sex and intimacy, and can explain many of the sexual dysfunctions that are reported by victims.

Other effects observed in victims of sexual abuse seem naturally grouped in relation to the dynamic of *stigmatization*. Child victims often feel isolated, and may gravitate to various stigmatized levels of society. Thus they may get involved in drug or alcohol abuse, criminal activity, or prostitution (Benward & Densen-Gerber, 1975; Briere, 1984; Herman, 1981; Reich & Gutierres, 1979). The effects of stigmatization may also reach extremes in forms of self-destructive behavior and suicide attempts (Briere, 1984; deYoung, 1982; Herman, 1981; Justice & Justice, 1979; Steele & Alexander, 1981; Summit & Kryso, 1978).

The psychological impact associated with these problems has a number of related components. Many sexual abuse victims experience large amounts of guilt and shame related to their abuse (Anderson et al., 1981; DeFrancis, 1969; deYoung, 1982). The guilt and shame seem logically associated with the dynamic of stigmatization, because they are a response to being blamed and encountering negative reactions from others regarding the abuse. Low self-esteem is another part of the pattern, as the victim draws the conclusion from the negative attitudes about abuse victims that they are "spoiled merchandise" (Benward & Densen-Gerber, 1975; Courtois, 1979; Herman, 1977; Justice & Justice, 1979; Steel & Alexander, 1981; Tsai & Wagner, 1978). Stigmatization also results in a sense of differentness, based on the (incorrect) belief that no one else has had such an experience, and that others would reject a person who had.

A number of the effects noted in victims seem reasonably to be connected with the experience of *betrayal* that they have suffered. The depression so widely noted in the literature (Adams-Tucker, 1981; Bagley & Ramsay, in press; Briere & Runtz, 1985; Benward & Densen-Gerber, 1975; Browning & Boatman, 1977; Jones & Bentovim, n.d.; Justice & Justice, 1979; Peters, 1984) may be in part an extended grief reaction over the loss of trusted figures. Sexual abuse victims suffer from a grave disenchantment and disillusionment. In combination with this may be an intense need to regain a sense of trust and security, manifested in some of the extreme dependency and clinging seen in especially young victims (Jones & Bentovim, n.d.; Lustig, 1966). This same need in adults may show up in impaired judgment about the trustworthiness of other people (Briere, 1984; Courtois, 1979; Justice & Justice, 1979; Steele & Alexander, 1981; Summit & Kryso, 1981; Tsai & Wagner, 1978), or in a desperate search for a redeeming relationship (Steele & Alexander; Summit & Kryso). As mentioned before, several studies of incest victims have remarked on the vulnerability of these women to relationships in which they are physically, psychologically, and sexually abused (Briere, 1984; deYoung, 1982; Fromuth, 1983; Herman, 1981; Miller et al., 1978; Russell, 1986). Some victims even fail to recognize it as sexual abuse when their partners become sexually abusive toward their children. This seems plausibly related to both overdependence and impaired judgement.

An opposite reaction to betrayal—characterized by hostility and anger—is seen also in sexual abuse victims (Briere, 1984; Courtois, 1979; Meiselman, 1978; Peters, 1976). Distrust may manifest itself in isolation and an aversion to intimate relationships. Sometimes this distrust is directed especially at men, and is a barrier to successful heterosexual relationships or marriages. Studies have noted marital problems among sexual abuse victims that also may represent the surfacing of mistrust and suspicion (Meiselman, 1978).

The anger stemming from betrayal is part of what may lie behind the aggressive and hostile posture of some sexual abuse victims, particularly adolescents (Adams-Tucker, 1981, 1982; Burgess & Holmstrom, 1978; DeFrancis, 1969; Justice & Justice, 1979; Reich & Gutierres, 1979; Tufts, 1984; Wisconsin Study, 1982). It may be a primitive way of trying to protect the self against future betrayals. Antisocial behavior and delinquency sometimes associated with a history of victimization are also an expression of this anger, and may represent a desire for retaliation. Thus betrayal seems a common dynamic behind a number of the observed reactions to sexual abuse.

There is also a configuration of effects of sexual abuse that seem plausibly related to the dynamic of *powerlessness*. One reaction to powerlessness is obviously fear and anxiety, as a person feels unable to control noxious events that are occurring. As we saw in Chapter 5, fear and anxiety are among the most common reactions to abuse noted among children. Nightmares, phobias, hypervigilance, clinging behavior, and somatic complaints related to anxiety have been documented repeatedly among sexually abused children (Adams-Tucker, 1981; Anderson et al., 1981; Browning & Boatman, 1977; Burgess & Holmstrom, 1978; DeFrancis, 1969; Gelinas, 1983; Goodwin, 1982; Justice & Justice, 1979; Kaufman et al., 1954; Peters, 1976; Sloane & Karpinski, 1942; Summit, 1983; Summit & Kryso, 1981; Tufts, 1984). Fears and anxieties are also prominent symptoms among adults (Bagley & Ramsay, in press; Briere, 1984), along with eating disorders (Oppenheimer et al., 1984) and dissociation (Briere & Runtz, 1985), which are probably related. The latter can easily be seen as attempts to combat anxiety and reassert some kind of control over unpleasant sensations.

A second major effect of powerlessness is to impair a person's sense of efficacy and coping skills. Having been a victim on repeated occasions may make it difficult to act in any other way than with the expectation of being revictimized. This sense of impotence may be associated with the despair and depression and even suicidal behavior often noted among adolescent and adult victims (Bagley & Ramsay, in press; Briere & Runtz, 1985). It may also be connected to the learning problems, running away, and employment difficulties noted by researchers, as victims feel unable to cope with their environments (Adams-Tucker, 1982; Anderson et al., 1981; Browning & Boatman, 1977; Herman, 1981; Kaufman et al., 1954; Meiselman, 1978; Peters, 1976). And finally, it seems readily related to the high risk of subsequent victimization (noted above in previous sections) from which sexual abuse victims appear to suffer: These victims may feel powerless to thwart others who are trying to manipulate them or do them harm.

Attempts to compensate for the experience of powerlessness may account for a third cluster of effects. In reaction to powerlessness, some sexual abuse victims may have unusual and dysfunctional needs to control or dominate. This would seem to be the case particularly for male victims, for whom issues of power and control are made very salient by male sex-role socialization (Groth, 1979; Rogers & Terry, 1984). Some aggressive and delinquent behavior would seem to stem from this desire to be tough, powerful, and fearsome if even in desperate ways to compensate for the pain of powerlessness. When victims become bullies and offenders, reenacting their own abuse, it may be in large measure to try to regain the sense of power and domination that victims attribute to their own abusers. All these effects seem related to the traumatic dynamic of powerlessness that is integral to the sexual abuse experience.

The preceding should give a sense of how the four traumagenic dynamics are connected to the common patterns of reactions seen among victims. It should be clear, however, that the reactions are multiply determined. Some effects seem plausibly connected to two or even three traumagenic dynamics; for example, depression can be seen as growing out of stigmatization, betrayal, or powerlessness. There is no one-to-one correspondence between dynamics and effects. It may be that depression that is stigma related has different manifestations, and therefore calls for a different therapeutic approach, than depression that is related to powerlessness. Such hypotheses suggested by the model are worthy of further clinical and empirical investigation.

## Clinical Assessment Using the Model of Traumagenic Dynamics

There are many possible uses for the conceptual model described here, but one obvious one is in making clinical assessments of the possible effects of abuse. Up to the present, clinicians have evaluated abuse experiences on the basis of unsystematic assumptions about what causes trauma. There have been some attempts to classify abuse experiences to aid in assessment. But these classifications have various shortcomings.

One common classification scheme looks at the characteristics of the offender: for example, whether the abuse was at the hands of a "regressed" or "fixated" abuser (Groth, 1978). However, this conceptualization gives little insight about the nature of the trauma to the child. More often, experiences have been classified according to simple dichotomies that reflect collective clinical judgment about what kinds of abuse are "more traumatic." Thus abuse is commonly distinguished by whether it occurred inside or outside the family, on the belief that abuse inside the family has more serious effects on the child. Abuse is also commonly categorized according to whether penetration occurred or not, and whether force occurred or not.

This approach to assessing the potential for trauma has real limitations. Beyond the fact that its assumptions are largely untested, there is the problem that the approach results in an overly simplistic classification of experiences as either more or less serious. Nothing about the *character* of the effect is implied. Nothing about how the trauma is likely to manifest itself is suggested.

The model of traumagenic dynamics proposed here allows for a more complex assessment of the potential for trauma. With the assistance of these concepts, the clinician can evaluate an abuse experience on four separate dimensions. The question is not "Was it more or less serious?" but "What are the specific injurious dynamics that were present?" The characteristics of the experience itself can be examined for their contribution to each of the traumagenic processes. On the basis of the configuration of traumagenic dynamics that were most present in this experience, the clinician can anticipate what would be the most likely type of effects.

Thus, once such a model was tested, a clinician might proceed through the model dynamic by dynamic, asking first: How traumatically sexualizing was this experience? Facts about the experience, such as whether or not intercourse occurred, how long it went on, and the degree to which the child participated, all might contribute to an assessment of the traumatic *sexualization*. Next a clinician would ask: How *stigmatizing* was the experience? Factors such as how long it went on, how old the child was, how many people knew about the events, and whether or not others blamed the child subsequent to the disclosure would all add to the assessment of this dynamic. Similarly, with *betrayal,* facts about the relationship between the victim and the offender, the way in which the offender involved the victim, and the attempts—successful and unsuccessful—of the victim to get assistance and support from other family members would all be taken into account. Finally, regarding the dynamic of *powerlessness,* the facts about the presence of force, the degree to which coercion was brought to bear, the duration of the abuse, and the circumstances under which the abuse was terminated would be particularly relevant to a determination of the degree to which powerlessness was a major dynamic.

Once an assessment was made about the experience according to the four traumagenic dynamics, a clinician should be able to draw inferences about what some of the predominant concerns of the victim would be, and also some of the subsequent difficulties that might be expected. An assessment based on the traumagenic dynamics would also be useful for formulating intervention strategies. If, for example, assessment suggested greatest trauma in the area of stigmatization, that might indicate interventions aimed specifically at reducing this sense of stigma. Such interventions might include involvement with a survivors group in which the victim could get support from other victims, or other self-esteem building activities to repair the sense of a stigmatized and devalued self.

### *Traumagenesis Before and After the Abuse*

Although the sexual abuse itself is assumed to be the main traumatic agent in victims, it is important to emphasize that any assessment approach to understanding trauma must take into account the child's experiences *prior to* and also *subsequent to* the abuse. Abuse will have different effects on children depending on their prior adjustment. And abuse will have different effects depending on how others respond to it. The conceptual framework being proposed here is easily adapted to this need.

The four traumagenic dynamics we have been discussing are not dynamics that apply solely to the abuse event. They are ongoing processes that have a history prior to and a future subsequent to the abuse. They can be assessed in each phase. In the preabuse phase, the traumagenic dynamics need to be understood particularly in relation to a child's family life and personality characteristics prior to the abuse. For example, if the child was a previous victim of physical or emotional abuse, he or she may already have been suffering from a disempowering dynamic before the abuse occurred. On the other hand, a child who was an eldest child with important responsibilities, living in a fairly healthy family environment, may have acquired a well-developed sense of personal efficacy and powerfulness. In such a context, the disempowering aspects of a sexual abuse experience may have only a minor or transient effect.

For another example, if the child had experienced an unstable family configuration, in which the loyalty of significant others was in doubt, then the dynamic of *betrayal* may already have been strongly potentiated. On the other hand, if the child had a sense of trust firmly established, the betrayal dynamic from the sexual abuse experience (involving a nonfamily abuser, at least) might be substantially less.

The operation of the traumagenic dynamics can also be assessed in the events subsequent to the sexual abuse. Two main categories of subsequent events have particular importance: (1) the family reaction to disclosure, if and when it occurs, and (2) the social and institutional response to the disclosure. For example, much of the *stigmatization* accompanying abuse may occur *after* the experience itself, as a child encounters family and societal reactions. A child who was relatively unstigmatized by the molestation itself may undergo serious stigmatization if friends later reject her, if her family blames her, or if the fact of her being abused remains a focus in her life for a long time. The dynamic of powerlessness is also greatly affected by a child's experiences subsequent to sexual abuse. If, for instance, a great many authorities become involved in the experience, the child is forced to testify, forced to leave home, forced to tell the story on repeated occasions, and subjected to a great deal of unwanted attention, this can also greatly increase the child's sense of powerlessness. If the child, on the other hand, has a sense of having been able to end the abuse and obtain support and protection, this may greatly mitigate any sense of powerlessness that resulted from the experience itself. Thus, in assessing the experience, the contributions of the pre- and postabuse situation must be included in relation to the four traumagenic dynamics.

### *Implications for Research*

The four traumagenic dynamics described in this chapter have implications for research as well as for intervention. Perhaps most important, they can be used as a conceptual guide in the development of assessment instruments. Up until now, research on child sexual abuse has been conducted using broad psychological inventories like the MMPI (Tsai et al., 1979), the California Psychological Inventory (Seidner & Calhoun, 1984), or else ad hoc, investigator-invented measures. The broad inventories have subscales such as neuroticism or self-acceptance that can assess a variety of pathological conditions, but these are not necessarily the pathologies related most closely to sexual abuse. The ad hoc measures, by contrast, are more sensitive to the specific pathology that may result from sexual abuse, but they are not based on any theory, and often suffer from lack of methodological rigor.

The model of four traumagenic dynamics outlined here can be the basis for the development of instruments specifically designed to assess the impact of sexual abuse. Sections of the instruments would be geared to tap each of the four dynamics. Two separate instruments might be developed, one for direct administration to the children and another for completion by parents or professionals with knowledge of the child. Forms of the instruments might be tailored for different age groups. Such instruments are seriously needed to further research on sexual abuse.

## *Conclusion*

This chapter has tried to suggest a framework for a more systematic understanding of the effects of sexual abuse. It has introduced four traumagenic dynamics, which are seen as the four links between the experience of sexual abuse and the sequelae that have been widely noted. Developing a conceptualization of these links will be a step in the direction of advancing our understanding of sexual abuse and mitigating the effects of these experiences on its victims.

# 7

# Designing New Studies

**David Finkelhor**

This chapter is intended to orient researchers, particularly those interested in studies of impact and treatment, to some important methodological issues in the field of child sexual abuse.

Child sexual abuse is a relatively recent topic for research, and thus poses some challenges for the new researcher. Much of the most up-to-date research has not yet been published or is difficult to obtain and individuals studying this problem do not all come from one discipline or methodological tradition. Thus there has been little chance for scholars in the field to come together and develop a consensus about methodology.

However, methodology is of utmost importance in this field. Sexual abuse, because of the shame and secrecy that surround it, is not an easy problem to study. The subject has been dogged by a history of myth and stereotype, and poorly designed studies in the past have only contributed to this confusion. Well-designed studies are very much needed.

This chapter tries to encourage improved designs by outlining some important methodological concerns any researcher in this field needs to consider, concerns related to defining abuse, choosing samples, creating a design, selecting instruments, and protecting research subjects. For the sake of economy and because it is a central element to much research in this field, this chapter limits itself mainly to research on the impact of abuse. Studies on offenders or risk factors for sexual abuse have other problems that will not be touched on here.

## *Definitions of Abuse*

Unfortunately for researchers, sexual abuse is not a uniformly defined entity. Different researchers have developed different definitions of this child welfare concept. Although some of this diversity is defensible and even healthy, it is important that researchers have strong reasons for choosing their particular definitions. Sometimes restrictive definitions are adopted simply to accommodate the nature of the population that may be conveniently at hand. However, that restrictiveness may not serve to advance knowledge in the field or the scientific question being investigated. This section is intended to give researchers some sense of the implications of different definitional choices.

### Defining Abusive Relationships

Almost all researchers include at least the core type of sexual abuse in their studies: situations in which a parent has sexual contact with a minor child (for example, Herman, 1981). The National Center on Child Abuse and Neglect, which has been very influential in defining the problem, employs a somewhat broader definition of abuse that includes sexual contact between a child and any *caretaker*. Thus studies based on child welfare samples have tended to be heavily weighted with this kind of abuse. However, it is important to recognize that there are other kinds of situations that have been included in other studies. (For added discussion of this issue, see Chapter 2.)

*(1) Abuse by Noncaretakers and Nonfamily.* In popular perception, sexual experiences between any adult and a minor child are abuse whether or not the abuser is a family member or care-

taker. Such experiences, which may constitute 30% to 50% of all adult-child contact (Russell, 1983; Finkelhor, 1979), are, however, less likely to come to the attention of child protective workers, and therefore are underrepresented in samples from such agencies. Thus less is known about them and their impact. Because they are such a frequent type of abuse, however, it is a good idea to try to include such cases. They show up more frequently in cases from sources connected with the criminal justice system than from child welfare agencies.

*(2) Abuse by Older Children.* It is increasingly recognized that there are many adolescents who abuse younger children both inside and outside their families. Because such cases are less likely to come to agency attention and because more information is greatly needed, it is important for researchers to include such abuse within their purview.

*(3) Abuse by Peers.* Children are sometimes abused by other children who are their own age or even younger, and Russell (1983) has urged that such experiences be included in studies of abuse. This runs against some tendency in the past to limit the term *sexual abuse* to acts committed by older perpetrators, but there is no strong rationale for this limitation. Although there is some evidence that abuse by peers has a different impact than abuse by older partners (Finkelhor, 1979; Russell, 1986), little is actually known about peer abuse. Of course, peer abuse needs to be defined carefully in order to exclude consensual sex. One way is to stipulate that the contact must occur as a result of force or be clearly unwanted.

There are two general arguments for limiting sexual abuse to cases of caretaker abuse or parent-child incest. First, these are the cases most seen by child welfare agencies, and therefore of immediate concern. Second, they have a certain commonality that makes them easier to analyze and to use as the basis for theory. But limiting the definition in such a way has serious risks. First, we may be ignoring serious types of abuse simply because they are less likely to come to the attention of agencies. Second, we may not be able to test certain presumptions about abuse without a more heterogeneous sample. In our judgment, at the current moment there is a strong need for studies that take a broad view of the phenomenon of sexual abuse. We urge researchers to include extrafamily, noncaretaker, and adolescent abuse within their definitions.

### Defining Abusive Acts

Another definitional issue concerns what kinds of sexual acts or situations should be included in the definition of abuse (see also Chapter 2). Researchers generally agree that abuse includes intercourse and attempted intercourse (anal or vaginal) and oral or manual contact with the genitals of either the child or the abuser. Some research has also included contact with buttocks, breasts, or thighs and even kissing that is of a sexual nature. Some research has included encounters with exhibitionists. One study included situations in which a child was allowed by a parent to have an unhealthy but consensual sexual relationship with a peer (NCCAN, 1981). Researchers must decide whether or not situations in which children are photographed for child pornography but not actually touched should be included.

Two factors are to be considered in trying to decide what types of acts to include:

(1) If researchers are too restrictive in the definition of abuse, they may never be able to test their own assumptions. Thus if encounters with exhibitionists are excluded on the grounds that this is not serious abuse, then the question of how serious such encounters are is never answered.

(2) On the other hand, if researchers are too liberal in their definition, their research may be rejected as meaningless by the public and professionals. Some researchers have included any childhood sexual experience that the subject felt was unpleasant, including seeing a parent naked or having a disappointing

first sexual experience. These seem beyond the pale of what is commonly defined as sexual abuse.

Given the embryonic status of the field, in our estimation, *investigators should be broad rather than narrow in their definition*. It is always possible to redo analyses with a more restrictive definition, but it is not possible to recover cases that were initially screened out. To deal with possible objections to too liberal a definition, investigators may wish to present analyses based on several definitions. Russell (1983) used this method very effectively in reporting rates for abuse based on several different definitions.

## Samples

### Studies of Initial Effects

Studies of the initial effects of sexual abuse generally look at cases that are being evaluated or treated by a mental health or child protective agency. Given that only a fraction of sexual abuse is reported or treated, it is doubtful that these cases are representative. However, to expect to obtain a representative sample of recently occurring cases, most of which would not have been reported, is unreasonable. What is reasonable is for investigators to make some special efforts to expand the composition of samples obtained through agencies and not to be content simply with whatever comes through the door.

Investigators should minimize selection bias and obtain samples that are as representative as possible. This means paying close attention to the kinds of selection mechanisms that are operating. Many agencies that treat sexual abuse, for example, get referrals primarily from certain sources, and investigators should be clear about the kinds of biases this exerts. Consideration should be given to supplementing a sample based only on one agency in which certain selection factors may be operating. Choosing cases from at least two or more different kinds of agencies may result in a broader sample. At the very least, in reporting the research the researcher needs to be as explicit as possible about the kinds of possible selection factors that may be present, because such factors may provide very important alternative explanations to some of the findings from the study.

One strategy for minimizing selection factors is to locate the study with an agency that is actively involved in case finding. Whereas treatment agencies often rely substantially on referrals for their caseloads, some prevention programs, for example, go out into the community, where they actively find and encourage reports. Research based within agencies that are locating cases may produce a better cross section of cases.

Another strategy for reducing selection bias is to try to obtain access to cases as soon as possible after they are reported. A great deal of selection occurs very quickly as cases drop out of the system. There is another advantage to assessing sexual abuse cases early after detection: Children and families have not yet been so profoundly affected by their contact with the system. One of the most interesting and pressing questions in the field of sexual abuse research is how contact with agencies after the disclosure affects the child and the family. Answers to this question can be found only by studying cases very soon after they enter into the system.

Although the above suggestions are concerned with broadening the samples to improve representativeness, there is at least one area in which investigators should consider narrowing their samples. Many studies of sexual abuse have looked at a very heterogeneous age range of children. However, it is becoming increasingly clear that the effects of sexual abuse differ a great deal depending on the child's age. Therefore, it may complicate the assessment of effects greatly when the sample is too heterogeneous. Researchers should consider focusing their research on a specific age group such as 7- to 9-year-olds, or 9- to 12-year-olds. Their findings may become much more clear-cut and interpretable when they take this narrower approach.

## Comparison Groups

One of the major shortcomings in previous research on sexual abuse is the absence of control or comparison groups. It is only through inclusion of such groups that investigators can find out how sexually abused children differ from other children. There are some obvious populations that can serve as comparison groups for samples of sexually abused children; for example, other students from the same schools or neighborhoods. This kind of comparison group has the nice advantage of controlling for many possible background and ecological variables. Detailed consideration should be given to matching procedures for choosing comparison groups. It may be a very good idea to match the children on certain variables such as presence of stepfathers, maternal absence, maternal employment, rural residence, parental income, and position in the sibship, all of which have been associated with risk for sexual abuse.

Another possible comparison group is children who are seen by agencies for problems other than sexual abuse. One nice feature of such a comparison group is that it may be possible to note the effects of sexual abuse that are not simply the function of being labeled as having a problem or having had contact with an agency. On the other hand, any problems that sexual abuse victims might share with the children with other problems, such as learning disabilities or anxiety, would fail to show up in such a comparison. Ideally, both an agency and a nonagency comparison group would be the best approach.

In either kind of comparison group, researchers have to be careful to investigate the possibility that some of the comparison children have suffered sexual abuse. To leave such children in the comparison group will work to mask differences between the groups and may lead to erroneous results.

Some studies deal with the issue of comparison groups by simply using normal instruments on which the sexually abused children can be scaled. The main problem with such an approach is that many of the outcomes that we are interested in with regard to sexually victimized children are not outcomes for which we know the norms. We do not know, for example, how frequent sexualized play is in ordinary children. Thus, even when using normed instruments, it may be very useful to have comparison groups.

## Studies of Long-Term Effects

Samples used in studies of the long-term effects of sexual abuse can be grouped roughly into three categories: random samples, volunteer samples, and clinical samples. Without any question, the best design is the random sample study, which should recruit the most representative selection of sexual abuse victims. It is quite clear now, as Chapter 1 has shown, that research on sexual abuse can be done in random sample surveys of the general population. However, Chapter 1 also shows that surveys require a great deal of attention to the training of interviewers, and very careful consideration to how sensitive questions are positioned and worded. Any researcher considering a random sample study of a community or other population needs to examine carefully the questionnaires in Chapter 1.

A major drawback of community surveys is their cost. Wyatt (1985) has shown that by making initial contacts by random-digit dialing and using much smaller samples, surveys do not have to be enormously expensive. But for those with even more limited budgets, samples can be drawn from other groups besides whole communities. Examples would include students, members of an organization, employees of a company or agency, members of a community health plan, or families enrolled in a medical practice. The more heterogeneous the group, the better, and it also is important that membership in the group is not plausibly related to the likelihood of being a victim of sexual abuse. This is not an easy requirement to meet, because the impairment to social functioning that may result from sexual abuse may affect a person's participation in virtually any social role or group. Nonetheless, samples of persons from such groups and organizations do provide a relatively good source of subjects at what can be a lower cost than a community survey.

A technique pioneered by Kinsey for such groups was to try to get 100% participation (Kinsey et al., 1953). To the extent that the participation rates can approach 100% in such organizations, these kinds of samples can have advantages even over community-based samples, in which the participation rates can run as low as 60% to 75%.

Some investigators (for example, Tsai et al., 1979; Baker, 1983) have recruited volunteer samples through ads, questionnaires in magazines, or posted notices on campuses or in public settings. Such samples are relatively inexpensive to assemble, but they can be extremely problematic because the investigator has little way of knowing what kind of a selection bias is at work. Especially in the case of sexual abuse, it seems likely that such volunteer samples recruit from among the healthy, a bias that may understate the extent of impact.

The most common kind of sample for impact and treatment outcome studies is a clinical group, usually patients at a mental health agency (for example, Briere, 1984; Meiselman, 1978; Herman, 1981). This can be an excellent group for studying the effect of treatment because it is the exact group of people—sexual abuse victims seeking help—for which the treatment is intended. However, such samples are not as good for studying the general effects of sexual abuse, because they tend to have an overinclusion of people with serious effects. As in the earlier discussion, the quality of the work will be improved if these samples are as inclusive as possible in recruitment. Even people coming simply for referral or one-time consultation should be included in the sample, so it is not solely long-term clients.

Other types of clinical samples have been drawn from prison populations, psychiatric inpatients, psychiatric outpatients, drug and alcohol treatment programs, child abusers, and residents of juvenile homes. However, subjects from some of these populations are not even representative of the pathology being treated. Thus incarcerated sex offenders are not representative of all sex offenders, and clients in drug and alcohol programs are not representative of all drug and alcohol abusers. Strategies for finding nonidentified, non-help-seeking members of deviant and stigmatized groups need to be developed.

In general, investigators must be as aware as possible of the kinds of selection factors that are at work in the samples they choose. Then they can at least describe these biases and, to some extent, they can try to compensate for them. They can make a special effort to include or recruit subjects from the ends of the spectrum that might otherwise be excluded. For example, in the case of mental health clinics, these might be the clients who come for only one visit or, in the case of a prison, these might be persons who are indicted and sent for evaluation, but not convicted.

## Comparison Groups

Here again, in studies of long-term effects as in initial effects, comparison groups are of crucial importance. When researchers sample from groups such as whole communities, organizations, or clubs, comparisons are automatically provided in the form of those participants who have not been victimized. For purposes of data management, one can sample again from the subset of nonvictims without a serious loss of validity.

It is with the clinical samples that the comparison group becomes particularly problematic. Often the comparison group is chosen from other members of the clinical population, the outpatients or the prisoners who were not victimized (Briere, 1984; Prentky, 1984). The problem here is that the members of the comparison group are likely to have been themselves traumatized in some other way, even if they have not been sexually abused. If this other trauma shares dynamics with sexual abuse, as is likely (for example, emotionally abused children may also suffer from betrayal at the hands of adults), then the full effects of the sexual abuse experience will not be highlighted in the study.

A good technique for dealing with this problem is to try to match the victims from the clinical group with nonclinical persons from similar backgrounds, matching on important variables such as social class, family structure, and parental characteristics. For example, it may be possible to look back to a victim's grade school records, and to follow up someone else from the same class and neighborhood with a similar background. For some of these same purposes nonabused siblings may also be used as comparison. However, this kind of comparison group has many of its own special problems.

### Stratifying for Sex and Race

In choosing samples for studying the impact of sexual abuse, not enough conscious attention has been paid to matters of sex and race. In some previous research, especially on children, boys and girls have been indiscriminately lumped together, in part because of the small number of boys in many samples. However, clinical work (Rogers & Terry, 1984) strongly suggests that boys react differently to abuse and grouping them with girls may muddle efforts to analyze effects. Clearly boys need to studied separately. However, the other risk is that boys will be neglected entirely. There has been only one study of long-term effects on boys (Wood & Deane, 1984). This is a question that is in serious need of more research.

Also neglected has been the study of possible racial differences in the nature of sexual abuse and its effects. Wyatt (1985) and Pierce and Pierce (1984) have compared black and white samples, both finding modest but not extraordinary differences. Our interpretation of the findings to date is that although researchers should be aware of racial differences in the samples they choose, and should make an effort to include mixed samples, it is not necessary to do all studies separately on white and black samples. Less is known about other racial and ethnic groups, however. For example, studies of sexual abuse in Hispanic communities are badly needed.

## *Design Issues*

Most studies of the effects of sexual abuse have been, and will no doubt continue to be, simple "one-shot," postabuse evaluations of victims. As the field develops, there will be increasing pressure for more sophisticated designs to answer some of the complex questions about sexual abuse. Investigators should consider some of the following alternatives for improving the designs that have been used until now.

*(1) Establishing a Preabuse Baseline.* A scientific evaluation of the effect of sexual abuse requires knowledge of what sexual abuse victims were like prior to the abuse. Some of what are seen as effects of abuse may be preexisting problems that were part of what created vulnerability to abuse. A child may have been emotionally deprived before the abuse occurred, and this may be what is largely responsible for later depressive or destructive behavior. Moreover, preabuse information is important because abuse may have very different effects on children depending on their preabuse status. Rutter (1982) points out that temperament plays a very important role in children's reactions to stressful events.

A design that deals with this issue would gather information on children prior to the period of highest risk for abuse, for example, by testing a large group of children in first grade and then following them up years later to find out which had been abused. No study has done this yet, although such a prospective longitudinal study is certainly possible and needed. However, because of the time and expense involved, consideration should be given in the interim to alternatives that provide more immediate, if somewhat less reliable, results. One obvious approach is to look for a cohort of children on whom a great deal of information has already been gathered, such as participants in some other study of child development. If such children are now old enough, an effort might be made to determine who within that cohort had been sexually abused, and to collect follow-up data that can be assembled together with the baseline information.

Even with children who have not been part of an earlier study, investigators should still give consideration to whether or not some useful baseline data on them may already exist. For example, records kept by schools, family doctors, and health maintenance organizations should be considered for possible use.

*(2) Preabuse Baseline Collected Retrospectively.* Even where baseline records are not available, one-shot evaluation studies can improve their design by collecting retrospective data about the child's situation prior to the abuse. In the past, not enough consideration has been given to the possibility that such conditions prior to the abuse may account for both the abuse and the subsequent impairment. A poor relationship with one's mother, for example, is associated with high risk for abuse (Finkelhor, 1984; Peters, 1984) and also with adult mental health impairment (Langner, 1962). Other possible antecedent variables include poverty, family disorganization, emotional abuse, and social isolation. Investigators can try retrospectively to establish the existence of these conditions and then include them in multivariate analyses with abuse and outcome data. Fromuth (1983), using this model, for example, found that much of the association between abuse and impairment as measured on the Hopkins Symptom Checklist washed out when controlling for a variable that measured degree of parental support. Peters (1984) found that the relationship between abuse and depression was substantially attenuated, but not eliminated, when controlling for a poor relationship with the mother.

Although this approach is crucial to one-shot assessment studies, it has substantial limitations that should be recognized. For one thing, it is possible that such retrospective reports about something as global and vague as parental support or closeness with mother are not very valid or reliable. Of most concern is the possibility that if children become victims of abuse, it may affect their retrospective accounts of their relationships with their parents or other background conditions. Every effort should be made to improve on the validity of such retrospective measures, for example, by getting confirmatory information from siblings, or by anchoring the accounts in very concrete behaviors.

Another problem with trying to control for conditions prior to abuse, however, is conceptual rather than simply methodological. Some kinds of sexual abuse may be so integrally related to deep and long-standing family patterns that it may never be possible to disentangle the effects of abuse from some of its antecedents. One simply may never find father-daughter sexual abuse in a situation in which a daughter has an excellent relationship with her mother. So it may not be very possible to determine whether or not the effects of the abuse are independent of the effects of the poor relationship. This suggests the importance of studies on *extrafamilial* abuse, in which prior family conditions may have less to do with whether abuse occurred or not.

*(3) Gathering More Complete Information About Events Following Abuse.* In addition to considering antecedents of abuse, investigators need to consider the effect of subsequent events as well. Although many studies gather information about how long the abuse lasted, who the offender was, and whether or not intercourse occurred, fewer have asked whether or not the abuse was reported to anyone, at the time or later; how disclosure was received; whether or not the child was blamed; whether or not the child was believed; whether or not friends, family, and community found out about the abuse; and so forth. Consideration needs to be given to the hypothesis that many of the effects of sexual abuse can be traced to its aftermath. Consideration needs to be given also to the hypothesis that some subsequent events, such as support from family, mitigate the effects of abuse. Multivariate analyses will be required to partition the effects of abuse and postabuse variables. A good sample for such a study is a group of children who suffer similar kinds of abuse (such as in a day-care setting), but whose disclosure is handled in different ways by parents and authorities.

*(4) Longitudinal Designs.* Some research on sexual abuse is beginning to use longitudinal designs (Conte & Berliner, 1984; Runyan, 1984), usually testing children shortly after disclosure and then again one year later. These longitudinal designs do allow answers to some questions that are not otherwise available, for example, concerning whether or not some effects of sexual

abuse are delayed. However, some effects may be *very* delayed, not showing up until the child reaches a stage of development in which some of these concerns—for example, related to sexuality—come to the fore. Recent research on divorce (Wallerstein, 1983) has found some effects that do not show up clearly for fifteen years. Obviously longitudinal studies with follow-ups of much greater than one year are needed.

The longitudinal design is also excellent for evaluating the effect of some specific postabuse events, such as court appearances, foster-home placements, or psychotherapy. Because such designs have a baseline measure of the children prior to these postabuse events, it may be possible to estimate the contribution of these events independent of abuse.

As one final advantage, longitudinal studies do allow for the measurement of effects at two points in time, something that may give greater reliability to assessments of pathology.

*(5) Multivariate Analyses.* Given the complexity of the problem of sexual abuse as we now understand it, all studies of the effects of sexual abuse should be oriented toward multivariate analysis. Researchers need to be able to look at the contribution of sexual abuse in an analysis that controls for demographic, social class, and family variables. And they also need to be able to assess the contribution of various kinds of abuse to trauma along with the contribution of such factors as whether or not the abuse was revealed and how it was dealt with.

Use of multivariate analysis also means that designs need to have large enough sample sizes. An often-cited rule of thumb is to have 10 cases for every variable to be included in the analysis. Studies based on 20 cases of abuse and 20 controls are hardly adequate. Investigators need to be thinking in terms of at least 100 *abuse* cases.

*(6) Conceptual Frameworks.* The most important component to a successful research design is a conceptual framework to guide the design. Conceptual frameworks give coherence to

the work, answer many questions, and provide a basis for interpreting results. For example, a conceptual framework regarding the developmental impact of sexual abuse should give suggestions about the appropriate intervals for follow-up. A conceptual framework about how sexual abuse fits into development will give suggestions about the appropriate variables to choose, and how to array them in multivariate analysis. Thus in embarking on any study, it pays for an investigator to develop a conceptual framework.

### Measurement and Instrumentation

The field of sexual abuse is still at an embryonic stage in matters of measurement and instrumentation. Different investigators use very different approaches and no consensus about instruments has emerged yet. There is a pressing need for some basic research in the field to settle such questions as the following:

(1) What is the best way to ask about whether or not sexual abuse has occurred?
(2) What assessment tools best capture the kinds of trauma associated with sexual abuse?
(3) What are the appropriate categories for grouping the sexual activities involved in sexual abuse?

Nonetheless, even as some of these questions are being settled by research and discussion, there are still some tentative guidelines investigators should keep in mind concerning instrumentation. Repeating a point made earlier, issues of instrumentation will be clearer and simpler for investigators who have a conceptual framework to guide their research. The conceptual framework should suggest the key variables that need to be measured, and should help in choosing or constructing instruments to operationalize these variables.

When choosing or constructing instruments, investigators should have some strong justifications for their choices. The fact that an instrument is reliable is not a sufficient justification in itself. A good justification might be that the instrument measures something that is theoretically related to abuse. Another good justification might be that the instrument has been used successfully by other investigators. Another might be that the instrument has discriminated trauma associated with sexual abuse from trauma associated with other problems in the population under investigation.

### Adult Measures

In the case of adults, certain measures have tended to be very popular—the MMPI, the Hopkins Symptoms Checklist, the Beck Depression scale, and the Rosenberg Self-Concept. These are widely used measures, with a strong record of validity and reliability in clinical research. They have utility in that investigators and readers are familiar with them, and their implications for clinicians are relatively clear. They are useful especially for exploratory work because they are broad general assessment measures and may indicate effects of sexual abuse that had not been previously noted.

On the other hand, these types of measures have some drawbacks that have already been encountered by the researchers who have used them to date. Most seriously, these measures were not designed to assess the particular impairments associated with sexual abuse. So they are not particularly sensitive to the matters of greatest concern to sexual abuse researchers. Using these scales as the main impact measures may not only dilute our sense of the impact of sexual abuse, but may also make it difficult to conduct sensitive analyses about the differential impact of different kinds of abuse. These scales simply may not tap the core effects of abuse. Peters (1984) found, for example, that the Beck Depression inventory did not discriminate sexual abuse victims from nonvictims, but her own more detailed questions about histories of depressive episodes did.

Moreover, general assessment instruments are sometimes used in a loose and atheoretical way that only adds to confusion in the field. For example, investigators, applying tests without any hypotheses, may find elevated scores on certain subscales, and take this as a sign of the pathological effect of abuse, even though no clear understanding exists of why abuse should have that impact.

Clearly instruments need to be developed that are based on a theoretical understanding of what impact sexual abuse has, such as that proposed in Chapter 6. Investigators are urged to try to develop instruments that have specific utility in assessing the impact of sexual abuse. Until such measures are developed, refined, and validated, it is probably a good idea for investigators to use a mix of measures: perhaps one general assessment, together with others developed specifically to look at certain theoretically anticipated impacts of sexual abuse.

**Child Measures**

Problems are even more acute in the area of child assessment because fewer instruments are available. Two that frequently have been used or considered for use by sexual abuse researchers are the Child Behavior Profile (Achenbach & Edelbrock, 1979) and the Louisville Behavior Checklist (Miller, 1967). These scales have the advantages of wide acceptance, norms for various populations, and forms for children of different ages. However, they also have the weakness mentioned earlier in regard to adult assessment instruments: They may be insensitive to the effects that are most closely associated with sexual abuse.

Both these checklists have an additional difficulty in that they are filled out by parents. All parent-completed instruments are problematic in that parents may have difficulty giving unbiased assessments. An emotional expectation of trauma may cause one parent to see trauma where it does not exist. Guilt-related denial may cause another parent to overlook signs of trouble when they actually exist. Such problems may be even more acute than usual in the case of sexual abuse, because parents may be intimately involved in the creation of the situation that brings the child into treatment.

A technique might be developed to correct for possible parental bias under these circumstances. Parents might be asked a general question about how much trauma they think sexual abuse causes. Those who seem oriented to expect trauma might be likely to see more trauma. If the expectation measure correlated with the actual observation measure, the expectation measure might be used like a "social desirability" scale to correct for parents' overexpectation of trauma.

Another general practice that ought to be used to guard against the weaknesses in parent-completed measures is for investigators always to utilize multiple-method assessment techniques. For abused children, it might be a good idea to combine parent ratings and therapist or professional ratings, as well as some form of self-completed instrument by the children.

## Measures of Sexual Abuse Experience

Unfortunately, there are as yet no "standard" instruments for asking about or coding the nature of the sexual abuse experiences themselves. However, investigators should pay careful attention to the conclusions from Chapter 1, which are based on the experience of previous researchers who have asked about histories of sexual abuse. We will reiterate the most important of the conclusions concerning question structure here.

(1) Investigators should use a series of questions (what we called "multiple screens") to inquire about a history of sexual abuse, rather than a single question.

(2) It may be valuable to ask a variety of questions that include mention of specific potential partners (what we called "relationship-specific questions") and specific sexual activities (what we called "activity-specific questions").

(3) Interviews, under most circumstances, are preferable to self-administered questionnaire formats.

We would like to make some additional recommendations about ways to improve the collection of data concerning histories of sexual abuse.

(4) Investigators need to gather sufficient detail on the sexual activity involved. In many cases, for example, investigators have made no distinction between the adult touching the child's genitals and the child touching the adult's. Information needs to

be gathered on whether the focus was on the child's genitalia or the adult's, as well as who was placed in the role of stimulator. In addition, the use of the term *fondling,* which has become widespread, is too vague. The data need to specify who was touched where. The terms *penetration* and *attempted intercourse* also need clearer definition. Russell's categories in regard to sexual activity merit close examination by those developing research protocols in this area (Table 7.1).

(5) Investigators need to gather more age-related data. Too often in studies, all that is known is the age of the child at time of assessment, the age at time of disclosure, or the age at time of onset. Research must record all this information as well as age at time of last sexual contact with the abuser.

(6) A greater degree of precision needs to be achieved in recording the exact relationship between the child and the abuser. Colloquial categories such as *neighbor* or *acquaintance* or even *relative* may be too vague because these terms do not capture the true nature of closeness or distance that researchers are attempting to gauge. In reality, some neighbors are accorded the trust level of close relatives, and others are virtual strangers. Some relatives may actually have little prior contact with a child because of geographic distance. Thus researchers should try to develop some measure of how much prior involvement a child had with the offender and in how much trust the offender was held by child and family.

(7) Better data need to be collected on the nature of the force, coercion, or trickery used to obtain a child's participation. Force and coercion tend to be vague categories, and are sometimes defined in strictly physical terms, but other times *force* is defined as having nonphysical as well as physical components. It is important for understanding the impact of sexual abuse that the physical and nonphysical components be separated, and that the nature of the coercion be specified.

**TABLE 7.1**

**Categories of Sexual Abuse**

| | |
|---|---|
| (1) | Rape—genital intercourse *by force*[a] |
| (2) | Genital intercourse *not by force* |
| (3) | Attempted rape |
| (4) | Attempted genital intercourse *not by force* |
| (5) | Fellatio, cunnilingus, analingus, anal intercourse *by force* |
| (6) | Fellatio, cunnilingus, analingus, anal intercourse *not by force* |
| (7) | Attempted fellatio, cunnilingus, analingus, anal intercourse *by force* |
| (8) | Attempted fellatio, cunnilingus, analingus, anal intercourse *not by force* |
| (9) | Genital contact (unclothed) including manual touching or penetration *by force* |
| (10) | Genital contact (unclothed) including manual touching or penetration *not by force* |
| (11) | Attempted genital contact (unclothed) including manual touching or penetration *by force* |
| (12) | Attempted genital contact (unclothed) including manual touching or penetration *not by force* |
| (13) | Breast contact (unclothed) or simulated intercourse *by force* |
| (14) | Breast contact (unclothed) or simulated intercourse *not by force* |
| (15) | Attempted breast contact (unclothed) or simulated intercourse *by force* |
| (16) | Attempted breast contact (unclothed) or simulated intercourse *not by force* |
| (17) | Sexual kissing, intentional sexual touching of buttocks, thigh, leg, or clothed breasts or genitals *by force* |
| (18) | Sexual kissing, intentional sexual touching of thigh, leg, or clothed breasts or genitals *not by force* |

SOURCE: Russell (1986).

a. *Force* includes physical force, threat of force, or assault when the victim is unable to consent because she is unconscious, severely drugged, or in some other way totally helpless. Note: It does *not* include the inability of a child to consent to sexual contact with an adult.

## Human Subjects

Any research on child abuse is, by its very nature, fraught with ethical problems. Researchers should give these problems serious consideration in advance and need to have well-rehearsed plans for handling them.

### Confidentiality and Reporting

Any study concerned with child abuse has a strong likelihood that it will uncover as yet unreported situations in which children have been abused or are in jeopardy. Handling these cases poses very serious dilemmas that the research community has not confronted adequately.

Many studies of child abuse, like other social science research, rely on promises of confidentiality to respondents. Many investigators believe quite passionately that, unless they promise such confidentiality, respondents will never reveal potentially abusive behavior and therefore valid research would be impossible. However, this contention has never been tested empirically.

If confidentiality is promised and cases of abuse are discovered, legal and ethical questions arise. In many states, *but not all states*, researchers fall into the category of those who are mandated to report cases of suspected and actual child abuse. Where reporting is mandated, researchers face the dilemma of not being able to promise confidentiality, of being forced to abrogate their promise of confidentiality in order to comply with the law, or of violating the law by not reporting cases of which they know. These are all difficult choices.

One partial solution to this dilemma is to apply for a Public Health Service Certificate of Confidentiality. These certificates are available from the office of the director of the Alchohol, Drug Abuse and Mental Health Administration under public law 93-282 (42 U.S.C. 242a(a)). The certificate of confidentiality, which originally was established to further research on drug abuse, allows for investigators in specially designated projects to gather from individuals information that may not be "compelled in any Federal, State, or local civil, criminal, administrative, legislative, or other proceedings to identify such individuals." This certificate of confidentiality does not take long to obtain. Investigators armed with such a certificate can promise confidentiality to participants in research with the confidence that even if they do encounter cases of abuse they are not under a legal obligation to report them.

However, although the certificate of confidentiality may solve certain legal problems, the ethical problems still remain. Can a researcher faced with the situation of child abuse ethically justify not reporting such a case? Researchers usually have defended nonreporting by saying that they were gathering valuable information that would be crucial to the prevention and treatment of many other cases of child abuse and that such information could not be gathered unless credible promises of confidentiality were given.

It would seem that for researchers to stop with this argument, however, would be an abdication of responsibility. Given the jeopardy that children may be in, the research community needs to go further than simply pleading for special treatment. Researchers should consider at least two alternatives. One is not to make promises of total confidentiality that would then preclude the reporting of cases of child abuse. The second is that when such promises of confidentiality are given to make contingency plans for special intervention initiated and supervised by the researcher. Promises of confidentiality do not preclude the possibility of the investigator performing some sort of intervention. At the very minimum, that intervention should include a great deal of encouragement to, and even pressure on, the respondent to report the case of abuse or to allow a report to be made.

### Avoiding Additional Trauma to Participants

Researchers in the area of child abuse need to take special precautions to avoid creating any additional trauma to victims of abuse. Most researchers do acknowledge this need. However, a full inventory of the variety of ways in which abuse victims may be traumatized further has not really been developed. Researchers need to give very careful thought to how their research design, interview, questionnaire, follow-up, and recruitment procedures might cause inadvertent injury to research subjects. Some examples of special concern follow.

Researchers must take care that involvement of abused children in a study does not put them at risk of further victimization. For example, victims of sexual abuse participating in a study on the effects of a prevention program for which parental permission is obtained may suffer from intimidation or retaliation from offenders—fathers or older brothers—to keep the child either from talking or from talking further. It was partly with this contingency in mind that recent revisions of NIH human subject guidelines *exempted* research on child abuse from the requirement to obtain parental permission. Investigators should always think very carefully about whether or not such requests for parental permission add to children's vulnerability.

Another way in which victims can be traumatized by research is if, in the process of research, the fact of their having been victims is revealed to people who were otherwise unaware. For example, in a recent study of the effects of sexual abuse (Conte & Berliner, 1984), it was decided not to obtain teacher evaluations of the school behavior of victimized children because such a procedure would have required revealing the victimization to some children's teachers who were not aware of it. Not enough is known about the effect of such labeling on a child, but it could be a potentially negative one. This problem also appears in studies of the long-term effects of abuse. Investigators need to be careful in contacting and interviewing adults molested as children, because these victims may not have told spouses or children about their abuse, and recruitment into a follow-up study may allow the fact of such victimization to be known. Care needs to be taken not to create suspicion among family through scheduling of appointments, letters to respondents, requests to officials for information, or visits by the subjects to the research site.

Research procedures themselves can traumatize victims. For example, it is important that all interviewers and all research personnel be well trained not to convey stigmatizing attitudes toward victims. It is also important that a presumption of serious effects not be communicated. A child or adult who is adapting well, and sees the abuse as a rather minor event, may be inclined to change or question his or her own view if investigators imply through questions or attitudes that sexual abuse should have serious long-term effects. Simply the length and complexity of a research protocol may convey alarm to a victim. As Lucy Berliner (personal communication, 1983) points out, "What message does a child take from being involved in two days of research because of an experience that lasted fifteen minutes?"

It is important that a presumption of trauma not be conveyed to the parents as well as to the children. Even if a child draws no particular implication from research participation, her parents may be led by the investigator to conclude that sexual abuse must be a horribly traumatizing event. They may then communicate their concern to the child.

There are various specific procedures in the course of research on sexual abuse that need to be used with caution. For example, asking children or adults to remember or relive events may in some cases provoke reactions. These kinds of concerns should not be seen as arguments against using such procedures; rather, they are mentioned here in order to sensitize investigators to possibilities that may occur in research, and that should be guarded against as much as possible in designing the research.

## *Conclusion*

This chapter has tried to provide a brief overview of issues that need to be addressed in designing research on child sexual abuse, and is not intended as a comprehensive methodological guide. Many other discussions of the problems are needed. The field is at a juncture where attention to methodology will have great payoffs in our ability to gain understanding. Sexual abuse is such an urgent problem that issues of research methodology can seem almost trivial compared to our needs for knowledge and action. But if we are to have a strong foundation of knowledge from which to build policy, this can happen only on the basis of conscientious and well-designed research.

# 8

# Prevention:
# A Review of
# Programs and
# Research

David Finkelhor

This chapter is a review of the field of child sexual abuse prevention. It is intended to serve as a short introduction to this field for those who are new to it. It also offers some criticism, recommendations, and research suggestions for those who are planning the direction the field should take.

Because of space limitations and the speed with which child sexual abuse prevention is developing, this review is not by any means an exhaustive inventory of ideas and programs in this field. Nor should it be used as a guide for setting up programs; many of the program guides are much better suited for that.

Sexual abuse prevention is a new field. Programs having prevention as their primary objective did not begin to appear until the late 1970s, several years after programs had been established to identify and treat sexual abuse victims. One of the earliest projects began in 1977 when the Sexual Assault Services division of the Hennepin County Attorney's Office (Minneapolis, Minnesota) received a private grant to develop a Child Sexual Abuse Prevention Project (Kent, 1979). It was not until 1980 that any federal funds (from the National Center for Child Abuse and Neglect) became available for prevention work.

In spite of the federal contributions, federal influence on the field has never been large. For the most part, prevention programs originated from the grass roots without government sponsorship. Most grew out of the volunteer efforts of rape crisis counselors, were sponsored by local social service agencies or police departments, or originated simply from the efforts of concerned educators and parents. By 1983, however, prevention programs were among the fastest-growing components of the movement to deal with child sexual abuse.

The rationale for prevention rests on a number of realities about child sexual abuse. First, as earlier chapters have shown, an important percentage of all children will suffer such abuse. Second, in spite of recent advances in the availability of treatment services to victims of child sexual abuse, it is clear that most child victims of sexual abuse will not be identified in the near future, let alone provided with service. Services are still scarce in most locales. More important, from all evidence, most children do not reveal their victimization, and, when they do, families are still unlikely to seek help (Finkelhor, 1984). Treatment programs can be expected to assist only a small percentage of victims. Some other broader approach is needed.

The logic of prevention has also grown out of experience working with victims of sexual abuse. Such experience suggested that many children could have been spared substantial vulnerability and suffering if they had had simple pieces of information, for example, about their right to refuse sexual advances or about the inappropriateness of the behavior that an adult was engaged in. It made obvious sense to try to provide children with such information to see if it could reduce the toll of victimization.

Thus prevention has great appeal as an approach to sexual abuse. It holds the potential of reaching a large number of children, short-circuiting some abuse before it occurs, and increasing the number of victims who get help. And it holds the potential of accomplishing these goals in a cost-efficient way, without the institution of major new social programs.

## *Audiences for Prevention Approaches*

Although the objective for all programs is to help children, not all prevention approaches have children as their exclusive or primary audiences. Some prevention is directed toward parents, and some toward professionals. We will discuss each of these audiences and some of their needs that have been identified by each approach.

### Children

Many prevention efforts are targeted directly to children through a variety of media. Programs like the Illusion Theater of Minneapolis and the CAP program of Columbus go directly into schools, where their trained staff conduct workshops for children at all grade levels. Children's authors have written storybooks and coloring books such as *Red Flag, Green Flag* to teach children how to avoid sexual abuse. A number of films, such as *Who Do You Tell* or *No More Secrets,* have been produced, primarily for use in the schools. In Seattle, ad campaigns with famous people, such as basketball star Bill Russell, have been used to teach kids to identify possible child molesters.

Although varying in their style and medium, the messages conveyed by most of these efforts to reach children have had some very common and basic themes.

(1) All the efforts have tried to educate children about what sexual abuse is. Although they sometimes call it by some name other than sexual abuse (especially with younger children), all have defined some behaviors as bad and have warned children to be alert to people who try to do such things to them. (We will give more discussion to the variety of approaches that have been used in a later section labeled "Current Concepts.")

(2) All the efforts have tried to broaden children's awareness about who potential sexual abuse offenders might be. In contrast to educational programs of earlier generations that warned exclusively about strangers, almost all current prevention programs let children know that potential offenders include people whom they may know very well and like.

(3) All the efforts have tried to give children some action that they can take in the event that someone tries to sexually abuse them. They encourage children to tell someone, especially someone they trust, and to keep telling until they are believed. In addition, some encourage children to leave, run away, say no, or resist in some fashion.

Prevention efforts have been directed toward a very broad spectrum of children. This strategy has been reinforced by two important facts emerging from contemporary research on sexual abuse. First, it is apparent that boys are subject to victimization as well as girls. Current estimates are that one boy is victimized for every two to three girls (see Chapter 2). Thus prevention education is usually conducted in mixed classrooms and both boys and girls are used as models in the media.

Second, children are victimized at an alarmingly early age (see Chapter 2). This emphasizes the need to bring prevention to quite young children. Just how early one can start to educate children about sexual abuse is not clear. General coping, assertion, and self-esteem skills are imparted to children very early in life, but what about the specific concepts involved in sexual abuse education? Although some programs claim success with children as young as age 2 (Snowdon, 1983), for the most part, programs limit themselves to school-age children, beginning at kindergarten. There has been less experience to determine what the capacities of younger children might be.

Of course, prevention efforts aimed at 5- and 6-year-olds cannot take the same format as efforts aimed at adolescents or preadolescents. Educational efforts have to take account of children's changing level of sophistication, their increasing knowledge about the world and about sexual behavior, as well as the different kinds of situations in which different aged children may be vulnerable. Linda Sanford (personal communication, 1983) believes there are essentially three childrens' audiences: kindergarten to third grade, fourth to eighth grade, and high school. Unfortunately, the differing needs of these audiences have not been defined clearly, although most programs acknowledge them in some way with the work they do. For example, the

Illusion Theater substantially shortens its program for younger children to accommodate their shorter attention span. The theater also found that certain terms, such as *incest,* were more confusing to the youngest groups and needed to be explained better or replaced by other words (Kent, 1979). One program deals with younger children by using more drawings; another deals with their greater impressionability by introducing role-plays as "pretend" stories (Olson, 1982).

Prevention efforts need to take account of other variables besides children's ages, such as differences in cultural and social class background. For example, the CAP Training Center of Northern California, working with many different ethnic groups, found that although the notion of an individual child's "right" to be safe (an important concept in the CAP program) was readily understood by black children, such ideas made little initial sense to Latin or Asian children (Cooper, Lutter, & Phelps, 1983).

There are also other special populations of children who need special approaches, including children who are handicapped and children who have already suffered victimization. For example, the Minnesota Program for Victims of Sexual Assault developed a prevention curriculum specifically for disabled adolescents that tries to take account of the fact that parents and the rest of society give such children less basic sex information (O'Day, 1983).

As for children who have already suffered victimization, many treatment programs began offering prevention education after they became aware that previously abused children were at high risk for reabuse and that prevention skills could be an excellent vehicle for restoring their sense of security and self-esteem (Berliner, 1983; Snowden, 1983). However, given that some victimized children will be present in any audience, all prevention programs have to take their special needs into account. Illustrating these special needs, Linda Sanford (personal communication, 1983) cautions against formulating prevention concepts, such as "never keep a secret," in a way that will make already victimized children feel worse because they did something they shouldn't have. She favors dealing with this problem by presenting children with options rather than absolutes.

## Parents

Prevention education directed toward parents has some advantages because of the central role parents play in children's lives. If parents learn to educate children themselves, children may receive repeated exposures to information from a trusted source, a situation that a special classroom presentation cannot parallel. Moreover, educating parents also holds out the possibility of dramatically increasing the detection of children who have become victims (because parents will become more sensitive to signs of abuse) and of improving the reactions of parents when they hear about or discover these victimizations.

The importance of educating parents is also underlined by the apparent inadequacy of what parents currently do to alert their children about sexual abuse. These practices were the subject of a earlier study of 521 parents of children ages 6 to 14 in the Boston metropolitan area (Finkelhor, 1984), which confirmed the concerns of many professionals in the field.

Some of the facts revealed by the study included the following:

(1) Only 29% of the parents said they had had discussions with their children specifically related to the topic of sexual abuse.

(2) Even when such discussions had occurred, in many cases they failed to mention important aspects of the problem. Only 53% of discussions, for example, mentioned the possibility of abuse by an adult acquaintance, only 22% by a family member. Only 65% mentioned the possibility of someone trying to take off the child's clothes.

(3) The discussions that did occur often occurred too late. Most parents believed the optimal age for discussing sexual abuse with a child is around age 9. Evidence from the parents' own childhood experiences revealed, however, that more than a third of all victims of sexual abuse would be victimized before age 9.

Why is it that parents have such difficulty in providing information about child sexual abuse to their children? The survey and the discussions with parents allowed for some understanding of this matter.

Some parents simply did not visualize sexual abuse as a serious problem, and therefore did not bring it up. However, this was not true of everyone. Nearly half the parents estimated sexual abuse to occur to one girl in ten or more often.

It is one thing to see the problem as widespread in the abstract, and another to see one's own child as at risk. The general problem then was for parents to imagine that their own children could be victimized. Parents tend to think of their own children as well supervised and able to avoid danger. Their neighborhood was thought safer than average by 61% and only 4% thought their neighborhood less safe. Other factors that keep people from imagining that their children are at risk are the images of sexual abuse as something that occurs only to lower-class families, or the image of potential sexual abusers as weird and conspicuous individuals. Clearly parents need to be educated not only that the incidence of sexual abuse is high, but, awful as it might be to imagine, that it could happen to their own children.

Another reason parents often give for not telling children about sexual abuse is the fear of frightening them unneccessarily. Parents say they are afraid both of creating additional anxiety for a child and of making the child suspicious of adults. Although these parents are certainly sincere in their concern, it is curious that virtually all parents warn children about the possibility of kidnapping. The idea that someone might try to take the child away from his or her home must certainly be a far more frightening idea to a child than the idea that someone might try to touch his or her genitals, particularly to children who have a very alarming awareness of separation but a rather vague one of sex. The contrast is particularly ironic insofar as kidnapping is far less likely in a child's life than sexual abuse. Yet parents all warn children about it. It suggests that part of the anxiety parents are trying to avoid is their own anxiety.

One reason kidnapping may be much easier to talk about than sexual abuse is that parents have ready-made formulas for discussing the subject. Every parent has heard phrases such as "don't get in a car with (or take candy from) a stranger," which he or she can repeat. Similar formulas have not existed in the past concerning sexual abuse. So a parent, confronted with the need to say something about sexual abuse, has to improvise, using his or her own confused knowledge about the subject, and this prospect has perhaps deterred many. Now efforts are being made by prevention educators, such as Linda Sanford (1980) and Carin Adams and Jennifer Fay (1981), to provide formulas for parents, and these may make the process easier.

A more profound problem for parents in talking about sexual abuse, and what differentiates sexual abuse from kidnapping, is that it concerns sex. Parents have a notoriously difficult time talking to their children about sexual topics of all sorts. This generalized difficulty with sexual topics has not been well investigated, but sex educators have posited a number of factors that are also probably at work in the case of sexual abuse (Roberts et al., 1978).

For one thing, parents often feel they lack the knowledge, vocabulary, and practice to speak about sexual matters. They fear embarrassing themselves in front of their children by appearing ignorant, tongue-tied, or confused.

Second, sexual topics trigger strong emotional feelings for parents, reminders of sexual embarrassments, traumas, or disappointments in their own lives.

Third, parents are unsure of their own values about sexual matters, and are aware that sexual discussions may oblige them to talk about matters of value, opinion, or even personal experience. All these concerns may be triggered when parents contemplate a discussion of sexual abuse with a child.

Sexual abuse educators have tried to circumvent this problem to some extent by fashioning ways of talking about sexual abuse that do not relate to sex. Certainly parents can do a great deal of educating concerning sexual abuse without having to discuss other sexual topics. Two questions, however, remain to be answered: (1) Can parents who continue to feel a great deal of anxiety about sexual matters in general be relied upon to raise the subject of sexual abuse in an ongoing and effective way, in spite of such anxiety? Or are efforts to take the sex out of sexual abuse education doomed for such parents because the subject cannot help but have sexual connotations for them? (2) Are such "denatured" discussions of sexual abuse (sexual abuse without references to sex) effective in informing children about the important features of the problem? Or do such discussions inevitably avoid certain matters that turn out to be crucial to a child's developing effective coping skills?

A question of some importance for parent education efforts is whether or not there are groups of parents who should be specially targeted. Obviously parents whose children may be at high risk of abuse are one such group. One consistent finding about risk is that children who live in stepfamilies are unusually vulnerable (Finkelhor, 1984; Giles-Sims & Finkelhor, 1984; Russell, 1984b). This suggests some special sexual abuse awareness information directed to parents who are remarrying. Another high-risk group is children with disabilities or emotional problems. Their parents also need to be alerted.

Another group of parents with some special needs may be those parents who were themselves victimized when they were children. Many workers in the field are of the opinion that children of such parents are at high risk, although no good research data have yet confirmed this point. Some of these parents undoubtedly have an extraordinarily difficult time raising these issues with their children because of the painful memories it stimulates. Certainly any program directed at parents needs to acknowledge openly that many former victims will themselves be present in the audience. However, an encouraging finding that appeared in the Boston survey was that parents who had themselves been victimized were one of the very few groups that had a better-than-average record in terms of providing their children with information. It may be that for some parents, the pain of their own victimization experiences makes it more difficult to talk with their children, whereas for others the close personal awareness of the subject impels them into taking some preventive action.

Undoubtedly parents from different ethnic backgrounds and different social classes need to be educated in a manner and with concepts that are consistent with their own specific backgrounds and needs. In a diverse country such as the United States, it is more difficult to design a single approach that can be effective with everyone. One interesting finding from the Boston study, however, was the uniformity with which parents of all classes and ethnic groups abdicated their responsibility. Parents who had more education or high occupational status definitely did not do a better job than poorly educated and lower-social-class parents. There were also no differences along racial, ethnic, or religious lines. This does suggest that equivalent if not identical problems confront parents in all social groups, and that no group should be assumed to be immune.

Although most education programs are directed toward parents in general, the reality is that prevention is done mostly by women. In the Boston survey, more than twice as many mothers as fathers had introduced the subject. Prevention educators say that their adult attendees are overwhelmingly women.

This fact raises important policy questions for the prevention movement. They do not discuss it explicitly in their literature, yet, by their silence on the subject, most programs appear to accept the fact that women inevitably will be the primary educators and the ones primarily motivated to learn about sexual abuse. To devote a great deal of energy toward recruiting men to attend sex abuse education programs and getting them to take responsibility for talking with their children may be a wasteful and inefficient use of resources. On the other hand, certain undeniable benefits might accrue from making it a priority to recruit men, one in particular being to discourage men from becoming abusers.

The goal of reducing the likelihood that adults will become abusers is important for prevention efforts, but it is one that goes

far beyond the scope of most prevention programs to date. By
and large, programs assume they are addressing adults who are
not abusers or potential abusers, but who are in a position to
identify others who may be. Even without specifically addressing the possibility that audience members might become abusers, however, it is likely that these programs do have an
important deterrent influence on anyone who is exposed to
them, if for no other reason than that they clearly reinforce the
norm that such behavior is exploitative of a child. Rich Snowden
(1983) is one prevention educator who stresses in his arguments
for prevention programs the fact that they may discourage men
and boys from committing abuse.

## Professionals

A third audience for prevention efforts is the professionals
who have contact with children. Four professional groups with
special strategic value in prevention efforts are teachers, physicians, mental health professionals, and police. Teachers especially have a lot of contact with children and already impart a
great deal of information concerning safety and coping with the
world. Moreover, they are professionals who, given prevention
education, could readily notice unusual behavior or changes in
behavior that might signify a child is suffering abuse.

Physicians have much less contact with children than do
teachers. But they occupy a special position in terms of the exper-
tise they hold in matters related to the body. This may allow them
the opportunity to raise questions concerning the possibility of
sexual abuse that other professionals and adults would not have.

Mental health personnel work with children who are troubled
in some way, a population that is at particular risk to abuse. Thus
better-prepared mental health professionals are in a particularly
strategic position to help prevent and uncover abuse.

Police often do not have a great deal of contact with children
prior to victimization, except through programs in which they
teach about community safety. However, police are very frequently involved in the investigation of sexual abuse after it has

occurred, and, if poorly trained, they can greatly compound the trauma of abuse for the child.

Professionals in recent years received a great deal of training dealing with sexual abuse, more of it geared toward intervention than toward prevention. However, in communities with prevention programs, professionals usually have received large doses of prevention education as well. Most of those groups who do sexual abuse education for children in the schools also will train teachers and other professionals in the schools. Several have produced manuals for training teachers and other professionals. There also has been a recent profusion of special workshops for professionals on the subject of child sexual abuse. Many mental health workers have participated in these. Physicians and police have received less exposure to such training, however.

It is certainly fair to say that education about child sexual abuse prevention is not part of the regular training that any professional receives. An important priority for educators in this field should be to try to affect the curriculum at professional schools to include material about sexual abuse.

### Current Concepts

Although there is some competition among groups espousing alternative approaches to sexual abuse prevention, what is generally striking about these approaches is their similarity. There are differences in philosophy, emphasis, vocabulary, and organizational style. But taken together, most groups have confronted a set of important challenges and resolved them in rather similar fashion.

The nature of the common challenges is outlined in the following paragraphs.

(1) Sexual abuse, as adults generally talk about it, is a complicated notion, involving concepts of appropriate sexual behavior, appropriate sexual partners, ethics, and social obligations. These concepts are not ones that are necessarily readily grasped by children, especially young children. Children have limited

knowledge about sex and certainly incomplete understanding of normative issues surrounding it. Prevention programs need to translate the notion of sexual abuse into concepts that make sense within the world of the child.

(2) The notion of sexual abuse is also one that has large and frightening overtones for adults. Thus they often have presented it to children in a way that makes an already frightening world just so much more so. As CAP educators point out, children who are made to feel only frightened and powerless may become even less capable of avoiding abuse. Prevention programs have had to find some way to avoid or moderate the potentially fearsome overtones of the issue.

(3) Sex education is a highly controversial matter in most communities in the United States. Some groups of parents have very strong objections to the idea that anyone but parents should talk to their children about sex, as well as strong ideas about what kinds of messages about sex their children should hear. As a result, teachers and particularly school administrators, who in most American communities are politically vulnerable officials, are very reluctant to permit anything that appears controversial in regard to sex to be included in the educational curriculum.

The solutions that prevention programs have used to confront these challenges have been creative. For example, how do you make sexual abuse meaningful to younger children? For the most part, educational programs have tried to relate the problem of sexual abuse to other kinds of problems that children readily grasp (Hutchinson & Chevalier, 1982; Crisci, 1983). The CAP programs start their explanations of sexual abuse by talking about bullies. They illustrate with a skit of an older child trying to coerce money from a younger child. Being the victim of a bully is presumably a kind of experience to which all children can relate. In this context, the explanation of sexual abuse (illustrated by a role-play in which an uncle tries to coerce a kiss from a little girl) is readily understood.

The Illusion Theater makes sexual abuse comprehensible by placing it in the context of what they call the Touch Continuum.

They start out by discussing the differences between touching that feels good (also called "nurturant" or "positive" touch), illustrated by hugs, pats, snuggles, and so on, compared to touch that feels bad (also called "exploitative," "manipulated," or "forced" touch), illustrated by hitting, bullying, or trapping. Illusion also has a category of what they call "confusing" touch ("touch that mixes you up or makes you feel funny") that includes touches that convey double messages. In this context they introduce sexual abuse as a form of touch that feels either bad or confusing (Kent, 1979). The Touch Continuum has been much borrowed and adapted, often ending up as a dichotomy between good touch and bad touch, or, as one adaptation puts it, "red flag versus green flag touches" (Williams, 1980). Obviously, "good and bad touch" is a vocabulary very readily understood by even small children.

The use of metaphors about bullies and touching has another function: It sets the discussion of sexual abuse outside the realm of sex education. Prevention programs usually have as their goals personal safety, assault prevention, or empowerment, not sex education. Although it varies from program to program and setting to setting depending on the sensitivities, most sexual abuse prevention programs are designed so that the subject of sex can be skirted tactfully. Words generally associated with sex or sex education do not have to be used explicitly. In many programs, sexual organs are not referred to. References are made instead to such things as "Private Zones" (Dayee, 1982), "molestation," "touching in private areas," "touching all over," "touching under the panties," and "places usually covered by a bathing suit." With some important exceptions, the formal curricula of most programs do not usually try to provide children with other kinds of sex education, such as information about sexual anatomy or vocabulary.

The tactful avoiding of sexual subject matter is generally well received by all participants. Parents and school personnel who screen these programs before they are shown to the children often arrive expecting to feel uncomfortable, yet find themselves quite relieved when they find how unobjectionable the programs are. Usually these screenings manage to undercut any potential objection that is based on fear that the programs will inject controversial sex education into the curriculum.

Another device that has been common to almost all programs has been to use humor and an entertainment format to convey ideas to children. The sexual abuse prevention programs have not been dry and serious. They have usually involved theater, role-plays, puppets, or coloring books. They have also been strongly participatory, asking children to take roles. This entertainment format has allowed a light tone. It has allayed adults' anxieties about frightening children.

Programs have also relied on other devices to undercut the potentially frightening element in discussions of sexual abuse. For one thing, they have tended not to illustrate (although sometimes they are mentioned in passing) the more frightening forms of sexual abuse, those that continue over extended periods of time or that involve great amounts of violence. The kinds of illustrations that are given in a variety of programs include such things as an older brother who always comes into the bathroom when a little girl is showering, an uncle who wants a highly sexual kiss, or a man who wants to put his hands into a child's pants (Hutchinson & Chevalier, 1982; Williams, 1980).

The programs have also tried to deal with the potentially frightening nature of sexual abuse by emphasizing positive actions children could take to handle such situations. Thus they give children suggestions for doing something about the problem.

In helping children avoid abuse, some programs emphasize encouraging a proper mind-set. Children are taught that they have "rights": the right to control their own bodies, the right to be "safe, strong, and free" (Cooper et al., 1983), the right not to have someone touch them in a way that feels bad, and the right to their private parts.

At the very minimum, programs instruct children to say "no" to abusers. In more methodical programs, they are also taught how to be assertive of their rights and their safety, even in the face of adults who insist otherwise. In the CAP program, they act out situations to help one another find ways to say "no." They brainstorm strategies for getting away from or out of dangerous situations. Some programs teach certain self-defense techniques, such as yelling and getting help from a friend. The CAP program has a special yell that children practice with all their classes.

All programs place a very strong emphasis on the idea that children must tell someone right away. This special emphasis reflects the reality that in the past most children have not told. To encourage telling, children are warned that offenders will usually tell them not to tell, but that they should ignore this. One of the concepts that has gained great popularity in prevention education is the distinction between a secret and a surprise (Sanford, 1980). Secrets, which you are never supposed to tell, are a bad idea, but surprises, which you will tell someone later in order to make them happy, are okay. Children are also sometimes alerted that not all adults will necessarily believe them but that they should continue telling until someone does. These avoidance, resistance, and help-seeking techniques are intended to help children avoid victimization and leave them feeling empowered rather than frightened. (Rich Snowden, 1983, has stressed the importance of giving illustrations of children being smart and effective and has criticized some programs for not emphasizing this enough.)

### Conceptual Dilemmas

Solutions to some problems often create other problems. Although the concepts developed by prevention programs demonstrate a great deal of creativity, they also create dilemmas. Some of these have been discussed in the literature on prevention, but some have not. A serious evaluation of the impact of prevention programs must eventually confront some of these dilemmas.

For example, prevention concepts have been used to simplify and make comprehensible the notion of abuse, but do these simplifications create a potential for misunderstandings of a new sort? The Touch Continuum teaches children to identify and reject touch that makes them feel bad or confused. Undoubtedly most sexual abuse does feel bad or confusing. But, there may be some situations in which sexual abuse does not feel bad or confusing, at least at the beginning; sexual abuse, or at least the attention and affection surrounding it, may actually *feel* good. Will children trained with Touch Concepts be unable to identify this?

At the other end of the spectrum, there is touch that may *feel* bad, but be good; for example, many things that doctors do to children. Some programs try to make exceptions for doctors, but this may be a nuance that is lost on children. Or, more likely, in order to get children to cooperate with doctors, parents may indoctrinate children with the message that sometimes people do things that feel bad, but that are good and important. Such a message may contradict all the benefits of a child's training in the Touch Continuum.

There are oversimplifications present in the CAP-type approaches emphasizing children's rights, too. There are times when children's feelings about their rights need to be overruled by adults, as there are times when adults' rights conflict legitimately with children's rights. CAP organizers maintain that "children intuitively distinguish between basic human rights (the right to eat, the right to sleep, etc.) and such issues as bedtimes and TV privileges. Teaching children that their right to be safe includes the right to say 'no' to an adult will not create stubborn or tyrannical children." But most parents, we suggest, would see this as a much more complicated issue, in which children's intuition cannot be relied upon automatically. Teaching children about "rights" probably does not make them tyrannical. But it is hard to know just what children "intuit" from such discussions.

The CAP vignettes, which start with the bully and move to the uncle who demands a kiss, also have possible shortcomings. They all present situations in which the child clearly is being intimidated. Unfortunately, some sexual abuse occurs in contexts in which children are feeling cared for and are offered very powerful incentives. The CAP vignettes, like the Touch Continuum vignettes, may not alert children to some of the more insidious forms of sexual abuse.

Nonetheless, we view most of these criticisms as minor in the face of the real contributions of Touch and CAP. As we indicated earlier, some simplifications are undoubtedly necessary to put sexual abuse into a context in which young children will understand it. Prevention education cannot realistically be expected to alert children to all possible situations. This is why children need to receive ongoing education about sexual abuse from a variety of sources, each of which can emphasize a somewhat different point.

A more troublesome problem from our point of view, but one whose real seriousness is difficult to judge, concerns the treatment of sex under the various prevention approaches. As we mentioned earlier, in order to deal with public squeamishness about sex education in schools, prevention programs have devised various ways for skirting more direct sexual references and discussions. Educators often can and do bring more sexual content into the programs (some programs that seem to make a particular effort include "Childproof for Sexual Abuse" [1981] from Washington state and "Sexuality and Sexual Assault: A Disabled Perspective" [1983] from Minnesota), but they often avoid it. The tendency to avoid may be particularly great when less experienced trainers selectively borrow concepts from other programs, or when the education is done in a setting where sexual subjects could be particularly controversial.

We see a number of possible negative consequences to sex abuse prevention that avoids sexual content. First, there is some question about whether or not children truly get the message about what sexual abuse is. Uncle Harry forcing a child to kiss him may not fully convey the kinds of behaviors that constitute sexual abuse. The same is true about the skits the Illusion Theater uses to convey confusing and exploitative touch. The problem is even more acute in some of the less graphic media in which stick figures are used or in which abuse is described as "touching all over" or the "uh-oh feeling." ("Uh-oh feelings" are used in the Renton, Washington, Sexual Abuse Prevention Program [1981].)

Second, in most of these programs, children do not receive practice in using words and phrases to talk about sexual activity. Nonetheless, there has long been a consensus among professionals in the field (emphasized quite clearly in Sanford's book, *The Silent Children,* 1980) that one thing that inhibits children from telling about abuse is that they do not have a vocabulary or past experience for discussing sex-related matters.

Third, this avoidance of explicit sexual content must be patently obvious to the children. Even in some wonderfully creative prevention programs, what they are seeing once again is adults using euphemisms and circumlocutions to talk about sex. The message behind the message for some children may be that, in spite of what adults say, they still do not want to talk in plain terms about sex.

Finally, it is worth being concerned about what other covert messages about sexuality children are receiving through these programs. It is possible that when adults talk to children only about avoiding the coercive forms of sexuality they leave children with the impression that sex is primarily negative. (For example, one wonders what underlying message is conveyed by the heroes of one program whose names are "Hands Off Bill" and "the Untouchables"; Martin & Haddad, 1981.) It is possible that through some of these programs children come to feel uncomfortable or guilty about childhood sex play they may have engaged in. Programs often try to leaven their approach by talking about positive touch, but almost never do they discuss what might be positive sexuality. We need to consider what the effects of this might be.

To their credit, professionals in the field of sexual abuse prevention are aware of these dilemmas. We have not encountered one who was not in favor of more general sex education in schools, and some, like the Illusion Theater, have made moves in this direction by developing programs such as their new play, "No Easy Answers," aimed at the junior and senior high school audience, that deal more explicitly with sexual topics. Some educators, such as Cordelia Anderson and Rich Snowden, say they are impressed with how little resistance they encounter when they introduce sex educational materials.

However, most sex abuse prevention educators also are very realistic. If sexual abuse prevention were to be linked too closely to a sex education focus, they acknowledge, fewer schools would adopt it and fewer children, especially young children, would be exposed. Most feel that prevention education could be improved with more sex education, but that under present circumstances children at least get valuable, if not exhaustive or complete, knowledge. Moreover, they feel that there is little evidence of actual harm caused by the compromises they have been obliged to make.

Nonetheless, the relationship between sexual abuse prevention and sex education is an important one that needs further exploration. When programs are evaluated, the question needs to be asked whether or not unintended negative consequences stem from the divorce of sexual education from sexual abuse prevention.

We are inclined to believe that the lack of sex education in these programs is a serious problem. Children cannot get adequate information about sexual abuse in a climate in which adults who have contact with the child feel constrained from ever talking about sex. People working in the sex abuse prevention field need to confront this. One way they can do it is to bring pressure, influence, and opinion to bear on behalf of more and better sex education. As their programs gain in reputation and credibility, such educators may come to be trusted enough to be allowed to initiate more sex education. By seeing their responsibilities as lying in the sex education area, too, they may make sure that they are not reinforcing, albeit unwittingly, the idea that children can be well protected from sexual abuse in a setting where adults are fearful of talking with children about sex.

## *Organizational Issues*

Programs to prevent child sexual abuse also confront what might be termed "organizational" challenges in developing an effective strategy. Three of the most important organizational challenges are listed below.

(1) Sexual abuse prevention runs the risk of provoking serious political opposition in many communities (depending, of course, on the region, the history, and prior experience with such programs). As was already mentioned, such efforts may resurrect the controversies about sex education that smolder in many communities. If sexual abuse prevention is not a problem with the parents who object to sex education, it may be with parents who are afraid of frightening children unnecessarily. Other parents may worry that teaching about sexual abuse will make children suspicious of their parents and relatives. Still others may be made uncomfortable by the association between the field of sexual abuse prevention and feminism. Sexual abuse is an unavoidably emotional topic and it is to be expected that some adults will find it potentially objectionable under any circumstances.

(2) A second organizational dilemma for those engaged in sexual abuse prevention concerns the uncovering of cases of sexual abuse. Although prevention programs may not have it as their goal, it is virtually inevitable that in any setting where adults openly discuss sexual abuse with children, some children will reveal either explicitly or implicitly that they have been victims. Anticipating such revelations, programs need to make some provision to deal with them.

(3) A third organizational problem concerns how programs can create a sustained impact. How much exposure to prevention ideas do children need before they truly incorporate them into their behavior? Unfortunately, little research has been done to answer this question. Some follow-up evaluation of school-based prevention programs suggests that a great many children do not retain for very long the information provided in a one-day

educational program (Wall, 1983). Prevention efforts have thus tried to create organizational frameworks for extending the effect of the educational programs.

Most prevention programs have devoted serious attention to how they were organized. Although this is not always an aspect of the programs that is easy to communicate or transfer to other communities as a package, it is a crucial part of the current prevention efforts. As in our earlier discussion of concepts, although a variety of organizational frameworks exists, one can find consensus about certain common elements that are seen as indispensable to prevention.

First, it is clear that the successful prevention programs define what they are doing not merely in terms of developing an educational program, but in terms of community organization. They have thought through political and organizational issues, and, although their ultimate goal may be the education of children, much of their initial effort is directed to the community.

Successful prevention programs generally do a great deal of work to create the proper climate for gaining entrée into a community. This includes developing a cadre of influential people who support the use of the program and who can lobby on its behalf. Of course, for long-established programs this is made easier by the reputations the programs may have developed on the basis of their prior work.

The Minneapolis Child Sexual Abuse Prevention Project developed sponsors for their program that included the district attorney and several other community notables. They identified key personnel within the school system and approached them individually. They worked on more progressive districts initially, so they could build a reputation before going into areas where their program would be more controversial (Kent, 1979).

For programs that work within the schools, one of the first steps, once school systems are interested, is to present the material to parents and to professionals in advance of any presentation to children themselves. These advance presentations can be used to diffuse any opposition and allay anxieties about the pro-

gram. They also educate other important audiences. Certainly
the entertainment format of the programs also assists in overcoming community resistance.

In addition to presenting material to professionals, prevention
programs usually recruit some local individuals to receive intensive training. This serves a number of functions. These individuals can assist the leaders in presenting the program to the
children. They are more likely to know the children (often they
are teachers or other school personnel) and thus give the program additional credibility. They are also instrumental in helping the program have a sustained effect because they are
individuals within the system who will continue to convey prevention concepts long after the trainers from the prevention program leave.

Another part of the community organization effort practiced
by sophisticated programs focuses on preparing the community
for reports of sexual abuse. Existing community agencies that
deal with child sexual abuse need to be alerted that the prevention programs will stimulate an increase in case reporting. In
some communities, referral resources need to be developed by
contacting professionals and agencies and assessing who has the
skills to receive reports. Then any professionals, including
classroom teachers or school guidance counselors, who are to
be involved in the prevention program or its follow-up need to be
trained in how to deal with reports from children. Some of the
prevention programs, like CAP, make their own staff available to
receive reports by scheduling time after the program when children who have special questions can come and talk privately.

There appears to be some difference of opinion in the field
over the advisability of incorporating prevention education
directly in the school curriculum. In Seattle, trainers for the Committee for Children train teachers who in turn present the
material to children. The trainers themselves appear in front of
classes only rarely. Donna James of the Committee feels that
this method is efficient, because trainers do not need to return to
a school each year, and effective, because students can get ongo-

ing instruction from a person they already know and trust, their teacher.

Other educators, such as Rich Snowden, prefer a model in which outside trainers come into schools and work with the children. This model ensures that the trainers will be true specialists in the field. Snowden also worries that schools will not give support and encouragement to their own staff who specialize in sexual abuse prevention and that these programs will suffer in times of budget cutbacks. After several years of experience, various communities will need to be compared to see whether one model or another is giving superior results.

### Research Findings

Systematic evaluations of prevention programs and the effects they have on children have been begun, but these efforts are still in their early stages. Nonetheless, it is useful to review several studies that have been done and some of the findings they have produced. Plummer (1984) evaluated the effectiveness of a three-day program on 69 fifth graders in a midwestern public school. The program under review was a curriculum utilizing the concepts of the Illusion Theater as well as the film *No More Secrets*. The students were evaluated with an instrument assessing their knowledge of and attitudes toward sexual abuse at four points: (1) prior to the program, (2) immediately following the program, (3) two months later, and (4) eight months later. The pre- and immediate posttest comparisons clearly showed that children had learned from the program. They showed particular gains in knowledge that sexual abuse is different from being beaten up, that child molesters could often be people known to them, and that boys are frequently victims. The evaluation also demonstrated that children did not have more negative feelings about touch between people in general at the completion of the program than before, although it is curious that 16% of the children at the beginning of the program said that touch between people is *never good*.

However, Plummer's most interesting as well as discouraging finding was that there appeared to be a substantial loss of learning over time, especially by the eight-month retest. In particular, children seemed to revert to their original notions that child molesters are primarily people they do not know. There was also a large increase in the number of children who felt that promises (such as a promise not to tell) should never be broken. Children seemed to return to their original confusion of mixing up sexual abuse with physical abuse, and there was also an increasing tendency among children to think that if they were abused, it would be their own fault. Not all the learning was lost, but Plummer's results point to the need for reviews.

Ray (1984) looked at the effectiveness of a workbook-based sex abuse prevention education program with third graders in Spokane, Washington. As in Plummer's study, the third graders showed, on a short test of questions about sexual abuse, that they had successfully learned concepts of child abuse prevention compared to their pretest scores, and this knowledge did seem to be maintained four weeks later when the groups were retested. However, there was some backsliding on two matters in particular: (1) the notion that sexual abuse may be at the hands of someone that they know, and (2) that boys have problems with sexual abuse as well as girls.

Conte, Rosen, Saperstein, and Shermack (1985) assessed the effectiveness of a prevention program established by the Cook County, Illinois, Sheriff's Office on a group of 40 children aged 4 to 10 years, enrolled in after-school programs in a Chicago suburb. The program was presented on three consecutive days for one hour each day and included instruction about various kinds of touching, assertive behavior, and role-plays, as well as showing the film *Better Safe Than Sorry*. The comparison of the children who received the training with a waiting-list control group showed that children who received the training did learn many prevention concepts and retained them for at least a week after the training. There was some indication that the older children, 6- to 10-year-olds, learned more than the younger children. Perhaps the most interesting finding of the study, however, was that the children seemed to learn only slightly more than half of the concepts the program was trying to teach and thus, even after the training, many misconceptions still remained.

Downer (1984) evaluated the elementary school curriculum, *Talking about Touching,* which was developed by the Seattle-based Committee for Children and is used extensively around the country. A group of 70 fourth graders who received the training (15 to 20 minutes per day for two to three weeks) were compared with 15 untrained students, using a 20-item multiple-choice questionnaire. The trained students did significantly better, particularly on questions showing knowledge of how to get help. There was no follow-up in this study, but 15 of the trained children (plus 13 of the untrained) were also tested in an interview using puppets and incomplete stories. The interview performance of the trained children confirmed the findings from the knowledge test. The students were able to demonstrate "assertive" verbal responses to threatening situations, but they were judged not entirely convincing in their tone of voice and body language.

Finally, a Child Safety and Protection Training project was conducted in California that evaluated 432 students from 13 schools (Toal, 1985). Three forms of the training were employed with the fourth, fifth, and sixth graders: the Child Assault Prevention Project program, the "No More Secrets" program, and the Personal Protection Workshop. A Child Safety Preparedness Test was administered three to four weeks after the training, and then in a follow-up five weeks later. Although the results showed children with the training did better than untrained controls even at the follow-up, there were no consistent differences among the three programs tested individually. (The study is, however, not finished and the program's administrators feel they simply need to use more sensitive outcome measures.) Perhaps the most interesting finding was that children who had reported being previous victims of assault seemed, when tested, to be the least prepared to avoid future assaults.

Given the few studies that have been done, it is obviously difficult to generalize from the results. Most studies have found that the training programs result in learning and in changed attitudes. Their optimism is cautious, however, insofar as one study indicated that the learning is far from thorough and two studies showed some significant decay in knowledge over time. It would appear that the idea that abuse can come from acquaintances is a concept particularly difficult to sustain, perhaps because it requires children to hold the cognitively dissonant values that people you know can be both good and bad. Overall, these studies have produced highly plausible findings and represent a good foundation on which to start to build research and theory in regard to sexual abuse prevention.

## Suggestions for Future Research

Additional studies on the effectiveness of sexual abuse prevention are bound to mulitiply rapidly. It is one of the aspects of the sexual abuse problem most amenable to research, and because a large number of programs are being implemented all over the country, the opportunities for studies are myriad. What follows are some suggestions for directions this research should take.

Research on sexual abuse prevention would benefit greatly from more thought and preparation on the question of how to evaluate the effectiveness of these programs. All of the studies to date have used questionnaires that tested the knowledge and the attitudes of the children about sexual abuse. But this approach needs to be refined and supplemented.

Of primary importance, effort needs to be spent creating sophisticated, valid, and reliable instruments. As Conte (1984) has pointed out, we need to know that these instruments can be read and understood by children. We need to be sure that they really test the concepts and information included in the programs. It would certainly assist evaluators in all parts of the country if researchers came quickly to develop and accept some standard test of sexual abuse prevention awareness.

However, tests of knowledge and attitudes are not enough; we have to keep in mind that the real purpose of these programs is to prevent sexual abuse, and we must develop designs to look directly at this task. Obviously, the ultimate test of prevention education is whether or not children with training are less likely to be abused. This suggests research designs that follow up children for several years after they receive training to see whether or not they are abused at rates different from their untrained peers. This means that we are going to have to look beyond the "quick" answers given by evaluation studies that test students a week or even a month after their training. The research conducted so far, which raises questions about the long-term retention of prevention concepts (Plummer, 1984), should caution us that long-term studies are really the ultimate test.

Nonetheless, short-term studies will continue to be done, and they will have some usefulness, especially if they, too, expand their scope. Conte (1984) has pointed out that these studies need to look not just at knowledge and attitudes, but also at *skills*. Children may know that they are supposed to say "no" to abusers, but whether or not they actually have the skill to do so is another question. Conte (1984) suggests a number of techniques for better assessing skills, including such methods as vignettes that ask children what they would do in various situations, role-plays in which children are actually called upon to enact the behaviors (for example, the puppet interview used by Downer, 1984), or even covert challenge situations, for example, in which children might be approached by adult confederates of the researcher (this of course raises important ethical considerations that would need extensive consideration). Researchers should also consider whether or not they might evaluate the impact of programs on children simply through observing them unobtrusively in their play and social life.

Another way in which these studies need to expand their concern is to focus more attention on possible adverse effects. As discussed earlier, questions have been raised about whether or not prevention programs might have such adverse effects as undermining parental authority, making children afraid of adults, or giving children negative messages about touching and sex. Such effects may be subtle and serious consideration should be given to their measurement. For example, it may be important to survey parents and teachers to find out if they noticed after the training any concerns and fears among the children that were previously not present. Efforts should also be made to look at the effects of the training on children's sexual attitudes and knowledge, although in many situations this is an admittedly controversial matter for researchers to ask about.

Even if they are very limited tests of the question of whether or not training prevents abuse, one value of short-term evaluations is their usefulness in analyzing the operation of prevention programs. For example, following the lead of the Child Safety and Protection Training Project in Sacramento, more studies ought to compare the relative merits of different programs. Perhaps more important, studies should try to look at the comparative effectiveness of different program components, regardless of the program or philosophy they come from. Thus, how do role-plays compare with film strips? How many hours of training are optimal to instill the concepts? How frequently do concepts need to be reviewed to be retained? Does the sex or the familiarity of the trainer make a difference?

Short-term evaluations can also look at how different programs match the needs of a variety of children and situations. Because some approaches are bound to fare better with some children than others, consideration must be given to the question of the children's age and sex. But it may also be the case that children of different social classes, ethnicity, and personalities learn better with different types of approaches. Thus studies should routinely try to look for interactions between children's backgrounds and the amount they learn and retain.

Finally, those interested in research on sexual abuse prevention need to move beyond program evaluation altogether. There are other research approaches that may give us a great deal of information on prevention and that should not be neglected. One approach is simply to study the attitudes, background knowledge, and behavior of children who have been sexually victimized for more clues about how to avoid abuse. The content of most current prevention programs was developed through clinical work with abused children and knowledge of the histories they recounted. But virtually no one has done a systematic analysis of such children, their knowledge, and their accounts of abuse for a better understanding of what the most important prevention steps might be. How many children actually did not know that what the abuser was doing was wrong at the time they were first approached? How many were afraid of being physically harmed? How many believed that if they told the secret something bad would happen to them?

A particularly fruitful approach might be to compare a group of victimized children with a group who were approached but escaped and told. It may indeed turn out that the abuse avoiders had more knowledge about abuse and more awareness about their rights. But it may also be that the avoiders were different in other ways that we do not currently understand.

Another line of research that may cast light on prevention is the study of child molesters themselves. As Conte has pointed out, careful study of the mode of operation of child molesters might reveal additional factors that prevention educators should take into account. Most molesters have had the experience of choosing which children to molest. Many have been foiled or resisted by some of the children they approached. Direct questions to molesters about what considerations led to the choosing of some children, and what it was that made them abandon others, could give us important clues about what to teach children.

In moving beyond the evaluation of school programs, another important broad area for research is parent-child interaction. Almost all professionals agree that parents are in the position to be the most effective prevention educators. So perhaps even more than school-based programs, programs to influence parents should be studied. Parents have been subjected to a great deal of information about sexual abuse since the Finkelhor (1984) survey. It would be important to know how parents are utilizing it. What do parents who have been educated about sexual abuse tell children that is different from information given by parents who have not been educated? And what do children take away from these conversations? An interesting research design, for example, would be to compare what parents say they have told children with what children say they have heard. There would undoubtedly be serious and interesting discrepancies. In fact, parents and children could be observed in conversations about sexual abuse in laboratory conditions to get even a third perspective on this communication. These are but some examples of other research approaches that need to be tried.

## *Conclusion*

Sexual abuse prevention promises to be one of the great social experiments of the decade. In response to the public discovery of sexual abuse, it has caught on all over the country and resulted in an enormous variety of school programs, books, pamphlets, films, television programs, plays, and lectures. Much of the content of this movement has great intuitive appeal, not simply to prevent sexual abuse, but also to give children more knowledge and confidence in coping with many situations. Whether or not these efforts have their desired effect remains to be seen. If enthusiastic response is any measure, one would have to say that positive effects are clearly apparent. However, more careful evaluations are also called for. Reasonable questions have been raised about whether or not this kind of education really protects children from most abuse, and about what some unintended consequences of the training can be, especially if done poorly. As efforts to protect children move into a more mature phase, careful planning and research should try to address these concerns. The payoff for such attention will certainly be a better understanding of the problem of sexual abuse and better ways of reducing its toll on children.

# References

Aarens, M., Cameron, T., Roizen, J., Room, R., Schneberk, D., & Wingard, D. (1978). *Alcohol, casualties and crime*. Berkeley, CA: Social Research Group.

Abel, G., Becker, J. V., Cunningham-Rathner, J., Renlean, J., Kaplan, M., & Reid, J. (1984). *The treatment of child molesters* (mimeo). New York: SBC-TM (722 West 168th Street, Box 17, New York, NY 10032).

Abel, G., Becker, J. V., Murphy, W. D., & Flanagan, B. (1981). Identifying dangerous child molesters. In R. B. Stuart (Ed.), *Violent behavior*. New York: Brunner/ Mazel.

Abel, G., Cunningham-Rathner, J., Becker, J. V., & McHugh, J. (1983, December). *Motivating sex offenders for treatment with feedback of their psychophysiologic assessment*. Paper presented at the World Congress of Behavior Therapy, Washington, DC.

Achenbach, T. M., & Edelbrock, C. S. (1979). The child behavior profile. *Journal of Consulting and Clinical Psychology, 47*, 223-233.

Achenbach, T. M., & Edelbrock, C. S. (1983). *Manual for the child behavior checklist*. Burlington: University of Vermont.

Adams, C., & Fay, J. (1981). *No more secrets: Protecting your child from sexual assault*. San Luis Obispo, CA: Impact.

Adams-Tucker, C. (1981). A sociological overview of 28 abused children. *Child Abuse and Neglect, 5*, 361-367.

American Humane Association. (1981). *National study on child neglect and abuse reporting*. Denver, CO: Author.

American Psychiatric Association. (1980). *Diagnostic and statistical manual of mental disorders* (3rd ed.). Washington, DC: Author.

Anderson, C., & Mayes, P. (1982). Treating family sexual abuse: The humanistic approach. *Journal of Child Care, 1*(2), 41-46.

Anderson, S. C., Bach, C. M., & Griffith, S. (1981, April). *Psychosocial sequelae in intrafamilial victims of sexual assault and abuse*. Paper presented at the Third International Conference on Child Abuse and Neglect, Amsterdam, The Netherlands.

Armstrong, L. (1983). *The home front*. New York: McGraw-Hill.

Atwood, R., & Howell, R. (1971). Pupillometric and personality test scores of female aggressing, pedophiliacs and normals. *Psychonomic Science, 22*(2), 115-116.

Badgley, R., Allard, H., McCormick, N., Proudfoot, P., Fortin, D., Ogilvie, D., Rae-Grant, Q., Gelinas, P., Pepin, L., & Sutherland, S. [Committee on Sexual Offences Against Children and Youth] (1984). *Sexual offences against children* (Vol. 1). Ottawa: Canadian Government Publishing Centre.

Bagley C., & Ramsay, R. (in press). Disrupted childhood and vulnerability to sexual assault: Long-term sequels with implications for counselling. *Social Work and Human Sexuality.*

Baker, T. (1983). *Report on reader survey: Child sexual abuse: "19" confidential survey* (mimeo). London: St. George's Hospital.

Bart, P. (1981). A study of women who both were raped and avoided rape. *Journal of Social Issues, 37*(4): 123-137.

Bell, A., & Hall, C. S. (1976). The personality of a child molester. In M. S. Weinberg (Ed.), *Sex research: Studies from the Kinsey Institute.* Oxford: Oxford University Press.

Bell, A., & Weinberg, M. (1981). *Sexual preference: Its development among men and women.* Bloomington: Indiana University Press.

Belsen, W. A. (1981). *The design and understanding of survey questions.* Aldershot, England: Gower.

Beneke, T. (1982). *Men on rape.* New York: St. Martin's.

Benward, J., & Densen-Gerber, J. (1975, February). *Incest as a causative factor in anti-social behavior: An exploratory study.* Paper presented at the meeting of the American Academy of Forensic Sciences, Chicago.

Berlin, F. S. (1982). Sex offenders: A biomedical perspective. In J. Greer & I. Stuart (Eds.), *Sexual aggression: Current perspectives on treatment* (Vol. 1); *Victim treatment* (Vol. 2). New York: Van Nostrand Reinhold.

Berlin, F. S., & Coyle, G. S. (1981). Sexual deviation syndromes. *Johns Hopkins Medical Journal, 149,* 119-125.

Bradburn, N. M. (1983). Response effects. In P. H. Rossi, J. D. Wright, & A. B. Anderson (Eds.), *Handbook of survey research.* New York: Academic Press.

Bradburn, N. M., & Sudman, S. (1979). *Improving interview method and questionnaire design.* San Francisco: Jossey-Bass.

Brassard, M. R., Tyler A. H., & Kehle. T. J. (1983). School programs to prevent intrafamilial child sexual abuse. *Child Abuse and Neglect, 31,* 241-245.

Briere, J. (1984, April). *The long-term effects of childhood sexual abuse: Defining a post-sexual-abuse syndrome.* Paper presented at the Third National Conference on Sexual Victimization of Children, Washington, DC.

Briere, J., & Runtz, M. (1985). *Symptomatology associated with prior sexual abuse in a non-clinical sample.* Paper presented at the annual meeting of the American Psychological Association, Los Angeles.

Brown, M. E. (1979). Teenage prostitution. *Adolescence, 14*(56), 665-680.

Browning, D. H., & Boatman, B. (1977). Incest: Children at risk. *American Journal of Psychiatry, 134,* 69-72.

Burgess, A., & Holmstrom, L. (1978). Accessory to sex: Pressure, sex, and secrecy. In A. Burgess, A. Groth, L. Holmstrom, & S. Sgroi (Eds.), *Sexual assault of children and adolescents.* Lexington, MA: Lexington Books.

Burnam, A. (1985). Personal communication concerning the Los Angeles Epidemiological Catchment Area Study.

Buros, O. C. (Ed.). (1970). *Personality tests and reviews*. Highland Park, NJ: Gryphon.

Cannell, C. F., Miller, P. V., & Oksenberg, L. (1981). Research on interviewing techniques. In S. Leinhardt (Ed.), *Sociological methodology 1981*. San Francisco: Jossey-Bass.

Carmen, E., Rieker, P. P., & Mills, T. (1984). Victims of violence and psychiatric illness. *American Journal of Psychiatry, 141*, 378-383.

Carnes, P. (1983). *The sexual addiction*. Minneapolis: CompCare.

Cavallin, H. (1966). Incestuous fathers: A clinical report. *American Journal of Psychiatry, 122*(10), 1132-1138.

Chaneles, S. (1967). Child victims of sexual offenses. *Federal Probation, 31*(2), 52-56.

Christiansen, K., Ellers-Nielsen, M., Le Maine, L., & Sturup, G. (1965). Recidivism among sexual offenders. In *Scandinavian studies in criminology* (Vol. 1, pp. 55-85). London: Tavistock.

Cohen M., Seghorn, T., & Calmas, W. (1969). Sociometric study of sex the offender. *Journal of Abnormal Psychiatry, 74* (2), 249-255.

Constantine, L. (1977). *The sexual rights of children: Implications of a radical perspective*. Paper presented at the International Conference on Love and Attraction, Swansea, Wales.

Constantine, L. (1980). Effects of early sexual experience: A review and synthesis of research. In L. Constantine & F. M. Martinson (Eds.), *Children and sex*. Boston: Little, Brown.

Conte, J. R. (1984, August). *Research on the prevention of sexual abuse of children*. Paper presented at the Second National Conference for Family Violence Researchers, Durham, NH.

Conte, J. R., & Berliner, L. (1984). *Impact of sexual abuse in children* (Report 1). (Contract No. PHS-1 RO1 M437133). Washington, DC: National Institute of Mental Health.

Conte, J. R., Rosen, C., Saperstein, L., & Shermack, R. (1985). An evaluation of a program to prevent sexual victimization of young children. *Child Abuse and Neglect, 9*, 319-328.

Cooper, S., Lutter, Y., & Phelps, C. (1983). *Strategies for free children*. Columbus, OH: Child Assault Prevention Project.

Courtois, C. (1979). The incest experience and its aftermath. *Victimology: An International Journal, 4*, 337-347.

Crisci, G. (1983). *Personal safety curriculum for the prevention of child sexual abuse*. Hadley, MA.

Cushing, J.G.N. (1950). Psychopathology of sexual delinquency. *Journal of Criminal Psychopathology, 49*, 26-34.

Dayee, F. S. (1982). *Private zone*. Edmonds, WA: Chas. Franklin.

Deitrich, G. (1981). Audiovisual materials with critique. In P. B. Mrazek & C. H. Kempe (Eds.), *Sexually abused children and their families* (pp. 257-259). Elmsford, NY: Pergamon.

Densen-Gerber, J. (1983). Why is there so much hard-core pornography nowadays? Is it a threat to society or just a nuisance? *Medical Aspects of Human Sexuality, 17*, 35.

DeFrancis, V. (1969). *Protecting the child victim of sex crimes committed by adults.* Denver, CO: American Humane Association.

DeLamater, J. (with McKinney, K.). (1982). Response effects of question content. In W. Dijkstra & J. van der Zouwen (Eds.), *Response behavior in the survey-interview.* London: Academic Press.

DeMause, L. (1974). *The history of childhood.* New York: Harper & Row.

deYoung, M. (1982). *Sexual victimization of children.* Jefferson, NC: McFarland.

Dillman, D. A. (1978). *Mail and telephone surveys: The total design method.* New York: John Wiley.

Downer, A. (1984). *The development and testing of an evaluation instrument for assessing the effectiveness of a child sexual abuse prevention curriculum: Talking about touching.* Seattle, WA: Committee for Children.

Ellis, A., & Brancale, R. (1956). *The psychology of sex offenders.* Springfield, MA: Charles C Thomas.

Farrell, W. (1982). *Myths of incest: Implications for the helping professional.* Paper presented at the International Symposium on Family Sexuality, Minneapolis.

Fenichel, D. (1945). *The psychoanalytic theory of neurosis.* New York: Norton.

Fields, P. J. (1981, November). Parent-child relationships, childhood sexual abuse, and adult interpersonal behavior in female prostitutes. *Dissertation Abstracts International, 42,* 2053B.

Finch, S. M. (1967). Sexual activity of children with other children and adults (Commentaries). *Clinical Pediatrics, 3,* 1-2.

Finkelhor, D. (1979). *Sexually victimized children.* New York: Free Press.

Finkelhor, D. (1980). Risk factors in the sexual victimization of children. *Child Abuse and Neglect, 4,* 265-273.

Finkelhor, D. (1984). *Child sexual abuse: New theory and research.* New York: Free Press.

Finkelhor, D., & Hotaling, G. (1983). *Sexual abuse in the national incidence study of child abuse and neglect.* Report to National Center on Child Abuse and Neglect.

Finkelhor, D., & Hotaling, G. (1984). Sexual abuse in the national incidence study of child abuse and neglect. *Child Abuse and Neglect, 8,* 22-32.

Finkelhor, D., & Redfield, D. (1984). Public definitions of sexual abusiveness toward children. In D. Finkelhor, *Child sexual abuse: New theory and research* (pp. 107-133). New York: Free Press.

Fisher, G. (1969). Psychological needs of heterosexual pedophiliacs. *Diseases of the Nervous System, 30,* 419-421.

Fisher, G. & Howell, L. (1970). Psychological needs of homosexual pedophiliacs. *Diseases of the Nervous System, 31,* 623-625.

Fitch, J. H. (1962). Men convicted of sexual offenses against children: A descriptive follow-up study. *British Journal of Criminology, 3*(1), 18-37.

Fraser, M. (1976). *The death of narcissus.* New York: Paul Hoeber.

Freund, K. (1967a). Diagnosing homo- or heterosexuality and erotic age-preference by means of a psychophysiological test. *Behavioral Research and Therapy, 5,* 209-228.

Freund, K. (1967b). Erotic preference in pedophilia. *Behavioral Research and Therapy, 5,* 339-348.

Freund, K., & Langevin, R. (1976). Bisexuality in homosexual pedophilia. *Archives of Sexual Behavior, 5*(5), 415-423.

Freund K., Langevin, R., Cibiri, S., & Zajac, Y. (1973). Heterosexual aversion in homosexual males. *British Journal of Psychiatry, 122*, 163-169.

Freund, K., McKnight, C. K., Langevin, R., & Cibiri, S. (1972). The female child as surrogate object. *Archives of Sexual Behavior, 2*, 119-133.

Friedman, P. (1959). Sexual deviations. In S. Arieti (Ed.), *American handbook of psychiatry*, (Vol. 1). New York: Basic Books.

Friedrich, W. N., Urquiza, A. J., & Beilke, R. (1986). Behavioral problems in sexually abused young children. *Journal of Pediatric Psychology, 11*, 47-57.

Frisbie, L. V. (1965). Treated sex offenders who reverted to sexually deviant behavior. *Federal Probation, 29*, 52-57.

Frisbie, L. V. (1969). *Another look at sex offenders in California* (Research Monograph No. 12). Sacramento: California Department of Mental Hygiene.

Frisbie, L. V., & Dondis, E. H. (1965). *Recidivism among treated sex offenders* (Research Monograph No. 5). Sacramento: California Department of Mental Hygiene.

Fritz, G. S., Stoll, K., & Wagner, N. A. (1981). A comparison of males and females who were sexually molested as children. *Journal of Sex and Marital Therapy, 7*, 54-59.

Fromuth, M. E. (1983). *The long term psychological impact of childhood sexual abuse*. Unpublished doctoral dissertation, Auburn University.

Gagnon, J. (1965). Female child victims of sex offense. *Social Problems, 13*, 176-192.

Gagnon, J. (1977). *Human sexualities*. Glenview, IL: Scott, Foresman.

Garbarino, J., & Stocking, S. H. (1980). *Protecting children from abuse and neglect*. San Francisco: Jossey-Bass.

Gebhard, P., Gagnon, J., Pomeroy, W., & Christenson, C. (1965). *Sex offenders: An analysis of types*. New York: Harper & Row.

Gelinas, D. J. (1983). The persisting negative effects of incest. *Psychiatry, 46*, 312-332.

Gigeroff, A. K., & Mohr, J. W. (1968). Sex offenders on probation: The exhibitionist. *Federal Probation, 32*(4), 18-21.

Giles-Sims, J. & Finkelhor, D. (1984) Child abuse in stepfamilies. *Family Relations, 33*, 407-413.

Gillespie, W. H. (1964). The psycho-analytic theory of sexual deviation with special reference to fetishism. In I. Rosen (Ed.), *The psychology and treatment of sexual deviation*. New York: Oxford University Press.

Glick, P. C. (1979). Children of divorced parents in demographic perspective. *Journal of Social Issues, 35*(4), 634-650.

Glueck, B. C., Jr. (1965). Pedophilia. In R. Slovenko (Ed.), *Sexual behavior and the law*. Springfield, IL: Charles C Thomas.

Goldhirsh, M. I. (1961). Manifest content of dreams of convicted sex offenders. *Journal of Abnormal and Social Psychology, 63*(3), 643-645.

Goldstein, M. J., Kant, H. S., & Hartman, J. J. (1973). *Pornography and sexual deviance*. Los Angeles: University of California Press.

Gomes-Schwartz, B., Horowitz, J., & Sauzier, M. (1985) Severity of emotional distress among sexually abused preschool, school-age and adolescent children. *Hospital & Community Psychiatry, 36*(5), 503-508.

Goodwin, J. (1982). *Sexual abuse: Incest victims and their families*. Boston: John Wright-PSG.

Goodwin, J., Cormier, L., & Owen, J. (1983) Grandfather-granddaughter incest: A trigenerational view. *Child Abuse and Neglect 7*(2): 163-170.

Goodwin, J., McCarthy, T., & DiVasto, P. (1981). Prior incest in mothers of abused children. *Child Abuse and Neglect, 5*, 87-96.

Goodwin, J., McCarthy, T., & DiVasto, P. (1982). Physical and sexual abuse of the children of adult incest victims. In J. Goodwin (Ed.), *Sexual abuse: Incest victims and their families*. Boston: John Wright-PSC.

Goy, R., & McEwen, B. S. (1977). *Sexual differentiation of the brain*. Cambridge: MIT Press.

Groth, N. A. (1978). Guidelines for assessment and management of the offender. In A. Burgess, A. Groth, L. Holmstrom, & S. Sgroi (Eds.), *Sexual assault of children and adolescents*. Lexington, MA: Lexington Books.

Groth, N. A. (1979). *Men who rape*. New York: Plenum.

Groth, N. A. (1983). Treatment of the sexual offender in a correctional institution. In Joanne Greer & Irving Stuart (Eds.), *The sexual aggressor: Current perspectives on treatment* (pp. 160-176). New York: Van Nostrand Reinhold.

Groth, N. A., & Birnbaum, H. J. (1978). Adult sexual orientation and attraction to underage persons. *Archives of Sexual Behavior, 7*(3), 175-181.

Groth, N., & Burgess, A. (1979). Sexual trauma in the life histories of rapists and child molesters. *Victimology: An International Journal, 4*, 10-16.

Groth, N. A., Hobson, W. F., & Gary, T. S. (1982a). The child molester: Clinical observations. In J. Conte & D. Shore (Eds.), *Social work and child sexual abuse*. New York: Haworth.

Groth, N. A., Longo, R. E., & McFadin, J. B. (1982b). Undetected recidivism among rapists and child molesters. *Crime and Delinquency, 28* (3), 450-458.

Gruber, K., & Jones, R. (1983). Identifying determinants of risk of sexual victimization of youth. *Child Abuse and Neglect, 7*, 17-24.

Gundlach, R. (1977). Sexual molestation and rape reported by homosexual and heterosexual women. *Journal of Homosexuality, 2*, 367-384.

Guttmacher, M., & Weihofen, H. (1951). *Sex offenses: The problem, causes and prevention*. New York: Norton.

Hamilton, G. V. (1929). *A research in marriage*. New York: Albert & Charles Boni.

Hammer, R. F., & Glueck, B. C., Jr. (1957). Psychodynamic patterns in sex offenders: A four-factor theory. *Psychiatric Quarterly, 31*, 325-345.

Harrison, P. A., Lumry, A. E., & Claypatch, C. (1984, August). *Female sexual abuse victims: Perspectives on family dysfunction, substance use and psychiatric disorders*. Paper presented at the Second National Conference for Family Violence Researchers, Durham, NH.

Hedin, D. (1984) *Sexual abuse in Minnesota* (mimeo). Minneapolis: Minneapolis Center for Youth Development.

Henderson, J. (1983). Is incest harmful? *Canadian Journal of Psychiatry, 28*, 34-39.

Herman, J. (1981). *Father-daughter incest*. Cambridge, MA: Harvard University Press.

Herman, J., & Hirschman, L. (1977). Father-daughter incest. *Signs: Journal of Women in the Culture and Society, 2*, 735-756.

Herman, J., & Hirschman, L. (1980). Father-daughter incest. In L. G. Schultz (Ed.), *The sexual victimology of youth*. Springfield, IL: Charles C Thomas.

Herman, J., & Hirschman, L. (1981). Families at risk for father-daughter incest. *American Journal of Psychiatry, 138*(7), 967-970.

Hite, S. (1981). *The Hite report on male sexuality*. New York: Knopf.

Howells, K. (1979). Some meanings of children for pedophiles. In M. Cook & F. Wilson (Eds.), *Love and attraction*. London: Pergamon.

Howells, K. (1981). Adult sexual interest in children: Considerations relevant to theories of aetiology. In M. Cook & K. Howells (Eds.), *Adult sexual interest in children*. New York: Academic Press.

Hutchinson, B., & Chevalier, E. A. (1982). *My personal safety book*. Fridley, MN: Fridley Police Department.

James, J., & Meyerding, J. (1977). Early sexual experiences and prostitution. *American Journal of Psychiatry, 134*, 1381-1385.

Jehu, D., & Gazan, M. (1983). Psychosocial adjustment of women who were sexually victimized in childhood or adolescence. *Canadian Journal of Community Mental Health, 2*, 71-81.

Jones, C. O., & Bentovim, A. (n.d.). *Sexual abuse of children: Fleeting trauma or lasting disaster*. Unpublished manuscript, Hospital for Sick Children (Great Ormond Street, London WC1).

Julian, V., & Mohr, C. (1980). Father-daughter incest: Profile of the offender. *Victimology: An International Journal, 4*, 348-360.

Justice, B., & Justice, R. (1979). *The broken taboo*. New York: Human Sciences Press.

Karpman, B. (1954). *The sexual offender and his offenses*. New York: Julian.

Kaufman, I., Peck, A., & Tagiuri, C. (1954). The family constellation and overt incestuous relations between father and daughter. *American Journal of Orthopsychiatry, 24*, 266-279.

Keckley Market Research. (1983, March). *Sexual abuse in Nashville: A report on incidence and long-term effects*. Nashville, TN: Keckley Market Research.

Kempe, R., & Kempe. C. H. (1984). *The common secret: Sexual abuse of children and adolescents*. New York: W. H. Freeman.

Kent, C. A. (1979). *Child sexual abuse project: An educational program for children*. Minneapolis: Hennepin County Attorney's Office Sexual Assault Services.

Kercher, G. (1980). *Responding to child sexual abuse*. Huntsville, TX: Sam Houston State University, Criminal Justice Center.

Kercher, G., & McShane, M. (1984). The prevalence of child sexual abuse victimization in an adult sample of Texas residents. *Child Abuse and Neglect, 8*, 495-502.

Kilpatrick, D. G. (1984, August). *Assessing victims of rape: Methodological issues* (Final report). Rockville, MD: National Institute of Mental Health, Department of Health and Human Services.

Kilpatrick, D. G., & Amick, A. E. (1984, August). *Intrafamilial and extrafamilial sexual assault: Results of a random community survey*. Paper presented at the Second National Conference for Family Violence Researchers, Durham, NH.

Kinsey, A. C., Pomeroy, W. B., & Martin, C. E. (1948). *Sexual behavior in the human male*. Philadelphia: W. B. Saunders.

Kinsey, A. C., Pomeroy, W. B., Martin, C. E., & Gebhard, P. H. (1953). *Sexual behavior in the human female*. Philadelphia: W. B. Saunders.

Knopp, F. H. (1982). *Remedial intervention in adolescent sex offenses: Nine program descriptions*. New York: Safer Society Press.

Kraemer, W. (1976). A paradise lost. In W. Kraemer (Ed.), *The forbidden love: The normal and abnormal love of children*. London: Sheldon.

Landis, C., Landis, A. T., Bolles, M. M., Metzger, H. F., Pitts, M. W., D'Esopo, D. A., Moloy, H. C., Kleegman, S. J., & Dickenson, R. L. (1940). *Sex in development*. New York: Paul B. Hoebert.

Landis, J. (1956). Experiences of 500 children with adult sexual deviants. *Psychiatric Quarterly Supplement, 30*, 91-109.

Langevin, R. (1983). *Sexual strands: Understanding and treating sexual anomalies in men*. Hillsdale, NJ: Erlbaum.

Langevin, R., Handy, L., Hook, H., Day, D., & Russon, A. (1985). Are incestuous fathers pedophilic and aggressive? In R. Langevin (Ed.), *Erotic preference gender identity and aggression*. New York: Erlbaum.

Langevin, R., Paitich, D., Freeman, R., Mann, K., & Handy, L. (1978). Personality characteristics and sexual anomalies in males. *Canadian Journal of Behavioral Science, 10*(3), 222-238.

Langmade, C. J. (1983). The impact of pre- and postpubertal onset of incest experiences in adult women as measured by sex anxiety, sex guilt, sexual satisfaction and sexual behavior. *Dissertation Abstracts International, 44*, 917B. (University Microfilms No. 3592)

Langner, T. (1962). *Life stress and mental health*. New York: McGraw-Hill.

Lewis, I. A. (1985). [*Los Angeles Times Poll #98*]. Unpublished raw data.

Loss, P., & Glancy, E. (1983). Men who sexually abuse their children. *Medical Aspects of Human Sexuality, 17*(3), 328-329.

Lustig, N., Dresser, J. W., Spellman, S. W., & Murray, T. B. (1966). Incest: A family group survival pattern. *Archives of General Psychology, 14*, 31-40.

MacFarlane, K. (1978). Sexual abuse of children. In J. R. Chapman & M. Gates (Eds.), *The victimization of women* (pp. 81-109). Beverly Hills, CA: Sage.

Maisch, H. (1972). *Incest*. New York: Stein & Day.

Mangione, T. W., Hingson, R., & Barrett, J. (1982). Collecting sensitive data: A comparison of three survey strategies. *Sociological Methods and Research, 10*(3): 337-346.

Marsh, J. T., Hilliard, J., & Liechti, R. (1955). A sexual deviation scale for the MMPI. *Journal of Consulting Psychology, 19*(1), 55-59.

Marshall, P. D., & Norgard, K. E. (1983). *Child abuse and neglect: Sharing responsibility*. New York: John Wiley.

Marshall, W. A. (1975). Growth and sexual maturation in normal puberty. *Clinics in Endocrinology and Metabolism, 4*, 3-25.

Martin, L., & Haddad, J. (1981). *What if I say no?* Bakersfield, CA: M. H. Cap.

Masson, J. M. (1984). *The assault on truth: Freud's suppression of the seduction theory*. New York: Farrar, Straus & Giroux.

Mausner, J., & Bahn, A. (1974). *Epidemiology: An introductory text*. Philadelphia: W. B. Saunders.

McAuliffe, S. (1983, March). Is sexual deviance a biological problem? *Psychology Today*, p. 84.

McCaghy, C. H. (1967). Child molesters: A study of their careers as deviants. In M. B. Clinard & R. Quinney (Eds.), *Criminal behavior systems, a typology*. New York: Holt, Rinehart & Winston.

McCaghy, C. H. (1968). Drinking and deviance disavowal: The case of child molesters. *Social Problems, 16,* 43-49.

McCord, J. (1983). A forty year perspective on effects of child abuse and neglect. *Child Abuse and Neglect 7*(3), 265-270.

McGuire, L., & Wagner, N. (1978). Sexual dysfunctions in women who were molested as children: One response pattern and suggestions for treatment. *Journal of Sex and Marital Therapy, 4,* 11- 15.

McGuire, R. J., Carlisle, J. M., & Young, B. G. (1965). Sexual deviations and conditioned behavior: A hypothesis. *Behavior Research and Therapy, 2,* 185-190.

McIntyre, K. (1981). Role of mothers in father-daughter incest: A feminist analysis. *Social Work, 26,* 462-467.

McLaughlin, L. (1982). Child sexual assault is your issue. *Aegis, 33,* 14-16.

Meiselman, K. (1978). *Incest: A psychological study of causes and effects with treatment recommendations*. San Francisco: Jossey-Bass.

Meyer, L., & Romero, J. (1980). *Ten year follow-up of sex offender recidivism*. Philadelphia: Joseph Peters Institute (112 S. 16th St.).

Miller, J., Moeller, D., Kaufman, A., Divasto, P., Fitzsimmons, P., Pather, D., & Christy, J. (1978). Recidivism among sexual assault victims. *American Journal of Psychiatry, 135,* 1103-1104.

Miller, L. C. (1967). Louisville behavior checklist for males, 6-12 years of age. *Psychological Reports, 21,* 885-886.

Miller, P. (1976). Blaming the victim of child molestation: An empirical analysis (Doctoral dissertation, Northwestern University). *Dissertation Abstracts International*. (University Microfilms No. 77-10069).

Mohr, I. W., Turner, R. E., & Jerry, M. B. (1964). *Pedophilia and exhibitionism*. Toronto: University of Toronto Press.

Money, J. (1961). Sex hormones and other variables in human eroticism. In W. C. Young (Ed.), *Sex and internal secretions VIII*. Baltimore, MD: Williams & Wilkins.

Morgan, P. (1982). Alcohol and family violence: A review of the literature. In National Institute of Alcoholism and Alcohol Abuse, Alcohol Consumption and Related Problems. (Alcohol and Health Monograph 1). Washington, DC: Department of Health and Human Services.

Murphy, J. E. (1985, June). Untitled news release. (Available from St. Cloud State University, St. Cloud, MN 56301).

Myers, H. F. (1982). Research on the Afro-American family: A critical review. In B. A. Bass, G. E. Wyatt, & G. J. Powell (Eds.), *The Afro-American family: Assessment, treatment, and research issues*. New York: Grune & Stratton.

Nakashima, I. I., & Zacus, G. E. (1977). Incest: Review and clinical experience. *Pediatrics, 60,* 696-701.

National Center on Child Abuse and Neglect (NCCAN). (1981). *Study findings: National study of incidence and severity of child abuse and neglect.* Washington, DC: Department of Health, Education and Welfare.

Nelson, J. (1981). The impact of incest: Factors in self-evaluation. In L. Constantine & F. Martinson (Eds.), *Children and sex* (pp. 163-174). Boston: Little, Brown.

Nelson, S. (1982). *Incest: Fact and myth.* Edinburgh, Scotland: Stramullion.

O'Day, B. (1983). *Preventing sexual abuse of persons with disabilities.* St. Paul: Minnesota Department of Corrections, Program for Victims of Sexual Assault.

Olson, M. (1982) *Personal safety: Curriculum for prevention of child sexual abuse.* Tacoma, WA: Tacoma School District.

Oppenheimer, R., Palmer, R. L., & Brandon, S. (1984, September) *A clinical evaluation of early abusive experiences in adult anorexic and bulemic females: Implications for preventive work in childhood.* Paper presented to the Fifth International Congress on Child Abuse and Neglect, Montreal.

O'Toole, R., Turbett, P., & Nalepka, C. (1983). Theories, professional knowledge and diagnosis of child abuse. In D. Finkelhor, R. J. Gelles, G. T. Hotaling, & M. A. Straus (Eds.), *The dark side of families: Current family violence research.* Beverly Hills, CA: Sage.

Pacht, A. R., & Cowden, J. E. (1974). An exploratory study of five hundred sex offenders. *Criminal Justice and Behavior, 1,* 13-20.

Paitich, D., & Langevin, R. (1976). The Clarke parent-child relations questionnaire: A clinically useful test for adults. *Journal of Consulting and Clinical Psychology, 44,* 428-436.

Panton, J. H. (1978). Personality differences appearing between rapists of adults, rapists of children, and non-violent sexual molesters of children. *Research Communications in Psychology, Psychiatry and Behavior, 3*(4), 385-393.

Panton, J. H. (1979). MMPI profile configurations associated with incestuous and non-incestuous child molesting. *Psychological Reports, 45,* 335-338.

Pelton, L. H. (Ed.). (1981). *The social context of child abuse and neglect.* New York: Human Sciences Press.

Person, E. S. (1980). Sexuality as the mainstay of identity. *Signs, 5,* 605-630.

Peters, J. J. (1976). Children who are victims of sexual assault and the psychology of offenders. *American Journal of Psychotherapy, 30*(3), 395-421.

Peters, S. D. (1984). *The relationship between childhood sexual victimization and adult depression among Afro-American and white women.* Unpublished doctoral dissertation, University of California at Los Angeles. (University Microfilms No. 84-28, 555)

Peters, S. D. (August, 1985). *Child sexual abuse and later psychological problems.* Paper presented at the American Psychological Association, Los Angeles.

Pierce, R., & Pierce, L. (1984, August). *Race as a factor in child sexual abuse.* Paper presented at the Second National Conference for Family Violence Researchers, Durham, NH.

Plummer, C. (1984, August). *Preventing sexual abuse: What in-school programs teach children.* Paper presented at the Second National Conference for Family Violence Researchers, Durham, NH.

Plummer, K. (1981). Pedophilia: Constructing a sociological baseline. In M. Cook & K. Howells (Eds.), *Adult sexual interest in children.* New York: Academic Press.

Prentky, R. (1984, August). *The correlative relationship between family instability in childhood and sexually aggressive behavior in adulthood.* Paper presented at the Second National Conference for Family Violence Researchers, Durham, NH.

Quinsey, V. L. (1977). The assessment and treatment of child molesters: A Review. *Canadian Psychological Review, 18*(3), 204-220.

Quinsey, V. L. (in press). Men who have sex with children. In D. Weisstub (Ed.), *Law and mental health: International perspectives.* (Vol. 2). New York: Pergamon.

Quinsey, V. L., Chaplin, T. C., & Carrigan, W. F. (1979). Sexual preferences among incestuous and non-incestuous child molesters. *Behavior Therapy, 10,* 562-565.

Quinsey, V. L., Chaplin, T. C., & Carrigan, W. F. (1980). Biofeedback and signaled punishment in the modification of inappropriate sexual age preferences. *Behavior Therapy, 11,* 567-576.

Quinsey, V. L., Steinman, C. M., Bergensen, S. G., & Holmes, T. F. (1975). Penile circumference, skin conduction, and ranking responses of child molesters and "normals" to sexual and nonsexual visual stimuli. *Behavior Therapy, 6,* 213-219.

Rada, R. (1976). Alcoholism and the child molester. *Annals of New York Academy of Science, 273,* 492-496.

Rada, R., Laws, D., & Kellner, R. (1976). Plasma testosterone levels in the rapist. *Psychosomatic Medicine, 38*(4), 257-268.

Radzinowicz, L. (1957). *Sexual offences.* New York: St. Martin's.

Ramer, L. (1977). *Your sexual bill of rights: An analysis of the harmful effects of sexual prohibitions.* New York: Exposition.

Ramey, J. (1979). Dealing with the last taboo. *SIECUS Report 7,* 1-2, 6-7.

Ray, JoAnne (1984, August). *Evaluation of the child sex abuse prevention project.* Paper presented at the Second National Conference for Family Violence Researchers, Durham, NH.

Reich, J. W., & Gutierres, S. E. (1979). Escape/aggression incidence in sexually abused juvenile delinquents. *Criminal Justice and Behavior, 6,* 239-243.

Renton School District, No. 403. (1981). *Sexual abuse prevention: A unit in safety.* Renton, WA: Department of Curriculum Instruction.

Roberts, E., Kline, D., & Gagnon, J. (1978). *Family life and sexual learning.* Cambridge, MA: Project on Human Sexual Development.

Rogers, C. (1982). Child sexual abuse and the courts: Preliminary findings. In J. R. Conte & D. Shore (Eds.), *Social work and child sexual abuse.* New York: Haworth.

Rogers, C. M., & Terry, T. (1984). Clinical intervention with boy victims of sexual abuse. In I. Stewart & J. Greer (Eds.), *Victims of sexual aggression* (pp. 1-104). New York: Van Nostrand Reinhold.

Ronstrom, A. (1985, June). *Sexual abuse of children in Sweden: Perspectives on research, interventions and consequences.* Unpublished manuscript. (Radda Barnen, Box 27320, Stockholm, Sweden).

Rosenfeld, A., Nadelson, C., Krieger, M., & Backman, J. (1979). Incest and sexual abuse of children. *Journal of the American Academy of Child Psychiatry, 16,* 327-339.

Ruch, L., & Chandler, S. (1982). The crisis impact of sexual assault on three victim groups: Adult rape victims, child rape victims, and incest victims. *Journal of Social Service Research, 5,* 83-100.

Runyan, D. (1984). *Child sexual abuse: Outcomes and interventions* (Grant proposal to National Institute of Mental Health). Chapel Hill: University of North Carolina.

Rush, F. (1980). *The best kept secret: Sexual abuse of children.* New York: McGraw-Hill.

Russell, D.E.H. (1983). The incidence and prevalence of intrafamilial and extrafamilial sexual abuse of female children. *Child Abuse and Neglect, 7,* 133-146.

Russell, D.E.H. (1984a). *Sexual exploitation: Rape, child sexual abuse, sexual harassment.* Beverly Hills, CA: Sage.

Russell, D.E.H. (1984b). The prevalence and seriousness of incestuous abuse: Stepfathers vs. biological fathers. *Child Abuse and Neglect, 8,* 15-22.

Russell, D.E.H. (1986). *The secret trauma: Incest in the lives of girls and women.* New York: Basic Books.

Rutter, M. (1982). Stress, coping and development: Some issues and some questions. In N. Garmezy & M. Rutter (Eds.), *Stress, coping and development in children.* New York: McGraw-Hill.

Sandfort, T. (1981). *The sexual aspect of paedophile relations.* Amsterdam: Pan/ Spartacus.

Sanford, L. (1980). *The silent children: A parent's guide to the prevention of child sexual abuse.* Garden City, NY: Doubleday.

Sedney, M. A., & Brooks, B. (1984). Factors associated with a history of childhood sexual experience in a nonclinical female population. *Journal of the American Academy of Child Psychiatry, 23,* 215, 218.

Seghorn, T. K., Binder, R. J., Prentky, R. A. (n.d.). *Childhood sexual abuse in the lives of sexually aggressive offenders.* Bridgewater: Massachusetts Treatment Center (Box 554).

Seidner, A. L., & Calhoun, K. S. (1984, August). *Childhood sexual abuse: Factors related to differential adult adjustment.* Paper presented at the Second National Conference for Family Violence Researchers, Durham, NH.

Sgroi, S. (1978). Child sexual assault: Some guidelines for intervention and assessment. In A. Burgess, A. Groth, L. Holmstrom, & S. Sgroi (Eds.), *Sexual assault of children and adolescents.* Lexington, MA: Lexington Books.

Sgroi, S. (1982). *Handbook of clinical intervention in child sexual abuse.* Lexington, MA: Lexington Books.

Shepher, J. (1971). Mate selection among second generation kibbutz adolescents and adults. *Archives of Sexual Behavior, 1,* 293-307.

Shrum, R. A., & Halgin, R. P. (1984, August). *Gender differences in definitions of the sexual victimization of children.* Paper presented at the Second National Conference for Family Violence Researchers, Durham, NH.

Silbert, M. H., & Pines, A. M. (1981). Sexual child abuse as an antecedent to prostitution. *Child Abuse and Neglect, 5,* 407-411.

Sloane, P., & Karpinski, E. (1942). Effects of incest on the participants. *American Journal of Orthopsychiatry, 12,* 666-673.

Snowden, R. (1983). *Boys and child sexual assault prevention project.* Unpublished manuscript, CAP Training Center of Northern California, San Francisco.

Soothill, K. L., & Gibbens, T.C.N. (1978). Recidivism of sexual offenders: A re-appraisal. *British Journal of Criminology, 18*(3), 267-276.

Sorrenti-Little, L., Bagley, C., & Robertson, S. (1984). An operational definition of the long-term harmfulness of sexual relations with peers and adults by young children. *Canadian Children, 9*, 46-57.

Steele, B., & Alexander, H. (1981). Long-term effects of sexual abuse in childhood. In P. B. Mrazek & C. H. Kempe (Eds.), *Sexually abused children and their families*. Oxford: Pergamon.

Stokes, R. E. (1964). A research approach to sexual offenses involving children. *Canadian Journal of Corrections, 6*, 87-94.

Stoller R. (1975). *Perversion: The erotic form of hatred*. New York: Pantheon.

Storr, A. (1965). *Sexual deviation*. London: Heineman.

Straus, M. A., Gelles, R., & Steinmetz, S. (1980). *Behind closed doors: Violence in the American family*. Garden City, NY: Doubleday.

Stricker, G. (1967). Stimulus properties of the Blacky to a sample of pedophiles. *Journal of General Psychology, 77*, 35-39.

Stuart, V., & Stuart, C. K. (1983). *Sexuality and sexual assault: Disabled perspective*. Marshall, MN: Southwest State University.

Sudman, S., & Bradburn, N. M. (1974). *Response effects in surveys: A review of systems*. Chicago: Aldine.

Sudman, S., Bradburn, N. M., Blair, E., & Stocking, C. (1977). Modest expectations: The effect of interviewers' prior expectations on responses. *Sociological Methods and Research, 6*, 177-182.

Summit, R. (1983). The child sexual abuse accommodation syndrome. *Child Abuse and Neglect, 7*, 177-193.

Summit, R., & Kryso, J. (1978). Sexual abuse of children: A clinical spectrum. *American Journal of Orthopsychiatry, 48*, 237-251.

Swanson, D. W. (1968). Adult sexual abuse of children: The man and circumstances. *Diseases of the Nervous System, 29*, 677-683.

Symonds, D. (1978). *The evolution of human sexuality*. New York: Oxford.

Timnick, L. (1985a, August 25). 22% in survey were child abuse victims. *Los Angeles Times*, p. 1.

Timnick, L. (1985b, August 26). Children's abuse reports reliable, most believe. *Los Angeles Times*, p. 1.

Toal, S. D. (1985). *Children's safety and protection training project: Three interrelated analyses*. Stockton, CA: Toal Consultation Services (6333 Pacific Ave., Suite 261).

Tobias, J. L., & Gordon, R. (1977). *Operation Lure* (mimeo). Michigan State Police.

Toobert, S., Bartelme, K. F., & Jones, E. S. (1959). Some factors related to pedophilia. *International Journal of Psychiatry, 4*, 272-279.

Tracy, F., Donnelly, H., Morgenbesser, L., & Macdonald, D. (1983). Program evaluation: Recidivism research involving sex offenders. In J. Greer & I. Stuart (Eds.), *The sexual aggressor: Current perspectives on treatment* (pp. 198-213). New York: Van Nostrand Reinhold.

Trainor, C. (1984). *Sexual maltreatment in the United States: A five-year perspective*. Paper presented at the International Congress on Child Abuse and Neglect, Montreal.

Tsai, M., Feldman-Summers, S., & Edgar, M. (1979). Childhood molestation: Variables related to differential impact of psychosexual functioning in adult women. *Journal of Abnormal Psychology, 88*, 407-417.

Tsai, M., & Wagner, N. (1978). Therapy groups for women sexually molested as children. *Archives of Sexual Behavior, 7*, 417-429.

Tufts' New England Medical Center, Division of Child Psychiatry. (1984). *Sexually exploited children: Service and research project* (Final report for the Office of Juvenile Justice and Delinquency Prevention). Washington, DC: U.S. Department of Justice.

Van den Berghe, P. L. (1983). Human inbreeding avoidance: Culture in nature. *Behavioral and Brain Sciences, 6*, 91-123.

Virkkunen, M. (1976). The pedophilic offender with antisocial character. *Acta Psychiatrica Scandinavica, 53*(5), 401-405.

Wall, H. (1983). *Child assault/abuse prevention project: Pilot program evaluation.* Concord, CA: Mt. Diablo Unified Schools.

Wallerstein, J. (1983). *Children of divorce: Preliminary report of a 10-year follow-up.* Paper presented at the American Academy of Law and Psychiatry, Portland, OR.

Walters, D. R. (1975). *Physical and sexual abuse of children: Causes and treatment.* Bloomington: Indiana University Press.

Weinberg, S.K. (1955). *Incest behavior.* New York: Citadel.

Weiss, M. D., Rogers, M. D., Darwin, M. R., & Dutton, C. E. (1955). A study of girl sex victims. *Psychiatric Quarterly, 29*, 1-27.

Wenet, F. A., Clark, T. R., & Hunner, R. J. (1981). Perspectives on the juvenile sex offender. In R. J. Hunner & Y. E. Walker (Eds.), *Exploring the relationship between child abuse and delinquency.* Montclair, NJ: Allenheld, Osmun.

West, D. J. (1977). *Homosexuality re-examined.* London: Duckworth.

Williams, J. (1980). *Red flag, green flag people.* Fargo, ND: Rape and Abuse Crisis Center of Fargo-Moorehead.

Wilschke, K. (1965). Uber die kriminogene rolle des alkohols bei sittlichkeisdelikten [The criminogenic role of alcohol in sex offenses]. *Munchener Medizinische Wochenschrift, 107*(4), 176-177.

Wilson, G. D., & Cox, D. N. (1983). Personality of paedophile club members. *Personality and Individual Differences, 4*(3), 323-329.

Wisconsin Female Juvenile Offender Study. (1982). *Sex abuse among juvenile offenders and runaways* (Summary report). Madison, WI: Author.

Wood, S. C., & Dean, K. S. (1984). *Final report: Sexual abuse of males research project* (90 CA/812). Washington, DC: National Center on Child Abuse and Neglect.

Woody, R. H. (Ed.). (1980). *Encyclopedia of clinical assessment* (Vol. 2). San Francisco: Jossey-Bass.

Wyatt, G. E. (1985). The sexual abuse of Afro-American and White American women in childhood. *Child Abuse and Neglect, 9,* 507-519.

Wyatt, G. E., & Peters, S. D. (1986). Issues in the definition of child sexual abuse in prevalence research. *Child Abuse and Neglect, 10,* 231-240.

Zelnik, M., & Kantner, J. (1972). Sexuality, contraception, and pregnancy among young unwed females in the United States (U.S. Commission on Population Growth and the American Future, Demographic and Social Aspects of Population Growth). In F. Westoff & Parke, Jr. (Eds.), *Commission research reports* (Vol. 1). Washington, DC: Government Printing Office.

Zimbardo, P., Haney, C., Banks, W., & Jaffe, D. (1972). *The psychology of imprisonment: Privation, power, and pathology.* Unpublished paper, Stanford University, CA.

# Index

# About the Authors

DAVID FINKELHOR is Associate Chair of the Family Research Laboratory and Associate Director of the Family Violence Research Program at the University of New Hampshire. He has been studying the problem of child sexual abuse since 1977, and has published two books, *Sexually Victimized Children* and *Child Sexual Abuse: New Theory and Research*, and over two dozen articles on the subject. He has been the recipient of grants from the National Institute of Mental Health, and the National Center on Child Abuse and Neglect. His other research interests include elder abuse and sexual assault in marriage.

SHARON ARAJI is Assistant Professor of Sociology at the University of Alaska, Anchorage. Prior to taking a position at UAA, she was a post-doctoral fellow at the Family Research Laboratory, University of New Hampshire, where she collaborated with David Finkelhor on several papers that focused on child sexual abuse. Her current research interests concern child sex offenders, child sexual abuse prevention programs, and women's roles in developing countries.

LARRY BARON is Lecturer in the Department of Sociology at Yale University. He spent two years as a post-doctoral fellow in the Family Violence Research Program at the University of New

Hampshire and one year as a post-doctoral fellow studying the sociology of social control at Yale University. He is currently completing a book with Murray Straus on rape and its relationship to pornography, sexual inequality, and the cultural support for violence in the United States.

ANGELA BROWNE is a social psychologist specializing in family violence, particularly violence occurring in adult relationships between romantic partners. She was formerly a post-doctoral fellow and is currently a research associate with the Family Research Laboratory at the University of New Hampshire. Dr. Browne is editor of the interdisciplinary journal *Violence and Victims*. She has also published articles concerning battered women who kill their abusive mates, and is currently completing a book on this topic.

STEFANIE DOYLE PETERS is currently a Research Associate in the Department of Psychiatry and BioBehavioral Sciences at the University of California at Los Angeles, where she received her degree in Psychology in 1984. Her research has focused on the long-term effects of child sexual abuse on the psychological functioning of adult women. She is also the coauthor of several papers examining methodological issues in the study of sexual abuse.

GAIL ELIZABETH WYATT is Associate Professor of Medical Psychology in the Department of Psychiatry and BioBehavioral Sciences at the University of California at Los Angeles, and a Research Scientist Career Development Awardee. Her research has examined the relationship of sexual socialization to a range of subsequent sexual experiences and women's psychological well-being. Dr. Wyatt has developed sex education programs for children and parents and is also a sex therapist, specializing in human sexuality within a sociocultural perspective.